WINGED
SCALPEL

Dedication

To the brave men and women of Merlin

WINGED
SCALPEL

A Surgeon at the Frontline of Disaster

Richard Villar

PEN & SWORD
DISCOVERY

First published in Great Britain in 2012 by
PEN & SWORD DISCOVERY
an imprint of
Pen & Sword Books Ltd
47 Church Street
Barnsley
South Yorkshire
S70 2AS

ISBN 978 1 78159 168 0

A CIP catalogue record for this book is
available from the British Library

Typeset in Ehrhardt
by L S Menzies-Earl

Printed and bound in England
by CPI Group (UK) Ltd, Croydon, CR0 4YY

Pen & Sword Books Ltd incorporates the imprints of
Pen & Sword Aviation, Pen & Sword Family History, Pen & Sword Maritime,
Pen & Sword Military, Pen & Sword Discovery, Wharncliffe Local History,
Wharncliffe True Crime, Wharncliffe Transport, Pen & Sword Select,
Pen & Sword Military Classics, Leo Cooper, Remember When,
The Praetorian Press, Seaforth Publishing and Frontline Publishing

For a complete list of Pen & Sword titles please contact
PEN & SWORD BOOKS LIMITED
47 Church Street, Barnsley, South Yorkshire, S70 2AS England
E-mail: enquiries@pen-and-sword.co.uk
Website: www.pen-and-sword.co.uk

Contents

HAITI 2010

LIBYA 2011

Foreword

I blame the SAS. Without them I would not be writing this. I would have been someone different, enjoying a quieter life free from danger. The SAS changed me, pushed me to my limits, sometimes beyond.

I used once to think I was brave, that nothing would perturb me. I was sure I had a limitless source of courage that made me stand apart from the normal male. SAS service does that to you. It makes you feel special; it makes you feel proud, privileged and fortunate. The Regiment took me to actions and opportunities throughout the world. Terrorism in London, violence in Northern Ireland, conflict in central America, the deserts of the Middle East, the mountains of Pakistan and Afghanistan, and Far Eastern jungles. It took me up Everest, and down again in an avalanche. It took me to the Falklands War, nearly killing me in the process. In many respects the SAS made me the man I am today. Yet however proud I am of my time as an SAS surgeon, however much I realise that my experiences are perhaps unique, I now know that anything the Regiment showed me was but a prelude of what was to follow.

I left the SAS a changed man and then worked in England and overseas. To my patients I was an orthopaedic surgeon, one who handled problems with damaged bones and joints. Yet I did more, much more, in a world few have had the privilege to see. I worked in small hospitals in rural India and big ones in Nepal. I worked in Lebanon for the Palestinians, who taught me, surprisingly, about the futility of war. I even endured the siege of Sarajevo in a hospital so full of shrapnel holes we likened it to Swiss cheese.

Today, I form part of the United Kingdom's Emergency Response whenever there is a disaster. I work with a group called Merlin – Medical Emergency Relief International. I am often the first man in, when the buildings have collapsed or the bombs have dropped. I doubt you will have heard of me. Yet this job has taken its toll, not just on me but also on the others with whom I work. It is a difficult existence yet I hope my efforts have led to many lives being saved and much pain and psychological stress being abolished. If that is true, then my personal suffering will have been worthwhile; the nightmares, the domestic upheaval and the injuries I have sustained.

This is my story, at least part of my story. It tells of my time in Kashmir and its most horrifying earthquake when tens of thousands died in seconds and I was left to decide, on the remotest Kashmiri mountainside, who should live and who should die. I write of Java and its quadruple, simultaneous catastrophes of volcanic eruption, earthquake, bird 'flu and terrorism. I write also of Haiti, that earthquake of earthquakes, where I arrived only days after the event and was immersed fully into the tragedy and violence of that desperate land. Finally, I go to Libya and Tunisia, where I worked at the peak of NATO's bombing campaign, and where I evaded Colonel Gaddafi by crossing the border only hours ahead of his men.

Before I begin, I must pay credit to the many others who accompanied me on these adventures. They are unbelievably brave and motivated people. Wherever I went, whatever I did, Merlin colleagues who have in many cases become lifelong friends accompanied me. Mostly, in this book I have changed their names, sometimes even their location. This is because to provide aid in the wake of conflict and disaster is dangerous. Not everyone makes it home. Medical staff are killed, maimed, imprisoned and tortured throughout the world for a multitude of reasons. These are brave people who do so much for the tiniest financial reward. I am but one of many and it has been my privilege to be involved.

I was present at each of the events I describe and I am sure more will follow. Wars and natural disasters are an unhappy, inevitable part of mankind's existence. However, I doubt I would have seen any of them had it not been for the SAS. They deserve my thanks, too. You see, they say you can take a man out of the Regiment but you cannot take the Regiment out of a man. They are right. Read and you may understand.

* * *

Kashmir – October 2005
(EPI = Epicentre)

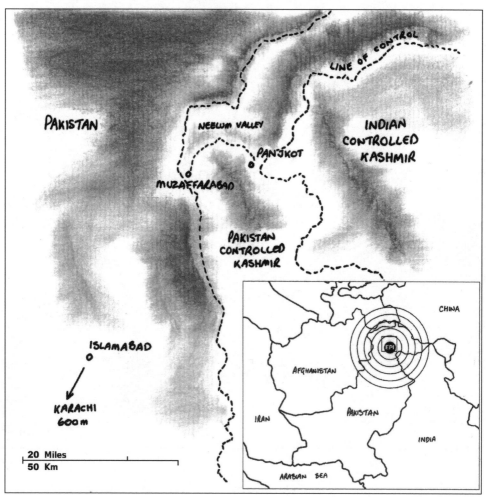

Java – May 2006
(EPI = Epicentre)

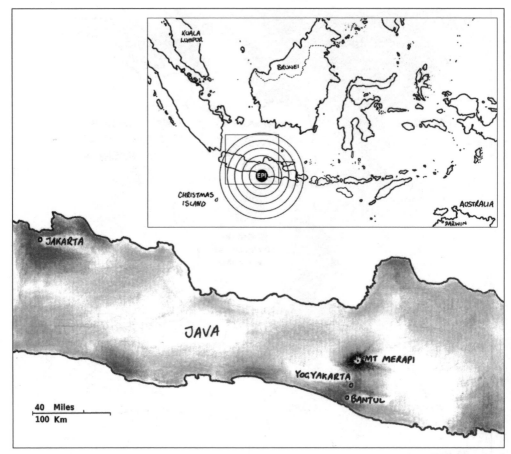

© Ben Coupland

Haiti – January 2010
(EPI = Epicentre)

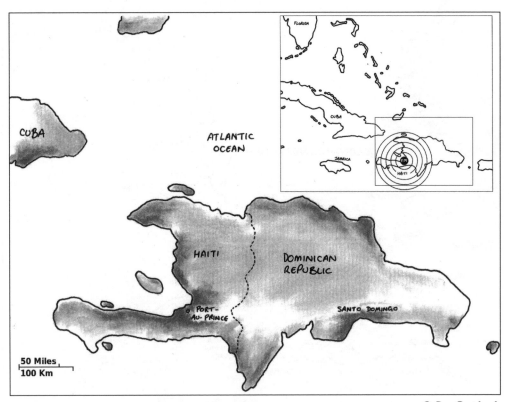

© Ben Coupland

Libya – April 2011

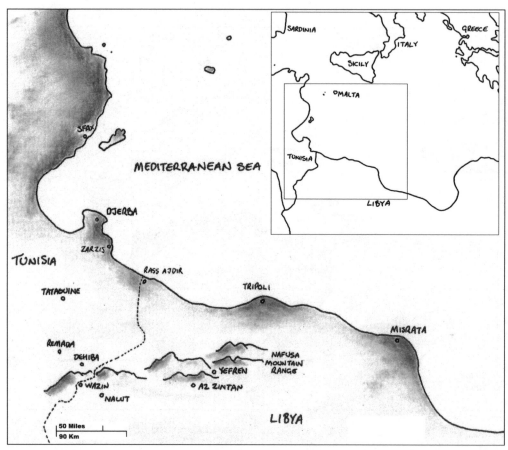

© Ben Coupland

Chapter 1

Nightmare

Different nightmares come and go but the terror, when it happens, is the same.

I wake up screaming, the sweat dripping from my drenched torso, my eyes wide open, arms flaying wildly in all directions. I turn, my trembling hand struggling for the bedside light. I fumble and I grope, frequently throwing the spindly lamp unintentionally to the floor. Then I find the tiny switch. For a brief second I wait, then I push. Instantly, from darkness, there is light. I sigh, I breathe deeply, throwing myself once more onto my back. I feel that distant sensation behind my eyes as the tears slowly well.

Rapidly the tiny drops become a torrent streaming down my cheeks. My body shakes, violent shakes, so forceful that the bed head thumps loudly against the wall. In the half smile, half grimace of distress, I raise my cupped hands to cover my face, as if to hide myself in shame. Always I say the same words, always my voice trembles, always I try to whisper and always I fail. 'Oh God!' I shout in panic. 'Oh God, why me?'

Then it is over, almost as quickly as it began. I relax, laying my arms limply down beside me. Yet the terror remains, the terror of a next time, the realisation that everything my dreams had shown was a horror I had actually seen.

The nightmare always follows the same pattern. I am walking down a rubble-strewn street in a destroyed city; somewhere primitive, somewhere poor, somewhere that tower blocks do not exist. It is early morning and the stench of death is everywhere. A shop sign dangles dangerously from a tilted post to my right, an elderly woman sits silently on an irregular boulder to my left. In the distance, at least as far as I can see through the thick, smog-like dusty haze in the immediate aftermath of an earthquake, I can see children running wildly in all directions, screaming for their parents, their friends, their brothers, their sisters. Yet whole families have disappeared, vanished without trace, and in a matter of a few seconds. The much-loved child has become an orphan in the time it takes to blink.

I stop to listen, but it is not the terrified children I hear. It is the voice, faint, remote, gasping, somewhere in the half-collapsed building behind me to my right. I turn and retrace my steps, just a few, but enough to hear the voice more clearly. Now I can make out individual words, they are more than just a mumble.

'Help me,' says the young female voice, 'Please help me.'

Through the haze I see the pile of broken rubble extending outwards from the concertinaed floors of the small apartment block. The boulders are strewn across the pitted road like a reptilian tongue, the line of rubble forked at its far end as it was thrown from the collapsing building with explosive force.

I come closer. Now I can see the girl. Her stained, pink, floral dress is crumpled up above her waist. She is about 16 years old, now face down in the dirt, her head forced agonisingly to the left by the large concrete boulder that is lying across her lower back and right shoulder. I can see the tiny trickle of blood coming from the side of her mouth and, through the dust, I can also see her blue, cyanosed legs now devoid of blood and crushed beyond all hope of salvage.

I approach the girl, I squat down beside her, I grasp her small, cold hand in mine. I whisper gently in her ear, 'I'm here to help you. My name is Richard. Who are you?'

For a moment I see the girl give a gentle half-smile. Her eyes flick towards me, imploringly, begging me to help. 'Please,' she says. 'I'm stuck. Please get me out of here.'

I look at the boulder that has pinned her to the ground, the boulder which has ensured she will never walk again. Probably, I suspect, the girl had almost escaped from the collapsing building during the earthquake. Another few feet and she would have been free. Yet she had perhaps stumbled and then the boulder had caught her, trapped her and crushed her to the ground.

I look harder at the boulder. One man, however strong, could not make it budge. It is massive, irregular, sharp-edged in parts, and has rusty and bent reinforcement wires protruding. Even if it could be moved, above us I see a large concrete slab held from its final descent by the boulder itself; one shift of the boulder and down the slab would come.

Yet it is not the slab that has now drawn my attention. The terror, the horror, the realisation develops inside me like some massive, frightening tidal wave. I look closer at the boulder that has trapped the girl. I had missed it until then. There, under the boulder, and to the girl's right, lies the crushed body of the child, perhaps four or five years old. The young creature is still tightly gripping the girl's right hand.

The child, I cannot tell whether it is boy or girl, is so clearly dead. I try not to show my distress as I know the girl, whose head has been forced to look away by the boulder, cannot tell what has happened. The child, I now feel certain, is the reason why the girl had not escaped. She would have stopped to rescue this tiny piece of mankind, perhaps a sibling, perhaps a stranger, but the girl's charity has been her own demise.

Then, as I look at the boulder, and the dead child, and then glance back to the girl's imploring eyes, I realise the situation is hopeless. What can I do? What can I say? Rescue is a million miles away, certainly many days.

I smile at the girl as I speak, squeezing her now clammy hand more tightly. 'It'll be fine,' I say, my voice as reassuring as I can muster. 'Just give me a few moments and I'll have you out of there.'

I see the girl smile. She is happier now. A stranger has come to help. Gently she nods her head as acknowledgement. Slowly I rise to my feet wondering what to do. Then Nature speaks, with a violence that makes mankind seem so insignificant.

The aftershock slams into the soles of my feet like a sledgehammer. I stagger awkwardly to my left almost falling to the ground. It is over almost as soon as it has started. Briefly there is silence. Then I hear the unmistakable sound of rubble shifting, of concertinaed floors subsiding, of already collapsed buildings collapsing further. I hear the shouts and screams of warning as those survivors who can run or stumble, dash to get clear.

I see the concrete slab above us shifting and instantly recognise I have milliseconds to live - unless I act. My survival process takes over; every reflex and every move is aimed at keeping me alive. To my instincts I have now become the priority. I turn rapidly and half dive, half stagger into the rubble-strewn street outside once more. As I roll headlong through the debris I hear the concrete slab come crashing down and see the girl's crushed frame disappear in a cloud of white dust. She has gone, now buried deeply beneath the debris, her pink dress already a memory.

I sit in the dirt, breathing in the contaminated air, only yards away from the girl. And then I wake up, and I cry, those same tears that have plagued me for so long. Those tears are for the girl, and the many, many thousands like her. Those tears are for the ones I could not save. Such is life with disaster.

* * *

KASHMIR 2005

Chapter 2

Shame and Upheaval

Much can happen in thirteen days, especially after an earthquake. That number and that delay are writ large in my mind even now. Writ large because I am horrified and ashamed that it took me thirteen days after the Kashmir earthquake to treat my first casualty.

Kashmir was a classic case of administrative chaos, and the world should take a lesson from it. Much is said at the time of a major disaster, much is promised and much may seem to be done. However, much is lacking when it comes to helping the folk who truly matter. Those are the casualties, the wounded, the diseased, the displaced. For Kashmir, the aid machine should hang its head in shame. The machine can be so willing and so well meaning, yet through sheer inertia can be so ineffective. This is my story of the Kashmir earthquake, a personal, sometimes emotional view.

On the morning of Saturday 8th October 2005, with me in central London, I awoke to hear the news from Kashmir. A Richter 7.6 tremor had hit a mountainous region northeast of the city of Muzaffarabad at 8.52 am, Pakistan time. The media were in full throttle. Casualty estimates were then unknown, but the earthquake had been major. Nobody could know that the end result would be more than 75,000 dead, many more injured, and three million homeless. The tremor had been a rough, rapid, vertical shock, which at its peak had lasted no more than three seconds. Three seconds – that was all. Yet the lives of so many had been destroyed or irreversibly changed. From London, Kashmir seemed so far away. The earthquake was bad news of course, but someone else's life, someone else's disaster and someone else's problem.

I tried to imagine the disaster and how it might appear. I knew the area well, having spent time in the North-West Frontier Province when Russia had been knocking on Afghanistan's door. Moscow had been one of many to believe it could tame the untameable. There is something almost romantic about the North-West Frontier. These are real mountains, rugged and hard, populated by a resilient and welcoming people.

A wimp would not last long in the North-West Frontier. The mountains are more than huge – Nanga Parbat in the Great Himalaya, sometimes called the Naked Mountain; or K2 to the north and part of the Karakoram range. I may be a medical man but I am also a mountaineer. To a true mountaineer the mere mention of Kashmir stirs the belly.

This was a busy professional time for me. I was relocating my practice from Cambridge to London and was right in the middle of the move. I had little time to spare for Kashmir and its tortured human load. The 8th October came and went, the stories fed by the media became more horrifying and yet more distant, while I was certain I would not be involved in the slowly awakening humanitarian aid machine. The television would show an occasional rescue team, each worker dressed in flashy uniform and carrying a spotless holdall, heading towards the earthquake zone. Often, their interviews were held on airport runways, in hotels, or on well-swept pavements. Rarely were they given in areas with damaged buildings, or in the mountainous region where the earthquake had occurred. Meanwhile Government spokesmen would announce generous offerings to Kashmir's victims, yet offer no detail of how the funds would be transferred, or when they would reach their intended destination. There was certainly no detail of how they would be used.

Anyway, for me, why did it matter, I thought? I had repeatedly offered my services in previous years to a succession of disaster charities. Few had replied and for those who had responded, none had given me a job to do. However much experience I might have gained as a Special Forces surgeon, the world of disaster relief appeared a closed shop. There was no way in, it seemed, without some major organisation supporting you.

It was on the 16th October, eight days after the Kashmir tremor, that my life irreversibly changed. I had taken a weekend off to escape London and walk in the soft and soggy hills of England's White Peak District, near to the village of Hartington. My mind was filled with the trivia of life. Kashmir to me then was a million miles away.

That was until my mobile rang, a piercing trill that brought me back instantly to the here and now. I moved to one side of the footpath, allowing a small group of walkers behind to pass and answered my telephone. I did not recognise the caller.

'Is that Villar the surgeon?' came an authoritative tone.

I suppressed a chuckle. 'Yes, this is Villar the surgeon,' I replied, half smiling. The use of my surname carried images of time spent with Her Majesty's Armed Services, so it was no surprise when the caller introduced himself as a Major General. The questioning then continued.

'The same Villar who was with the SAS?'

Here we go I thought. I had spent a considerable time with the SAS, I had even written a book about my time with the Regiment, but it was still not something I freely discussed with strangers on the telephone.

'Many years ago, yes.'

The Major General clearly understood my concern. 'Just checking you are the right chap. What do you know about mountaineering?' he asked.

I looked around me at the smooth contours of the White Peak's hills and smiled further. The Major General would of course have no idea from where I was speaking. 'A fair amount,' I replied. 'I have spent much of my life in the mountains.'

'And field hospitals?'

'Them too.'

'Then you are just the man for the job,' said the Major General.

'What is this about?' I queried, suspicion evident in my voice.

'Kashmir, man. It's all over the news. You must surely have heard?'

My mind instantly switched into overdrive. So this was how these things began. This was the first approach and how it was done. My name was registered with at least a dozen charities, each made aware that I would be happy to help in a disaster, that I could move fast, and that I had the relevant experience. It was now so long after the earthquake that I was sure I would not be required. Surely no aid machine could be this slow? Yet it was.

Briefly the Major General explained. Merlin, one of the UK aid organisations wished to position a field hospital near to the epicentre of the Kashmir earthquake. They needed someone with experience to help run the show in the field. Was I interested?

For an ex-SAS surgeon that was an unnecessary question. Of course I was interested and of course I wanted to go. Suddenly my worries about the trivia of a practice move disappeared. It was as if they had never existed. My focus instantly changed. Whether it was a search for adventure, whether it was a desire to help others, or a mixture of the two, the Kashmir call struck home. Irrespective of the upheaval it would create in my life, if Kashmir summoned I would go.

* * *

Chapter 3

Seat 28A

With a shaking hand I dialled the number given to me by the Major General. It was a London code, somewhere near the City. I had half jogged, half stumbled back to my Hartington hotel before making the call. The clouds above were darkening rapidly as England's Peak District began to do what it did so well. Rain.

I listened to the telephone ring for what seemed an age. No answer. I tried again, no answer then, too. On the third attempt I was through. My mouth was dry with excitement as I licked my lips with an ineffective tongue. I did not know what to expect but imagined a dark, dusty office, desks piled high with reference books and papers, behind which would sit an overweight, balding and elderly man wielding a Bakelite telephone. The ringing suddenly ceased and the telephone was answered. This was no elderly man. Instead I heard the delicate voice of someone I would soon learn was Suzie.

'Hello? Merlin here,' came the reassuring female voice.

'Umm…umm…umm,' I began. 'Umm…' I struggled to make any sound at all. So certain had I been that a gruff male voice would reply that Suzie's flower-like voice had rendered me virtually mute.

'Hello?'

Silence. I simply could not speak.

'Hello?

More silence.

'Come on, whoever you are.'

Still more silence.

'Well bugger off then.' And the line went dead.

I sat on the edge of my bed in the hotel room, my head in my hands with disbelief. What an idiot! I was ex-SAS, had seen countless conflicts and dealt with human misery in so many forms. Theoretically I was prepared for anything, and with a confidence to match. Yet I had been struck dumb by a voice or, perhaps, the excitement of the moment.

So I tried again. On this occasion it worked.

Suzie was my Merlin handler and never learned that I was the speechless one. An ex-laboratory technician, she was a charming girl, with plenty of disaster experience herself. She laughed when I asked, 'Why me? Surely you must mean someone else?'

'No, Richard,' came her insistent reply. 'Only you. Our advisers say you are what we need.'

No pressure, I thought. Someone, not me, had built up her expectations. Now I had to deliver.

As we talked, as Suzie painted the tragic picture of Kashmir, it was evident Merlin needed help. Brilliant though it was at providing care to remote lands during normal times, the construction of an emergency field hospital in the wake of a major disaster was way outside its normal role. To create a tented hospital in a valley is hard enough. Stick it on a mountainside and the problems are far greater. Merlin had been struggling to find someone of sufficient experience to handle the matter and had come across my name by chance.

I refrained from saying that I had volunteered my services some years earlier but had received no reply. I imagined my records had long since disappeared into a bottom drawer, never to see daylight again.

'You'll be leaving any moment,' said Suzie. 'Get yourself jabbed up.'

'No problem,' I replied.

'I'll be in touch.' Again the line went dead.

First stop the next morning was a travel inoculation centre in an unprepossessing area of south London. I had received a late-night telephone call from Merlin to say that my appointment had been booked. The centre was similar to Doctor Who's Tardis; drab and dirty on the outside but sparkling, modern and efficient within. There, I had more needles inserted into me by a smiling Polish blonde than a hedgehog has spines.

'Just a pre-e-eck,' she would say. 'And another. Oooh! And here's another.'

By the time the blonde had finished I was feeling much the worse for wear. My immune system had withstood the vaccine-inflicted simultaneous onslaught of polio, yellow fever, typhoid, cholera, tetanus, rabies, meningitis and Japanese encephalitis B. Clutching several packets of antimalarials, water purification tablets and the world's tiniest mosquito net, I wobbled and weaved my way through the London underground to the Merlin offices for my pre-mission briefing. There, for the first time, I met Suzie.

She looked at me over the top of tiny reading glasses, her brown eyes matching her brunette hair almost exactly. I guessed Suzie was about 35 years old. Tight turquoise jumper above, equally tight light blue jeans below, telephone jammed firmly between ear and shoulder, she extended her right hand and arm as I approached. I could see she had much to say and much to do. Suzie was the definition of multitasking. Telephones shrilled, fax machines whirred and emails pinged continually. The entire Kashmir relief project seemed to pass through her desk and yet she was completely relaxed. There are simply not enough Suzies in the world.

'Hi,' she mouthed, eyebrows rising in welcome as our hands touched briefly. Then her thumb jerked backwards, indicating over her shoulder. I glanced up to see an arm waving from behind a desk at the far end of the warehouse-like office. There was a black-and-white sign at the arm waver's station. I squinted hard. 'Human Resources' it read, so I walked quickly across, nodding my thanks to Suzie.

The Merlin offices were a hive of activity. Casually dressed aid workers were dashing left and right, documents were being prepared, and line drawings in red, black, blue and green were being scribbled haphazardly on white boards. Meanwhile tiny meeting rooms held small groups of earnest individuals in obvious and deep discussion. Kashmir was most definitely the focus. On several desks I could see images of collapsed buildings, photographs of crying adults and children, and many photographs of corpses. This was a far cry from England's Peak District, or my practice, even the Polish blonde. This was a terrible and tragic disaster.

My pre-mission briefing was conducted at pace while I was seated at the Human Resources desk.

'Sign here, please,' the officer instructed, pointing to the dotted line at the bottom of a pre-completed form that she slid towards me. I saw the bold heading 'Contract of Employment' and smiled. Merlin now had me on its books, certainly for the present. I signed, taking the document's contents on trust. I had to. There was no time at this stage for complex employee negotiations.

Meanwhile, a tall Australian, the country director for Pakistan, mumbled rapidly into my right ear. Quickly he described whom I was to meet when I arrived in Islamabad, my would-be point of entry to the disaster zone. Then he tapped his watch face. 'Your flight leaves in six hours. It's British Airways but you will need a visa before then.'

As the Australian spoke, so did the thin, wiry Cumbrian logistician standing to my left.

'We've a problem with oxygen requirements for the field hospital,' he said. 'What can you tell us about those?'

'Nothing,' I replied.

'And power? How much electricity will we need?'

'God knows,' I answered.

'Do you speak Urdu?' the arm waver then asked, her pen poised to write my answer on a clipboard.

'Sorry, not a word,' I replied. I felt increasingly useless. Although I knew much about surgery and survival, I knew almost nothing about the things that really mattered; those behind-the-scenes activities that keep hospitals supplied, alive and thriving.

'Suzie!' I shouted and watched her turn. 'Are you sure you need me? I seem to have none of the skills you seek.'

She laughed, half raising her hand as if to say, 'Don't you worry.' Then she returned to her work.

Sixty minutes later, my ears buzzing with endless instructions and my head fit to burst, I emerged from the office building into the chilled and polluted air of an overcast London. I was missing two vital items. One was a map, the other a visa. Both were critical to success.

Maps are frequently in short supply for disasters. Invariably the event has occurred somewhere remote, in a location that sees little consumer demand for mapping. My favourite location for finding the things was Stanfords, near London's Covent Garden. It had served the great and good for generations. The moment you walk inside you feel like a real explorer. Big maps, small maps, medium-sized atlases, lie beside charts and guidebooks of almost every location.

My first visit to Stanfords had been three decades earlier before a trip to the North-West Frontier Province of Pakistan. Then, I had sought a map of the remote Rumbur Valley that stretched westwards from Pakistan to Afghanistan. The valley was about as uninhabited and remote as one could be. Yet in a flat and dusty drawer, buried deeply in a dark area of the farthest corner of Stanfords, lay the map. An elderly man with a huge limp and congenitally curved spine had produced exactly what I had sought. With a flourish he had placed the crisp document on the wide table and had stroked the map flat with a loving caress. As I had looked at the tight contour lines of the steep and rugged mountains, I could almost smell the valley. Hear it, too. The fresh pine resin, the distant tinkle of goat bells and, way in the distance, the rush of the valley's stream. All those years ago, when I had bought that map in Stanfords, in my mind I was already in Pakistan. So, with great confidence I entered the shop once more, sure it would come to my rescue.

My disappointment, however, was total. No longer was Stanfords the dark, unkempt, almost haunted establishment, a centre for pondering, browsing, daydreaming and armchair travel. Now it was a brighter place filled with all walks of life, not just ambitious explorers. There were mothers with pushchairs wrestling with uncontrollable children, grannies with wicker baskets and puffed out hair, there were school children playing tag between the counters and plenty of non-English-speaking tourists seeking to find maps of London. The explorer types were there, of course, but in far smaller numbers; Stanfords had a supermarket air about it. It was clearly competing successfully in a competitive world but it was no longer the Stanfords I had known. Furthermore, my man with the limp and curvy spine had long disappeared and, more importantly, there were no maps, absolutely none, of the Kashmir earthquake area. The few they had once displayed were now well gone, purchased by aid agencies and individuals already on their way to the earthquake zone.

I had little time to prepare. British Airways flight 129 to Pakistan's Islamabad took off barely five hours later and I was on it. At least I would be if I could obtain a visa. I knew that would be a challenge. The normal waiting time for a work visa to Pakistan was three months. I had less than three hours to obtain one.

So, clutching an already half-crumpled letter from Merlin, certifying me to be a true and upright character as well as a citizen of the United Kingdom, I entered the front door of Pakistan's High Commission in London's Lowndes Square. I strode confidently up to the handlebar-moustached security guard sat to one side of the building's entrance corridor. He looked studiously at my convict-like passport photograph stapled firmly to the top right corner of the hand-completed visa form. I could almost hear him ponder. First he turned the form clockwise, then anticlockwise, then upside down. Finally he held it up to the light.

Next he glanced at me through thick glasses, then back to the photograph and then back to me. He did this at least a dozen times. No wonder, I thought. I photograph terribly and would never make it to a Hollywood screen.

As I watched the security guard struggle and reflect, I wanted to shout, 'Come on man! It's your country I am trying to help!' The clock was ticking steadily and I was trying hard not to hop from foot to foot.

Eventually the guard was satisfied. With a sigh he scribbled a few words on the application form – 'Sir, for your orders please' - and I was ushered through into a large, mahogany-lined office.

Behind a plush ruby leather-topped desk sat a manifestly more senior character; this was the Consul himself. He looked at me intently, too. Next came the multiple glances between my photograph and me. Satisfied I was not a fundamentalist in disguise, without a word he signed my application form, thrust it back across the desk and pointed towards the door. 'Good luck', he whispered, almost conspiratorially.

I rose quickly to my feet, smiled, nodded my thanks and headed from his office. I was done, documented, and on my way to Heathrow.

I was fortunate. Not all were. As I hastened from the Consul's office I could hear the complaining wails of two female aid workers from another aid organisation. The security guard was on his feet and shaking his head, the tips of his handlebar moustache quivering as he did so.

'You must come back tomorrow. We are closed,' he said, clearly the immovable object.

'But our flight leaves in a few hours' time,' the two workers complained in near unison.

More head shaking. 'We are closed, my ladies.'

'But...'

'Closed.'

And that was it. The one-sided negotiation was complete. I had been given my visa by the narrowest margin, walked guiltily past the aid workers and left the building. The women had missed their flight. For me, with Consular blessing and a fortuitous tail wind, three months had been reduced to six minutes. Throughout the entire visa process only two words had been said. 'Good luck' from the Consul.

Heathrow was chaos with passengers and baggage everywhere. For flight BA129 disaster relief was clearly the order of the day. There was the Norwegian Red Cross, Convoy of Hope, The Orphan Child, Oxfam, Médecins Sans Frontières (MSF), the Danish Red Cross, plenty of other aid organisations and, of course, me. Everyone was arguing and bartering for extra baggage allowances and most were permitted.

Disaster relief is a strangely motivating feeling, particularly when the world is in support. You do sense people behind you. Meanwhile, media reports arrive thick and fast. That was certainly the case for Kashmir. One word dominated the majority of bulletins – delay. Delay in countries donating funds, delay in aid being sent, delay in wounded being extracted, delay, delay, and delay.

Yet Heathrow had a positive feel that day. Aid worker would talk to aid worker, even if the two had never previously met. Ground staff would spontaneously stop, place a caring hand on a shoulder, and wish some scruffy individual with a red cross on a battered rucksack all the very best. Business class lounges were made available without a murmur of discontent and even discounts were negotiable in some of the already cheap duty-free shops.

There are also strange contrasts in disaster relief. In the earthquake zone lay thousands of helpless individuals in terrible suffering. Elsewhere in the world meanwhile, were many thousands of aid workers, some excited to fever pitch, who had now been given the chance to visit and to help. One man's misery was another's adventure. It was strange, almost unkind, but a reality.

Seat 28A on flight 129 was manifestly too small for anyone other than a midget. I am more than six foot one in old English. As the Boeing 777's door thumped to a close, I signalled the stewardess, seeking permission to change my seat to one with more legroom nearby. She smiled and nodded, so I quickly moved to an adjacent seat, this time with plenty of space. Briefly I stretched out my legs in enjoyment but rapidly my pleasure turned to despair. I should have checked my next-door-neighbours. To my front sat a six-year-old boy who cried throughout the eight-hour flight while behind me an elderly lady continually vomited. All credit to the stewardess, who spent much of the journey piling tissues onto the pools of dribble and vomit that surrounded me. I looked longingly at Seat 28A on several occasions during the flight. The moment I had left, a sleeping First Officer had immediately filled it. There was no going back for me.

*   *   *

Chapter 4

I See Helicopters

What is it about baggage reclaim areas? Does the world suffer from the same problem as me? My bag is always the last to appear or so it certainly feels.

That morning, at 6 am Islamabad time and eleven days after the earthquake, I felt lonely as I watched my fellow passengers stride purposefully forward to collect their baggage. One by one they disappeared towards the Arrivals Hall, luggage in tow, leaving me abandoned. My battered, black, rugged North Face bag, filled to the brim with aid supplies, was the last item to appear. By then I had already eyed up the lost baggage counter. Some might regard it as unusual, but that morning I could be found talking to my North Face bag as if it were a long-lost friend.

Once through Customs I emerged into the broad Arrivals Hall. It was humming with activity. People scattered here and there, disaster relief teams dotted about wherever I looked. Most were wearing smartly pressed uniforms and many were posing for team photographs. Power dressing was de rigueur and disaster tourism had arrived. Immediately to my left was a Korean Rescue Team in their bright orange overalls while to my right were the dark blue uniforms of the Bomberos Unidos from Spain. My already stained, white T-shirt and equally tatty beige climbing trousers could not compete. I lowered my head and scurried quickly away to one corner of the hall. Anyway, I was alone and needed to stand away from the crowd. Once in my corner I scanned the area for any sign of welcome. I saw nothing. No sign, no flag, no waving hand. No one had come to meet me.

Merlin understood these situations and provided all its workers with a Constant Companion. This was a small sheet of paper, prepared in London, which carried the contact details of anyone and everyone involved in a disaster relief programme. A Constant Companion is guarded to the death. It is as valuable as a passport. Mine was hidden carefully in the back of my tiny black notebook, and was an aide memoire that I carried with me everywhere.

The Constant Companion suggested I should telephone someone called Paquito, Merlin's logistician in Islamabad. In fact the moment I pressed the call button on my mobile I saw a small-framed, balding individual weave his way rapidly between the numerous aid teams. He headed in my direction, occasionally glancing at a photograph held in one hand, then at me, then back to the photograph. I smiled. This was just like the security guard at Pakistan's High Commission in London. Then, stopping barely a yard in front of me, the new arrival gave a broad smile on his weathered face and extended a calloused hand in welcome. I shook it firmly and noticed the strong grip in return.

'I'm Paquito. You Richard?' The accent was Spanish.

'Yep.'

'It's good. You look just like your photo. Normally they do not. Anyway let's go.'

With that, Paquito turned rapidly on his heel and headed back towards the exit door on the far side of the Arrivals Hall. I scurried after him, my North Face bag slung awkwardly across my shoulder.

Despite his brief introduction, Paquito turned out to be very talkative. Logisticians are a key part of any aid programme. They ensure a team is kept supplied, watered and fed. They bargain with locals to win the best price, they book air tickets, they speak multiple languages, and order transport. In fact, logisticians do almost everything. Without a decent logistician, an aid programme is destined to fail.

Being in his fifties, Paquito had seen much of the world. By the time he had delivered me in his battered minibus to the tiny Islamabad guesthouse, I knew most of his life story. Three wives, each from a different country, seven children and a mother who was desperately ill in Madrid. Paquito had seen it all and done it all, or so it appeared. It is the way of things in disasters. Hearts are poured out to complete strangers in seconds. It is almost a confessional. I was to learn that Paquito was a good, hard-working guy, with his heart in the right place, and impossible to fluster.

The guesthouse had clearly taken its fair share of earthquake damage, despite the epicentre being 150 kilometres away. Its rough, cream-painted concrete walls carried numerous cracks. Shattered glass lay on the ground and, as I walked into a gloomy reception area, it was clear that mains electricity was nowhere to be found. Somewhere in the distance I could hear the chug of a diesel generator, the likely source of power of the flickering lamp to one end of the mica-topped reception desk. A bored clerk, a man in his mid-thirties, carefully wrote longhand every detail about me from my passport into a massive ledger. He tried six different ballpoint pens before finding a seventh with sufficient ink to complete his task. When it came to red tape and record keeping, Pakistan was hard to beat.

The guesthouse was Merlin's headquarters. From there everything was planned subject, of course, to London's approval. As I unpacked my North Face bag into the tiny wood-wormed chest of drawers in my equally tiny first floor room, I felt excited. I could not imagine I would be in Islamabad for long. Every newspaper headline I had seen en route, every bulletin I had heard or viewed, said the same thing. Kashmir was in big trouble; aid was taking forever to reach it, while casualties and corpses were still everywhere to be found. I was sure Merlin would want me in the mountains almost the moment I had arrived and I was looking forward to the opportunity to start. Inside I had a real feeling of urgency. Every second counted.

My pre-mission briefing had told me to report to a Dorotea, head of station in Islamabad and Swedish by birth. I had not been told her surname. 'Dorotea will tell you everything you need to know,' London had advised. So the moment I had unpacked I left my room and headed down the single flight of stairs to seek out Dorotea. It did not take me long.

To one side of the reception was a large open-plan lounge area that had been converted to an office. Beyond were two French windows that led to a small walled garden. Incongruously for a disaster zone, the garden appeared well tended. A white board, covered in illegible red handwriting, stood awkwardly on a tall easel to one side of the lounge area. Nearby, on one wall hung several long sheets of white paper, A4 in size and secured end to end with gaffer tape, carrying the lists of equipment that I imagined had been ordered by Paquito. There were two broad mica tables positioned end to end across the centre of the lounge, their surfaces almost invisible due to the papers scattered over them. Meanwhile around the table were at least eight plastic chairs, some slid in and some slid out, evidence of at least one recent meeting. A blank, unpowered computer, covered by a thin layer of white dust stood neglected in one corner. But I was not alone. Along the badly painted wall to my right was a further, single mica table. At it sat two people, one male, one female. Precariously perched on their plastic chairs, they were fully immersed in each other. Fully immersed and arguing.

'I'm surprised you are not looking at your messages,' said the female in a schoolmarm-type voice.

'That's because I am too bloody busy doing more important things,' came the muttered, irritated, male reply.

For a moment I hesitated. I did not wish to intervene. It was clearly tense and I had arrived at precisely the wrong time. It was as I vacillated that the arguers turned, realising they were no longer alone. Both looked surprised. The schoolmarm spoke first. I could see the residual fire burning in her brown eyes.

'Hello! And you are...?'

'Richard Villar. I've just arrived from London.'

The schoolmarm forced a smile. 'Ah yes, the surgeon,' she said, as if I was an incidental. 'I'm Dorotea, head of station. Welcome.'

Her companion reached across the table to shake my hand. 'Hi,' came the confident tone. 'I'm Mike.'

Mike, I was soon to learn, was a classic in disaster relief and just what was needed when trouble appeared. A qualified doctor, he was a man both of action and decision, a colleague who was trustworthy to the hilt. If you sought someone for a sensible view when times were rough, you looked no further than Mike. He was at his best when the rest of the world was struggling. Yet such a character could create problems too, as it did not always sit comfortably alongside a more traditional aid worker's approach.

There are two types of aid worker in my view. There are those who defer to authority for all decisions and will not take risks. They are most happy in peaceful times. This was the category for Dorotea.

Then there are aid workers who are happy to make decisions independently and who sometimes know they must take risks. In the aftermath of a disaster this latter category is most use and was exemplified by Mike. Mike believed, as did I, that there was one thing worse than making the wrong decision. That was to make no decision at all. I could see instantly why there might be friction between Dorotea and Mike and why, when I had arrived, they had been arguing.

Mike, with a local Pakistani colleague Akram, had just returned from a brief assessment trip to the Neelum Valley. This was a 206-kilometre rift that passed north from the city of Muzaffarabad, then headed east to cross the Line of Control between Pakistan and India. From the Neelum Valley came several smaller valley offshoots, headed north and south.

Mike and Akram had focussed on a southerly offshoot, the Panjkot Valley, immediately beside the Line of Control. There, building destruction had been total and the valley's limited health facilities had also been completely destroyed. The Pakistani Army was there in force, as might be expected in a war zone. This was an extremely dangerous area for many reasons, the earthquake being but one. Sanitation was non-existent and ruptured supply pipes meant that villagers had to walk for one hour to find water. The assessment had estimated that there were 5,000 injured in the one small area of the Panjkot Valley and that 2,000 were in need of urgent surgical attention. The case for a field hospital on site was indisputable. Mike and Akram's final report, completed barely forty-eight hours earlier, was the reason I was there.

I turned to Dorotea. 'I need to check the equipment for the field hospital. Where would I find that?' I asked.

'You can't,' Dorotea replied.

'Can't?'

Mike intervened. 'It's not here yet,' he said.

'Not here? Why not?'

I saw Dorotea's eyes lower to the ground as if to study the pattern on the guesthouse's carpet. She remained silent. Mike continued.

'I wish I could say this hasn't happened before. Part of the hospital is at the Pakistan-India border and part is in Dubai. None of it is here yet.'

'Not here?' I asked incredulously. 'What am I supposed to do?'

'Exactly,' replied Mike. 'Welcome to disaster relief.'

Naïve I may have been but I felt it was reasonable the field hospital should have been in Pakistan. What was the purpose of summoning a surgeon if there was nowhere for him to work? Field hospitals are huge affairs. Multiple tents, lorry loads of equipment and boxes, water supplies, anaesthetic machines, wards, operating theatres, X-Ray and even a mortuary. They do not grow on trees and must be assembled from multiple sources, often over many weeks and months. This needs to be done well ahead of time. It was clear from the media reports alone, added to Mike and Akram's assessment, that we did not have weeks and months available. People were dying as we spoke.

There was also the problem of access. The earthquake area was inaccessible by road. The choices were by helicopter or on foot. That meant helicopter. Helicopter? I had not flown in one since my time in the Army. During the Falklands War I had lost more than twenty friends when a Sea King had plummeted into the sea during an inter-ship transfer. Predictably, I had taken against helicopters and had vowed I would never fly in one again.

Four years earlier, I had visited a fortune-teller during a friend's stag weekend near London. Shut away in a darkened room down one end of a long corridor, the fortune-teller, a girl with misaligned eyes, had taken my watch and studied it intently for several minutes. It was, she had said, to develop a feel about me. The only feeling I had experienced was an urgent need of a chaperone.

After a lengthy silence, the fortune-teller had leaned back in her chair, looked up at the ceiling, and declared, 'I see helicopters.'

I had shaken my head in disbelief. 'Not a hope,' I had said.

Yet the fortune-teller had insisted, repeating herself several times. 'I see helicopters, I see helicopters, I see helicopters.'

Nothing happened over the following four years, I thought she had been making it all up and forgot all about her. Then Kashmir appeared. It was clear that the only sensible way to travel was by helicopter. Nothing else would do. If Panjkot was to be my location, and it seemed that was the case, helicopters would once more form a major part of my life. I made a mental note to return to the fortune-teller one day and tell her. Helicopters it would have to be.

* * *

Chapter 5

Meetings, More Meetings

The Pakistan Institute of Medical Sciences, PIMS, was frantically busy the next morning. Patients awaiting treatment lined the corridors, helicopters came and went, while new wards had opened up in passageways and outpatient clinics, such was the pressure of work.

I followed Dorotea as she made her way through the melee to the Health Emergency Operation Centre, deep inside the 20-year-old PIMS building. She had insisted we attend one of the emergency planning meetings held there each day. The Institute, a large teaching hospital, acted as a focal administration point for the Kashmir relief programme as well as a major casualty treatment centre for those who had been evacuated from the mountains.

As a new boy, I had no idea what to expect, so sat silently to one corner at the back in yet another uncomfortable plastic chair. Dorotea sat beside me, pencil and notebook poised. I looked around. There were more than fifty delegates present in the cramped room. They represented a large number of organisations; United States Navy, United Nations Humanitarian Aid Service, World Health Organisation, United Nations, Qatar Red Crescent, refugee organisations, rehabilitation bodies, children's charities and many others. Everyone appeared the same, pencils and notebooks at the ready, one leg crossed over the other, gazing intently forward. We waited for the first utterance from the row of five Pakistani officials - one was the Minister of Health - sitting behind a table at the front of the room.

My mind wandered as we waited. That morning Mike and I had happened across each other en route to the guesthouse breakfast 'What's this about, Mike?' I had asked. 'Why a meeting? Why are we not out there in the mountains? Isn't that why we are here?'

Mike had laughed openly. 'That's all this lot does,' he had declared. 'Every disaster is the same. Meet and talk, meet and talk. They're good at it. But don't let them see a patient. They wouldn't have a clue what to do…whoops…quiet!' His voice had died rapidly to a whisper as Dorotea brushed past us.

At PIMS I was about to lean across to Dorotea to ask when we would be headed to the epicentre when a deep, resounding voice stopped me. 'Quiet, please!' it said. I looked towards the table, where one of the Pakistani officials was now on his feet. He was a tall, broad individual, well dressed in dark grey suit, waistcoat and light grey tie. He looked as if he had just returned from a wedding. 'I have an announcement. Please stand,' he continued.

Obediently, the entire audience rose to its feet. There was not a whisper of discontent. No one, other than the official, spoke.

'I regret to announce the deaths of two aid workers yesterday, both decapitated by the rear rotor blade of their helicopter. Silence in their memory, please.'

For two minutes the audience remained motionless. Everyone was deep in thought. Delivering aid was a dangerous activity and becoming more so by the year. Somewhere in the world one aid worker was killed every week and three times as many injured. One was kidnapped every fortnight. The decapitated individuals highlighted the problem. However noble the act of providing aid, however well meaning the motive, some folk never made it home.

'Thank you,' boomed the official at the end of the two-minute period. 'Please be seated.' Then, one by one, his colleagues stood and delivered their own disaster update.

The meeting was not happy listening. The body count was climbing by the day and was now over 55,000. The number of homeless had reached more than three million and the frequency of amputations was rising. More amputations meant a greater need for rehabilitation facilities as well as artificial limbs. Meanwhile there was a desperate shortage of anti-tetanus vaccine, bird 'flu had appeared and the number of available helicopters to airlift supplies was ludicrously small. It was approaching two weeks after the tremor and the United Kingdom, for one, had no helicopter presence in Kashmir at all. The situation was critical and becoming worse rather than better.

As the officials spoke, each taking his turn, the number of attendees gradually swelled. People shuffled in from the sides and back of the room. Every spare chair had an aid worker on it, in some instances two. The late arrivals sat on the floor, or half knelt or crouched uncomfortably, wherever they could find space. There was barely room to breathe.

I glanced towards Dorotea and saw that her notebook remained empty; she had not written a word. I wondered why, although guessed she, too, was feeling overwhelmed by the enormity of the project. She sensed my glance and, almost guiltily, covered the small book with the palm of her hand.

Hastily, I looked towards the front table once again, catching the tail end of the final official's report.

'... made 25,000 hospital beds available. Finally, the Belgian hospital will be leaving shortly.' Then the official sat down.

Leaving? Why were agencies leaving at this critical stage? Then I realised. The official had not meant a Belgian hospital but B–FAST, the Belgian First Aid and Support Team. They act so quickly that if you blink you can miss them. The earthquake had occurred on the 8th October, B–FAST had been mobilised on the 9th and was at work in Pakistan by the 12th. They had already treated 2,000 earthquake victims, twenty-seven per cent of whom had been under the age of 12 years. They had finished and were headed home. It was now the 19th and we had not even started.

'What do you think?' asked Dorotea as we drove back to the guesthouse. There was no confidence in her eyes at all. I had learned something of her background from both Mike and Paquito. Dorotea had plenty of experience in delivering aid to remote regions but never in the face of on–going conflict or disaster. A different mentality is needed for such things. Dorotea did not have that. She was best suited to a gentle, safe environment where everything could be planned months ahead. Delivering aid to a remote mountainside at an earthquake epicentre 150 kilometres away appeared outside her comfort zone. While at her meetings, Dorotea was content. At the disaster front line she was distinctly uneasy.

'There's much work to do,' I replied. 'Tomorrow I should go to Panjkot.'

'But the hospital hasn't arrived. We have nothing to offer even if we can reach the mountains.'

'That doesn't matter. We have ourselves and we have the will. Even if we cannot help medically, we can surely help with reconstruction.'

Dorotea shook her head. 'No,' she said, her thin lips now tightly pursed. 'As station director I cannot allow that. We should discuss it with the Pakistanis at tomorrow's meeting.'

At that moment I wanted to turn, grab her by the neck and shake her. Did she really mean another meeting? Did she not realise how many casualties were dying while we pondered, reflected and talked? Dorotea was out of her depth and she knew it. Yet as station director it was not a fault she could confess.

Back at the guesthouse I was saddened to learn that Mike had returned to England, his job now done. In my room's pigeonhole behind the reception desk were some papers, my personal copy of Mike's report. On the front page, written in large capitals and a clearly confident hand, was a brief message. 'Go for it Richard! Give 'em hell!' it said.

So give 'em hell I would.

That evening, when the Merlin staff were relaxed and chatting, most lounging casually in the few armchairs spread randomly around the lounge area, I talked to each one individually. Dorotea had not appeared. To my surprise, I soon realised that I was not alone. Paquito was the first to confirm my views.

'Good day?' he asked.

'Interesting,' I replied. 'But shouldn't we be out there?'

'You should.'

'Then why aren't we?'

'No one will make a decision.'

'Then let me,' I declared, a mischievous smile on my face. 'Mr Paquito, please find me a helicopter and then let's go!'

Paquito looked at me quizzically with a deeply furrowed brow. Is this man serious I could see him thinking? What he did next I did not expect. After a brief hesitation he rose rapidly to his feet. His furrows had totally disappeared. Then he spoke, emphasising his words by hand in a classically Hispanic way. 'You're right!' he cried. 'Let's do it! Dr Richard, one helicopter coming your way!'

With that Paquito had gone, striding purposefully through the guesthouse doors. Seconds later I heard the chug of his diesel engine as he headed away towards the airport.

It was as if Paquito's outburst had lit a fuse leading to a huge firecracker. Suddenly, everyone was saying the same thing.

'You're right.'

'I agree.'

'Let's go now.'

'We're no use here.'

Each Merlin member had a similar view. The group's frustration was palpable. I could touch it, feel it, smell it; I could almost see it. The irritation was collective and real.

One of the support staff, Nadia, who would never normally go into the field, even volunteered to help. 'Can I come with you when you go?' she asked.

So intent were we on the problem, so immersed in our discussion, that no one noticed the shadowy figure of Dorotea standing quite still by a concrete column immediately behind. I sensed rather than saw her, and then I turned.

'Hello,' I said, feeling instantly guilty.

I was about to explain, half expecting to be sent home the following day. Yet Dorotea had clearly heard every word. There was no need for me to speak. She said nothing, turned on her heel and walked slowly down the corridor towards her room. Her rounded shoulders and hanging head said all. It was as she had turned that I saw the tiny tear well gently in the inner corner of one eye. I wanted to go after her, to apologise for my insubordination, but before I could rise fully to my feet she had disappeared.

*   *   *

Chapter 6

Panjkot Valley

It was a new day and with it came a new atmosphere. For the Merlin staff in Islamabad change and optimism were now in the air. There was a spring to everyone's step, although by 10 am Dorotea still had not appeared. It was now twelve days after the earthquake, far too late already, but nevertheless time to do business.

Privately I was worried. We had no transport and no medical supplies. All I had was a first aid kit, perhaps good for a few blisters and an ingrowing toenail, but no use for treating major casualties. Meanwhile the hospital was still en route from multiple locations. Even Paquito could not say where it was. London had also advised that a surgical team would be arriving imminently although they could not say when. So far there was nowhere to put the team members, no equipment to use and no means of transporting them to the mountains. I knew well what each member would have sacrificed at home to make the journey to Pakistan possible. One look at how little had been done in time for their arrival and I would not be surprised to see them turn around and return to the United Kingdom immediately.

My first stop that morning was the United Nations Air Cell, a prison-like name to describe a small office, with an even smaller desk, from which the entire helicopter support operation was run. Behind the miniscule desk sat Rafael, a Spaniard drafted in for the task. At that moment, Rafael was the most powerful man in Pakistan, with control of everything that happened in the mountains, or elsewhere. You did not upset Rafael. You were doomed if you did so. It helped that Paquito was Spanish.

Rafael had very few helicopters available of the right sort. The United Kingdom had promised two Chinooks, while a number of other countries had pledged the same. However, a Chinook is big and heavy – when empty it weighs ten tons - so cannot land in muddy fields. It also has a huge downdraft and can easily blow over rickety, half-collapsed wooden buildings. It can totally destroy tents. Smaller helicopters would be needed and there were very few of those.

The trick to guarantee helicopter space was to keep Rafael sweet. He was snowed under with work. Within minutes of entering the Air Cell, I could see the impossibilities of his role. Hanging precariously on one wall was the helicopter tasking whiteboard. The multiple smudged red entries covering its surface showed the problem instantly. Every helicopter was booked for several days to come. It was impossible for Rafael to satisfy all demands with the handful of helicopters available to him. Aware of this, the Pakistan Government had already issued an announcement to earthquake survivors to make their own way down the mountains to the nearest town in order to seek help. There was no way of knowing whether this announcement had been heard.

'*¡Hola! Buenos días!* Hello! Good morning!' I said that day as I entered Rafael's tiny kingdom. My knowledge of Spanish had already nearly reached its limit. Paquito came to my rescue. For several minutes the two Spaniards talked at pace in their own tongue. I could tell they were talking of politics and women, nothing of disaster. Then Rafael turned to me.

'You want a helicopter?'

'Yes, please. Sorry...umm...*por favor.*' How I wished I had been properly able to speak Spanish at that moment. Several years earlier I had taken Spanish lessons back home. Unfortunately, my tutor had been in the middle of a particularly messy divorce, so the only vocabulary I had learned were words such as custody, affidavit and subpoena. I knew nothing of the vocabulary of disaster.

Rafael grinned. 'English is better. OK?'

'OK'. I smiled and could see Paquito smile, too.

'What is available?' I asked. 'We need to leave today. Tomorrow by the latest.'

Rafael shook his head. 'That will not be possible. Look, I have nothing for the next five days.' He indicated the whiteboard almost with contempt.

'Nothing at all?'

'Nothing.'

I was about to turn, to say I would be back, when I noticed the spindly writing at the upper left corner of the whiteboard. It was in black rather than the usual red and had clearly been written in a different hand. 'What's that?' I asked, pointing to the illegible scrawl.

Rafael hesitated and then frowned. 'I don't know,' he said, peering closer at the black scrawl. 'I didn't write that. Wait a minute…yes, of course. That's it!'

'That's what?'

'One of those can be yours,' he said. 'Look closely at the writing. It says Mi-8. I had forgotten. We have two Mi-8s expected from the Ukraine at any moment. You can take one.'

I could barely restrain myself. In two short strides I had reached Rafael and placed a hand gently on each of his shoulders. I looked into his startled eyes. '*Muchas gracias mi amigo*. Thank you very much my friend,' I said, sincerity in my tone. 'This is excellent. Is a mid-day departure OK?'

'Mid-day is fine.'

The Mi-8 was the world's most-produced helicopter and had been manufactured by Russia for more than fifty years. It had an incredible track record. Widely used during the various Balkan conflicts it was a highly adaptable machine. It was even employed to drop radiation-absorbing materials into the Chernobyl reactor in 1986. Many Mi-8 carcasses, and their pilots too, lay in the machines graveyard near Chernobyl as a result. The Mi-8 was just what was needed for the Kashmir earthquake programme. Even better, its Russian aircrew were ex-military, having seen service in Afghanistan, so could fly higher, sometimes lower, frequently faster, than almost any pilot in the business. The Mi-8s were gold dust, as were the men who flew them. We had fallen on our feet.

At least I thought we had until I was walking through the front doors of the guesthouse thirty minutes later, Paquito immediately behind. We were both in very high spirits and desperate to share the good news with our colleagues. Merlin was on its way and the mountains beckoned.

Then my mobile rang. I reached into the military-style thigh pocket of my beige trousers and retrieved the device. I answered, my mind still on how best I should phrase the announcement to the staff as well as how to tell Dorotea. I recognised Rafael's voice immediately.

'I have a problem,' he said. 'You have a problem.'

I stopped in my tracks instantly. I half guessed what was to follow. 'Tell me.'

'The Mi-8 crews are being held at the Afghanistan-Pakistan border. There is no chance of a sortie today.'

I felt instantly depressed. 'When will they be released?' I inquired.

'No idea. I will ring you the moment I receive news.' Then the line went dead.

This situation was not good. The frontier between Afghanistan and Pakistan was a security nightmare. To be stopped there could mean a delay of days or weeks. Yet I had to accept it. There was no alternative. Unfortunately, without a helicopter, Merlin might as well pack and go home. This is so often the pattern of disaster relief. You fluctuate between bliss and despair in seconds.

Paquito and I decided not to tell the staff full details of what had happened. It seemed easier that way. 'The omens are reasonable,' I announced to the small group seated around the conference table, 'but they are not guaranteed.' Many heads nodded as they returned to their discussions about sanitation, water, vaccinations, and the multiple other items that support a disaster relief project. I noted that Dorotea was still nowhere to be seen.

For the rest of the day I moped. I was on the verge of real despair. I had stepped out of line to negotiate transport and Dorotea had gone to ground as a result. So much depended on Rafael and what he would next tell me. There was little else to be done. The entire project hinged on an ability to reach the mountain valleys of Kashmir quickly. To go overland would take a month.

When my mobile rang a second time, at approximately 4 pm that day, I almost dropped the thing in my haste to respond.

'Yes?' I snapped, instantly regretting my tone. My hand was trembling, my forehead was sweaty and I felt very nauseated.

'Doctor, it is me. Rafael. You OK?'

'No. I'm terrified of what you are going to say.'

'No worry,' came the accented reply. 'All OK. The helicopters are through. Be here at 6 am tomorrow.'

'Rafael, you're a star.'

From that moment events moved rapidly. While I had been moping, Paquito had been far from depressed. He had been in overdrive. Out and about in deepest Islamabad, he had purchased a huge quantity of medical supplies. He also proudly announced that some tarpaulins had arrived from the United Kingdom. These were being rapidly packed by airport staff into individual bundles, each bundle containing twenty bright blue tarpaulins. At least we now had something to offer the injured. One glance at Paquito's logistics board, however, showed how much equipment was still outstanding. He was waiting for nineteen individual equipment deliveries, from nineteen different locations, and only two had arrived.

The remaining deliveries included tents, biscuits, blankets, medical kit, stretchers, generators, hospital beds, and so much more. We were still a long way short of creating a full field hospital.

The next morning, the 21st October and day thirteen after the earthquake, I awoke early. Actually, I am not sure I woke up at all. I had been awake most of the night, my mind whirling furiously. What if…? What about…? Have I…? Imagine…?

Consequently, I am unsure who sounded the grumpiest when I received my 4 am alarm call, the guesthouse receptionist or me. Once I had stumbled down to the still-darkened reception area, it seemed best that we both apologised to each other for our discourtesy. We did, and I received a free cup of coffee as a result plus the life story of the receptionist. I regretted having to cut him short, my mind on the tasks ahead, as he had such an interesting tale to tell. Political intrigue, secret police, missing family, torture, and a long and arduous walk across the mountains from persecution by a distant relative.

To see the helicopter parked to one side of the airport runway that morning was truly wonderful. Although the dawn was inexplicably cold and slightly damp, the ancient white Mi-8 was the clear focus of attention. Its sagging rotors, chipped and dented bodywork clearly in need of a clean, showed it to be a workhorse of the sky. Its two crew, pilot and navigator-cum-loadmaster, were charmers. Although the Russians were outwardly unfit, overweight and balding, they were most definitely up for the task ahead. Both smiled widely as I approached and immediately gave me the title of Dr Richard. For some reason no one ever uses my surname in the field. I glanced through the rear door of the Mi-8 to see an empty vodka bottle and five beer cans rolling haplessly around the helicopter's cargo area. I laughed and pointed at them, turning to the pilot and his colleague as I did so.

'Yours?' I queried.

'Of course, Dr Richard,' said the pilot. 'We are Russians. Our country's success depends on the quality of its vodka.'

'*Davai*. Let's go,' I said using the one of the few Russian words I knew.

'Hey! You speak Russian?' asked the pilot.

I smiled and shook my head furiously in reply. Anyway, right then, language was the last thing on my mind. I was about to fly to an earthquake epicentre in an ancient Ukrainian helicopter piloted by two alcoholic and overweight Russians. Yet somehow that did not worry me. Somehow the crew exuded trust.

That first flight, which lurched precariously past the seemingly limitless peaks of Kashmir, was humbling. Muzaffarabad, with a population of about 750,000 souls, was at least half destroyed. Most of the official buildings and many of the bridges had been decimated. The city was on the banks of the Jhelum and Neelum Rivers and it was along the Neelum River that we flew.

I am no geologist but some of the information that had filtered through to Islamabad became clearer as we headed north and then east towards Panjkot. Geologically, northern India is being thrust under the Himalayas and, as this happens, so the mountains increase slowly in height. Earthquakes like Kashmir in 2005 were how the Himalayas originally formed. Kashmir was unusual as it was a surface rupture, the first ever reported in the Himalayan range. The rupture extended for seventy-five kilometres, caused 3,000 individual landslides and shifted the ground more than sixteen feet.

From the air it was impossible to miss the geological and humanitarian tragedy unfolding below. At one point I saw a massive, one-kilometre length of mountainside that had subsided onto part of a city beneath it. Many tens of thousands of people died, not as a result of the initial earthquake, but from the landslides that followed. Nor could I ignore the huge number of tents now beginning to take shape in an area immediately outside Muzaffarabad, clear evidence of a refugee crisis in progress. The power of Mother Nature when she acts is indescribable, uncontrollable, and puts tiny mankind into perspective.

Flying in a Mi-8 as a passenger is a noisy experience. With me were Paquito, Akram and Nadia. Paquito because he was the only one who understood the equipment he had ordered; Akram, because he had been in Panjkot before as part of the assessment with Mike; and Nadia because, quite simply, she had asked to go. The least she could do, I thought, was to act as my assistant. In flight, we were shaken about furiously and, although the cargo compartment was padded, the soundproofing was negligible. Seat belts and take-off drills were not a feature of disaster-relief helicopter flights so it was possible to move about the compartment whatever was happening. Turbulence was constant and it was easy to end up in a heap somewhere in the far corner. I landed on Akram's lap on three separate occasions. Nor was this the time to turn off mobile telephones; mostly they had no reception anyway. It was certainly not an opportunity to watch a Miss World lookalike don a flimsy, orange lifejacket in the interests of in-flight safety.

To my left, and separating me from the cockpit, was a large pile of Paquito's blue tarpaulins, several boxes of water and some rudimentary medical kit packed loosely into a small cardboard box. Although the official medical supplies had not arrived, at least we could offer something to the people of Panjkot.

My original intention had been to land at Nauseri, a village to the west of Panjkot. Mike and Akram had visited the area and felt this would be a suitable location from which to run a relief programme. Unfortunately, although Nauseri had a military helipad, perfect for the delivery of supplies, a Korean aid and rescue team had already set up shop. There would be no room for two.

Forty-five minutes after take-off, the Mi-8 turned hard right, banking steeply, and entered the Panjkot Valley. At any other time the area would have been a perfect holiday destination. Around me were the rugged outlines of irregular tree-covered mountain ridges, perfectly farmed and contoured terraced fields, and light blue water in the river below with the occasional bubbly turbulence of rapids. Small communities of timber-framed houses were dotted haphazardly around, sometimes in ones and twos, occasionally in twenties or more. Tragically, every house had been destroyed. There was not one standing, wherever I looked.

As the Mi-8 levelled out from its steep banking turn I shouted across to Akram, trying hard to make myself heard above the din of the rotors. 'Akram! Akram!' I yelled.

Akram leaned towards me, frowned slightly and raised his eyebrows, as if to say 'Yes?'

'Where shall we put down?' I shouted. 'Where was it you visited with Mike?' I had already given Mike's co-ordinates for Panjkot to the helicopter pilot, but they were only approximate readings taken from Mike's satellite telephone.

Akram turned to look through the opaque and dirty helicopter window behind him. Resting his head against it while cupping his hands around his eyes to reduce reflection, I saw him search the ground below. He frowned, then squinted, frowned, squinted, frowned and squinted once more. I could tell he was having difficulties. He found it hard to identify from the air what he had seen earlier from the ground. This is a skill that pilots develop over many years. It does not come naturally.

After several minutes, Akram turned back towards me, frustrated by his struggles. 'I don't know!' he shouted. 'I can't tell! It all looks different!'

I nodded. There was no purpose in being angry, as I fully understood Akram's dilemma. I raised my hand in friendship towards him, as if to say 'No problem', and then rose unsteadily to my feet. I leaned over the large pile of tarpaulins, put my head through the open cockpit door and shouted to the rear views of the pilot and his companion.

'Where can we land?' I shouted. 'Where are we now?'

The navigator-cum-loadmaster was sitting to the pilot's left, a tatty aerial map spread across his knees. Briefly, he half turned towards me, raised his hand to acknowledge he had heard, and then adopted the same attitude as Akram, gazing intently through the Mi-8's cockpit window, a glare-protective hand to his forehead. It did not take him long to glance back over his shoulder, smile and place a stubby forefinger on the map. I looked closely. The Russian was pointing at a large letter 'H' immediately beside the village of Panjkot. The letter 'H' is map shorthand for a helicopter-landing site.

I looked through the cockpit window. Beneath us I could see a white letter 'H' emblazoned on the ground, matching that shown on the map. That was good. What was not so good was that at many other locations on the mountainside I could also see the letter 'H'. There were at least twenty. Beside each emblazoned 'H' stood groups of local people waving. Sometimes the groups were small, maybe only two or three individuals. Sometimes they were larger, twenty, thirty, perhaps more. They were waving anything they could find; blankets, a brightly coloured plastic bag and, at one location, even an old pink dress. Wherever I looked I could see groups of locals trying to attract our attention.

It was impossible to tell which 'H' matched the location found by Mike and Akram during their assessment. The survivors had rapidly realised that the only way of receiving help was to make it possible for a helicopter to land near their property, or at least that portion the earthquake had allowed them to keep.

I had no idea what to do. Wherever we landed, someone would be ignored. The flying time between the various emblazoned landing sites may have been only seconds but walking between them could take the best part of a day. This was mountainous territory, landslides were everywhere and regular pathways had been destroyed. There was no hope of any casualty making it on foot to a central location, unless their injuries were minor. Aid would have to be taken to them.

Instantly I could see the entire logistic nightmare of the Kashmir relief programme spread before me. Earlier I had been offered the free services of a United Kingdom Mountain Rescue Team, but had refused them because I had been uncertain how such individuals might have helped. Now I regretted my decision. The Kashmir people are a mountain people. To help them fully you need to be a mountain person, too.

In my hesitation, the decision of where to land was made for me by the pilot. Wind direction and ground conditions were the determining factors. For many of the impromptu landing sites the survivors had not allowed for nearby trees or the slope of the mountainside. When landing a helicopter, a pilot requires as much room as possible for clearance of his main and tail rotor blades. Flat surfaces, or slightly uphill ones are acceptable. Downhill inclines court disaster.

With a rackety clatter from the Mi-8, the Russian pilot made his final approach. He was totally within his comfort zone and clearly happy to land anywhere. As we descended towards the large flat expanse surrounding the chosen letter 'H', I guessed this was the official Panjkot landing site anyway. It had certainly been expertly prepared.

The nearby wooden houses, or what was left of them, became more obvious as we hovered several hundred feet above the ground. Immediately to one side of the landing site was a concertinaed property, its now twisted and tortured corrugated iron roof lying helplessly to one side. Around the collapsed building stood a crowd of at least 200 locals. Every single one was waving frantically at us.

The Mi-8 descended slowly, almost inch by inch, the pilot in total control. Then, as we came nearer, the downdraft from the main rotors hit the ground. Suddenly, frighteningly, dust and dirt whipped up and the corrugated iron roof began to lift, its sharp edges threatening all those around. I saw the group scatter in every direction. The Panjkot people had seen the danger and were now running for their lives.

'*Nyet!* No!' I shouted.

But I need not have worried. The pilot had seen it, too. Gradually he moved the Mi-8 across the sky, watching the corrugated roof carefully as he did so. As the helicopter slid sideways, so the thrashing of the corrugated iron reduced until it gave barely a twitch. Then, with seamless professionalism, the pilot lowered his charge to the ground, cut the engines and we were there, the first Mi-8 to reach Panjkot since the disaster.

*   *   *

Chapter 7

Manohar

As a helicopter lands, there is a brief period when your blood pressure settles, in tandem with the steady drop in engine tone. It is a wonderful feeling and so pleasant when the engine stops. The rotors, which have for so long been a blurred outline above, now become heavy blades alongside as they dangle towards the ground. For the pilot and his colleague, there was still much to do after landing. In particular, the compacted-earth landing surface looked as if it might struggle under the weight of a fully laden helicopter. The pilot was first out, making certain his 12,000-kilogramme Mi-8 did not sink too far into the ground.

He had clearly chosen the correct landing site, as in less than a minute a smartly uniformed military officer, three pips on his epaulettes, was first to the helicopter's now open side door.

'Welcome to Panjkot gentlemen…and lady,' said the smiling face as he belatedly identified Nadia who was sitting behind the massive pile of tarpaulins. 'I am Captain Mungavin, Pakistan Army. Who is in charge?'

There was silence. Who was in charge? I had no idea. The Armed Services have a clear rank structure. Everybody knows who reports to whom. Civilian aid organisations are different. There is a theoretical structure that does not always function perfectly in the field. Merlin considered Dorotea to be the chief, so everyone should have reported to her. Unfortunately, Dorotea had gone to ground and was nowhere to be found. She certainly was not on board the Mi-8.

I saw Captain Mungavin's eyes dart between us. 'Surely one of you must be in charge?' he queried.

'He is,' said Paquito, pointing in my direction.

'Him,' added Akram, again pointing towards me, closely followed by Nadia who did the same.

Awkwardly, I rose to my feet within the tight confines of the Mi-8's cargo area, reached across and shook the officer's hand through the open side door. Then, one by one, we stepped into the Panjkot sunlight. It was a hot, clear mountain day. Fifty metres away, and surrounding the landing site, was a large throng of local people, at some points up to five deep. These were the survivors. Many were injured. Some were standing, some were sitting, and at least twenty were lying on makeshift stretchers. Most were men, or children. There were few women to be seen. I had no idea why.

There are two ways in and out of a Mi-8. There is a side door on the left, generally used by passengers and crew, and a broad rear door, or tailgate. The tailgate allows access to the entire cargo compartment and it is through this that the helicopter is loaded and unloaded. I heard Captain Mungavin shout a brief order and immediately four soldiers clambered on board through the tailgate and started to unload cargo. The tarpaulins were piled neatly on the ground to one side of the helicopter.

As I watched the tarpaulins being unpacked I heard the sound of commotion behind me. I turned to see a soldier, baton in hand, about to strike a survivor. The injured man was trying to run towards the helicopter, perhaps to climb on board, or even to take a tarpaulin. He had no chance. With a resounding crack the baton struck forcibly at the survivor's thigh and he went down hard, yelping like a wounded dog. Slowly he crawled back to the edge of the landing site to join his people. The throng fell completely silent. The military had control.

Captain Mungavin was perhaps in his late twenties. Of medium height he was a manifestly intelligent individual as well as being smartly dressed, confident and the archetypal gentleman. His English was perfect. His eyes were firm, almost unblinking, while his handshake had been strong and his stride confident. It was clear that his men respected him. You did not argue with Captain Mungavin.

It is at such times that I am thankful to be ex-military. It has allowed me to talk the talk and walk the walk when needed. I am comfortable when surrounded by armed soldiers. Many of my civilian colleagues are not. Panjkot was a stone's throw from a war zone. Only the very best in the Pakistan Army were there.

The village was extremely close to the Line of Control. This was the military control line between the Indian and Pakistani-controlled parts of the former state of Jammu and Kashmir. It was not an internationally recognised border, more a de facto frontier that had existed since 1972. On the Indian side, India had erected 550 kilometres of double electrified fencing up to twelve feet high and had mined the gap between them. This was the Indian Kashmir barrier to which Pakistan frequently objected.

Kashmir had been a trouble spot for decades before the earthquake. Kashmiri separatists sought either an independent Islamic state, or unification with Pakistan. About 25,000 insurgents had died there since their struggle began in 1990, although India had stated their barrier had reduced insurgencies by up to eighty per cent.

India did not intend to stop there. Only three years before the earthquake, it had declared its desire to create the longest, fully fortified border in the history of the world. Its aim was to seed the entire 1,100-mile length of its Pakistan border with landmines, in places with minefields up to three miles deep. This was before Pakistan announced that it, too, would do the same. These minefields were in addition to those created during the three Indo–Pakistan wars that had been fought since partition in 1947. Landmines are a scourge for any medical aid worker. Worldwide up to 100 million are still in place, and they kill or injure as many as 20,000 people every year. As a medic, a landmine is a catastrophic military device.

Briefly, rapidly, I told Captain Mungavin more detail of why we were there. I explained I was a doctor and this would be a short visit, no more than an hour. My objective was to establish where I could position a field hospital.

Captain Mungavin nodded. 'You will have time to see patients while you are here?' he asked.

One glance towards the throng of casualties gathered around the landing site showed what an impossible task this would be. All I had was a pile of Paquito's tarpaulins, some bottled water and a tiny medical kit. The expectations of Captain Mungavin and the survivors were far beyond what I could provide. In addition, my primary task was not, on this occasion, to treat casualties. I was in Panjkot to plan their future. Yet how could I say that to the mass of humanity around me? Each survivor was now waiting patiently, each was quiet. Yet each was also watching my every move. I would have to do some medical work, even if all I had was a boxful of plasters, crepe bandages, slings and a few pills.

I turned towards Akram, who was standing immediately to my right.

'Can you start?' I asked. 'We need a site for medical tents and staff accommodation. It should not be far away.'

Akram nodded, smiled briefly and started to turn.

'One more thing,' I added, the near miss with the corrugated iron roof being fresh in my mind. 'Don't put the tents too close to the landing site. They won't stand a chance in a helicopter downdraft.'

Akram chuckled and went on his way.

I then turned to Captain Mungavin, while pointing towards the casualties. 'The patients? Shall we see them now?'

Captain Mungavin nodded and then smiled. He looked towards the casualties too, making a wide sweeping movement with his arm as if to say, 'After you.'

So I immediately started to walk towards the survivors, Nadia hurrying to my side, the cardboard box of rudimentary medical supplies in her arms. I could see this was why she had come.

Slowly, I walked through the mass of casualties, my eyes darting from one to another. I made sure to smile throughout. A smile is the best equipment any aid worker can carry in a disaster. Not a funny smile but an optimistic one. There is a difference. People want to know what you really feel and will scan your expressions for this. Nadia kept pace with me, stepping nimbly between or over the casualties who were lying or sitting on the ground. Many of the men were wearing the traditional *pakol* headgear of the North-West Frontier and Kashmir, a flat woollen hat, usually mid-brown. I wished I had brought my own, still in a drawer in England, evidence of my first visit to the area many decades earlier. Worn summer and winter, the *pakol* keeps its wearer cool in one and warm in the other. Meanwhile, to my right and paralleling my course was Captain Mungavin and two soldiers. Both were armed. I was glad they were there as we were very vulnerable. To have an impromptu bodyguard was a lifeline. I nodded my thanks to the captain as we walked; briefly he nodded back. Wherever I glanced, someone would raise a hand to attract my attention, or point to another lying on the ground alongside.

Everyone wanted me to stop, everyone wanted to be the first treated. However, it was Nadia's voice that grasped my attention. It was firm and demanding. 'This one!' she cried, as she pointed to a small boy lying on the ground to her right.

The young fellow, no more than six years old, looked terrified. He was sprawled sideways across a man's lap. The man looked desperately sad. I guessed he was the boy's father. Perhaps in his early thirties, he displayed an irregular, small, black moustache and was not wearing a *pakol*. I stopped and knelt slowly to the ground beside the boy. Suddenly it was if all the other casualties had disappeared, such was my focus on this little character.

Gently, I touched the boy's shoulder, glanced up towards his father, then down to the little boy once more.

'*Nam kya hai?* What is your name?' I asked. Hindi seemed the simplest language to try. India, after all, was not far away.

'Manohar,' replied the father, smiling down at his son. I had guessed right. Hindi seemed to work, certainly for the most basic of questions and greetings.

'*Dhanyawad*. Thank you,' I said. My Hindi knowledge was now rapidly reaching its limits.

I looked carefully at Manohar. He was wearing a patterned purple cardigan and loose, light blue trousers that stopped just above the knee. He was not moving his left leg at all and his left ear carried a deep laceration that was clearly infected. While I was examining little Manohar, his father waved his hand continually to keep the flies away. It is impossible in such surroundings to work in a fly-free environment. Once, in a central Indian mission hospital, I had required a nurse positioned in the operating theatre throughout the day. Her only task was to stop flies crawling into the wound while I operated. She was largely successful but not always so. In Panjkot meanwhile, the flies were there in force and Manohar's left ear was their target.

Despite its mucky appearance, it was not the ear that greatly concerned me, but Manohar's left leg. There was no movement in the foot and the limb was cold, not blue, just cold. The right leg was perfectly warm. The left leg was also positioned oddly, twisted inwards, and significantly shorter than the other side. The diagnosis was clear. The earthquake had dislocated Manohar's left hip. It had now been dislocated for almost two weeks and would need surgery to put the joint back into position. Sometimes dislocated joints can be manipulated into place by pulling and twisting on them. This needs to be done early, usually within hours of the injury. Two weeks was far too long, so an open operation would be needed. With flies everywhere and nothing more than a cardboard box of simple medical equipment, that was impossible to do on a mountainside in Panjkot. Manohar would need evacuation to a fully equipped hospital as soon as possible.

I knew what I needed to do. I turned towards Captain Mungavin who had also stopped to look at the tragedy of little Manohar. He raised his eyebrows as if to ask what I was recommending.

'Let's take this boy out,' I said, nodding towards the Mi-8. 'Out to Islamabad. And fast.'

* * *

Chapter 8

Too Many Casualties

The simple assessment visit to Panjkot had now turned into a major casualty evacuation operation. With the tarpaulins unloaded, there would be space in the Mi-8 for about fourteen passengers. That did not mean fourteen patients, as each casualty required one person to accompany them. There was also the Merlin team to consider.

My rough calculation was that there would be room in the Mi-8 for up to six patients. I looked around me. How could I decide? From the air, my estimate of 200 survivors surrounding the landing site looked wrong. As Nadia and I slowly made our way through the mass of injured I guessed that my estimate would have to at least double. There were more like 400 casualties waiting patiently and inspecting my every move. I was sure that each would want both treatment and evacuation to a place of safety. I glanced again at Captain Mungavin and wondered if he had made the same calculation as myself. I was willing to wager that he had. Six happy patients headed in a helicopter to Islamabad meant 394 unhappy ones. That would be sufficient to start a major riot so I had to tread carefully.

Slowly, Nadia and I worked through the casualties, stopping to apply a dressing here or to clean a wound there. It was impossible to see everyone. Anyway, I could not do much as the medical supplies were limited, but it gave me the opportunity to assess those who needed treatment in a major hospital and those who could be left safely behind.

From the corner of one eye I could see the pilot becoming restless. He was glancing continually towards the wheels of the Mi-8, which I could see was slowly settling into the ground. Only the top half of the wheels was now visible. It would not be long before a take-off would be impossible. The pilot caught my own glance and raised his hand in warning. I nodded. It was time to leave. 'Come on,' I whispered urgently to Nadia, inclining my head towards the helicopter. 'Let's choose who we can and get going. We haven't long.'

For a brief moment Nadia hesitated, her forehead wrinkled. I could see she wanted to protest. Then a tear appeared in the corner of her right eye. 'But...these people. There are still so many to see,' she stuttered.

'The helicopter,' I again whispered. 'Look at it! We'll be going nowhere if we don't hurry.'

I wanted to point at the Mi-8 to emphasise my words, yet did not want to attract the attention of the survivors to what was rapidly becoming a transport emergency. I wanted also to lay a gentle hand on Nadia's shoulder, both in reassurance and insistence. However, in this strongly Islamic region, to even touch a woman in public would be dangerously unacceptable.

Nadia looked towards the helicopter but clearly did not understand the predicament. I saw no alarm in her eyes at all. Then, unexpectedly, she raised her head, pulled back her shoulders in military style and declared. 'If we cannot treat them, let's leave some money. That is the least we can do.'

I could see that Nadia was fully overcome by her surroundings. She wanted to do what she could. Untrained medically, yet with deep care and passion, to leave money would be her contribution. I saw her hand reach towards the patterned cloth shoulder bag that was thumping gently against her hip as she walked.

'No!' I whispered insistently. 'You cannot do that! You'll start a riot if you produce any money here.'

For a moment Nadia looked confused. I continued, 'Give some to one and you must give it to the others. Anyway, where would they spend it? Look around you. The place is destroyed.'

Nadia stopped. Her hand was inside the shoulder bag and I could see her fumbling for her wallet. Then she hesitated and the frantic hand movements inside the bag ceased. Her shoulders sagged and, very slowly, she pulled her hand from the bag. The hand was empty. I relaxed, sighing imperceptibly. Nadia had understood.

Panjkot was indeed destroyed. There was not one building standing, wherever I looked. The village was situated either side of the steep-sided Panjkot Valley, terraced fields occupying much of the area. Our helicopter landing site, and impromptu clinic, was a thousand feet up on one side. Way down in the bottom I could see a clear river and, somewhere in the air was the sound of the water's rush. Yet there was also the smell of death. Temporary graves were scattered both sides of the valley, graves that were only small mounds of earth, some marked and some not. So far away from Muzaffarabad, Panjkot was the last place to be rescued. For the massive global aid machine, Panjkot was out of sight and out of mind. Merlin was the village's only hope.

Quickly, Nadia and I continued our work with the main body of casualties, Captain Mungavin and his men keeping a careful eye on what we did. They had already loaded little Manohar onto the helicopter, using one of Paquito's tarpaulins as an improvised stretcher. Manohar's father would be headed towards Islamabad too. One glance at my watch and further glances at the subsiding Mi-8 showed that I had only minutes remaining on site. I could see the Russian pilot was becoming extremely anxious, fidgeting continually and clearing the earth from around the helicopter's wheels with his bare hands.

To travel with Manohar I selected a young girl with a broken right shoulder and a man in his mid-twenties with a broken spine and paralysed legs. There was also a pregnant woman who had been paralysed by falling debris although her baby was still alive; and a five-year-old boy with a broken thighbone. Finally, there was a teenage girl with a broken pelvis. The bone had clearly been properly smashed. When I laid my hand on one side of the pelvis I could feel the whole bone float free. The girl was lucky to be alive as pelvis fractures can cause major blood loss. She could easily have bled to death.

By now, Captain Mungavin also sensed the urgency. He stepped nimbly between the casualties and came to my side. 'You have to go now,' he said.

'I know. But we'll take these people when we go.' I pointed towards the five further casualties I had selected.

Captain Mungavin understood immediately, turned to his men who were grouped to one side of the crowd and shouted rapid-fire orders in a tongue that escaped me. His words had their effect. Twelve soldiers immediately sprang to work.

One-by-one, the selected casualties were carried through the tailgate of the helicopter and placed gently on the cargo compartment's floor. A total of six injured survivors, each with a companion, made twelve Panjkot villagers in the cargo compartment of the Mi-8. Add to that four Merlin staff and we now had sixteen passengers rather than the maximum of fourteen. The pilot noticed this instantly. I saw his disapproving look, his shaking head, as the pregnant woman was placed as the final casualty on the cargo compartment's floor. 'Too many, Dr Richard,' he said, still shaking his head. 'She must go.' He pointed directly at the pregnant woman.

'How can we leave her here?' I protested. 'She is paralysed, too.'

'We will all be paralysed if this helicopter crashes,' came the reply. 'Leave that one behind.' He jabbed his finger directly at the woman as he spoke. She looked up towards me, terror in her eyes. She could not understand one word of what was being said but could certainly see the anger in the pilot's eyes.

As with the captain of a ship, the pilot of a helicopter is boss. What he says is gospel. Yet how could I stand by and allow the woman to be abandoned? I could not. There was only one solution.

'OK. Take her and leave me.' I was not bluffing. I picked up my small emergency pack and headed towards the helicopter's side door. In reality I had no idea what I would do next, but felt Captain Mungavin would probably find me somewhere to sleep. If the pregnant woman was abandoned, she and her baby would most likely die.

The pilot stepped to one side to let me pass but the moment I did so he grabbed me gently by the left shoulder. I stopped where I was. 'You win,' the pilot said. 'I'll try. Now sit down and let's go.'

I instantly did what I was told and nodded my thanks to the pilot. He had returned to the cockpit where I could see a heated discussion underway with his colleague. I knew what the subject would be. Then, slowly, the tailgate door closed and I waved through the still-open passenger door to Captain Mungavin. He waved back and smiled. Beyond, I could see his men struggling to hold back the crowd of locals, each of whom had hoped to be on the Mi-8 as well. I could hear the arguing, the shouting, the shoving and the occasional raised, threatening hand. The military had the upper hand, but it was a tense situation. It would not have taken much for the crowd to overrun the helicopter.

The rotors of the Mi-8 sprang into life, the pilot revving the engines furiously. The helicopter felt as if it would shake into a thousand pieces at any moment. The din was unbearable, yet nothing happened. The Mi-8 failed to climb a single inch. Slowly the engine noise decreased as the pilot briefly reduced the strain on his craft. Then he tried again. The noise picked up, as did the rotor speed, while the helicopter shook violently from side to side. I hung on tightly to the edge of the bench-like seat. I could barely keep my balance even though I was sitting down. This time it was different. Millimetre by millimetre I sensed the wheels drag themselves from the mud, yet they could not quite come free. A vice had clamped us down. I could see the crew shaking their heads in frustration and disappointment. The pilot flicked switches, adjusted bevelled knobs, and continually glanced left and right, up and down. He was clearly very worried. But slowly, ever so slowly, the vice-like grip diminished and the Mi-8 worked itself free. First the left wheel, then the right, and finally we were in the air.

At least we were until the hand appeared. It was an old and sinewed hand, the fingers gripping the side door's frame, the knuckles whitened as they held tightly on to the helicopter. As they gripped, so a face appeared, the face of a white-bearded old man, his eyes wide open, pleading. Somehow, the old man had bypassed Captain Mungavin's soldiers and half-dashed, half-limped to the helicopter, grabbing hold as it had begun to lift. For a brief moment I hesitated, then I saw the pregnant woman look towards the old man. Her eyes brightened and she smiled, shouting something I could not understand. Then she stretched her arm towards him. Instantly I understood. This was the girl's grandfather, or even her father. Age estimations with these tribal people were, to me, almost impossible. Quickly, I leaned across, placed one hand under the old man's armpit and heaved him on board. With a weakened kick of his legs he lurched and half sprawled face first onto the Mi-8's floor. We headed upwards rapidly, the old man's legs still dangling from the door as we rose. Then we were up and away.

With the old man safely on board I closed the side door and then looked towards the cockpit. The pilot had turned almost fully in his seat and was smiling broadly. Now we were in the air and the intense shaking had settled, he looked more relaxed. 'Dr Richard,' he shouted over the terrible noise. 'You're crazy!'

Briefly, the Mi-8 circled Panjkot. Beneath I could see the sprawling, destroyed houses that formed the village, spread over the mountainside. The half-harvested maize on the terraced fields, the sparkling river deep in the valley bottom, and the lush green vegetation were truly picturesque. It was impossible to imagine how, two weeks earlier, the area had been such a place of terror. Way below, I could see the crowd of casualties slowly move, as the injured and their companions made their way back to shattered properties. From the air, Captain Mungavin's soldiers appeared relaxed; there was no sign of continuing struggle. Then we were away, heading towards Islamabad with our very human cargo.

* * *

Chapter 9

Missing and Unidentified

The flight through the Kashmir valleys to Islamabad was magical. The weather was good, the sky bright blue and cloudless, and there was no turbulence in the air. Looking through the helicopter's windows, I could almost forget there had been an earthquake. Yet looking immediately around me, I could not.

In the cargo compartment of the Mi–8, we busied ourselves with the casualties. The two paralysed patients, one the young man, the other the pregnant woman, had no control of their legs, which would flop around helplessly whenever the helicopter banked left or right. Meanwhile Manohar and the little five-year-old with the broken thighbone were both in considerable pain. The medical kit only contained paracetamol as a painkiller and then in tablet form. For younger children it is best to give paracetamol as a liquid as they may have problems swallowing a tablet. So I crushed some paracetamol tablets with the back of a metal spoon in the bottom of a plastic cup, added a little water, and tried to persuade Manohar and the five-year-old to drink my improvised preparation. I failed, as the most of the liquid dribbled down their cheeks and onto the compartment's floor. It was almost impossible to keep the cup steady in flight. Anyway, judging by their distressed faces the moment the cup touched their lips, the medicine tasted filthy. The final two patients, the young girl with the broken shoulder and the other with the smashed pelvis, were fine. I had expected them to be in pain but they were not. This situation is common when broken bones are neglected. Initially the break is extremely painful, but even when left untreated and ununited, pain can slowly settle.

As we flew, occasionally the pilot would circle a cluster of destroyed houses, or a remote mountain-top property lying collapsed on its side, while his colleague would write down the co-ordinates for its location. These details would be handed to United Nations staff in Islamabad so that aid could be targeted later, so long as Rafael had sufficient helicopters.

Meanwhile I too was planning Merlin's project in Kashmir, so to overfly the area was a perfect opportunity. I wrote furiously in my small and battered notebook as we flew, the shaking of the Mi-8 making it hard to keep a steady hand. I decided that my aim should be to develop a series of facilities   along the Neelum Valley, from Panjkot at one end to Muzaffarabad at the other. Three or four separate locations would do it. Panjkot could be the first.

There was little conversation on the flight and I could see Nadia occasionally wipe a persisting tear from her eye. She was not medically trained. As a medic you perhaps become hardened to these things and forget the effect that human misery can have on those who are unaccustomed to seeing it.

I was so far away in thought and planning that I totally missed the change in engine tone as the helicopter came into land. It was only when it touched the ground at Islamabad's PIMS landing site that I realised the journey was complete. Then there was chaos. The moment the tailgate was lowered I could have been a startled rabbit. I had no idea what was happening. Suddenly, more than a dozen locals stormed into the cargo compartment, each wearing a surgical facemask, and started to unload the casualties. They asked no one. With much talking, jabbering, shouting and arguing between themselves, with much pushing and pulling, the casualties were rapidly placed onto patient trolleys and taken at pace into the PIMS building, almost 300 yards away. In less than a minute the cargo compartment was empty.

PIMS had employed a small army of volunteers to act as porters, auxiliaries, clerks, handymen, and receptionists. Everyone wished to be involved, to carry a patient through the PIMS front doors, to be the first to reach the Accident and Emergency Department and to be the first to save a life. It was mayhem. First off was Manohar, screaming loudly for his father who had been left behind. Then the pregnant woman was manhandled onto a stretcher, strange hands firmly gripping her swollen belly, her paralysed legs flopping wildly from side to side. Her elderly companion was left to hobble behind her, the distance between them ever increasing.

'Slow down! Wait!' I shouted.

No one paid any attention. The volunteers were off and there was no way anyone would hold them back. Quickly I escorted Manohar's father towards the hospital's front entrance, as we chased after his son. The father was frantic with distress, tears streaming down his face as he shouted the little boy's name. In the distance I could hear Manohar, on his trolley, also scream for his father. We had still not caught up with the jogging porters by the time I saw the trolley pass rapidly through the PIMS main doors.

Once inside the building I could see the scene. There were patients everywhere, admitted from towns and villages throughout the earthquake zone. The wards had spilled out into the hospital corridors and into all the main public areas. Doctors, some male, some female, were weaving their way slowly from bed to bed. But apart from the din created by the overenthusiastic volunteer porters and Manohar's screams for his father the atmosphere was one of calm organisation. PIMS was pulling out the stops and, from what I could see in this fleeting visit, had not been found wanting.

It took me ten further minutes to reunite father and son. I found Manohar in the X-Ray department at the far end of a dark and gloomy corridor. On one of the viewing boxes I could see the X-Ray film of the boy's left hip. The joint was indeed dislocated. Surgery would, more than likely, be the next step. But to see father and son together once more was wonderful. They hugged, they cried and the father endlessly stroked his little boy's forehead. At least they would be together, I thought as I turned to leave, when they both faced such an uncertain future.

I slowly retraced my steps, out through the main hospital doors and towards the Mi-8. Already its rotors were beginning to turn and I could see the pilot through the cockpit glass as he flicked his switches and checked all around, readying his craft for take-off. I had wanted to thank him, to shake his hand, for taking risks where others would have fled, but could see that his mind was now set on other things. As the wheels of the Mi-8 lifted free of the ground I managed a brief wave and thumbs-up sign, which I could see being returned, and then the helicopter was up and away.

When a helicopter leaves you alone on a landing site it is one of the loneliest feelings in the world. When it lands, when it is unloading, when it is preparing to take off, a landing site is exciting, stimulating and busy. But when the helicopter departs you feel abandoned. Suddenly you have lost a great friend. As the Mi-8 climbed higher into the sky that day, I felt that loneliness. I had felt it so many times before in my military days when Her Majesty landed me in some far-flung, strange location and then left me to my own devices. It is at the point the helicopter leaves that you realise you are on your own.

I walked back towards the main PIMS building once more. An occasional ambulance would come and go, doors opening and closing noisily as another casualty was unloaded. To one side I could see a large noticeboard. Pinned to its face, side by side, every tiny space occupied, were the photographs of many dozens of patients; male, female, boy, girl, young and old.

Standing towards one end of the noticeboard I could see a man, perhaps in his mid-thirties. He was smartly dressed in a spotlessly white *shalwar qameez*, the national dress of Pakistan, India and Bangladesh. I drew closer. As I did so, I could see he was crying, although he was trying hard not to show his despair.

'Can I help?' I asked.

The man turned towards me. I looked directly into his bloodshot eyes. He wiped the tears from his face with the back of one hand and then spoke. 'I'm sorry. It's just that I cannot find her.'

'Who?'

'My mother.'

'Why are you looking here?'

'Because they brought her here from the mountains. These are the photographs of the injured people. My mother is not among them and she is not in the hospital. I am sure she is dead.'

Then the man broke down. He took a few unsteady paces towards some low, wide concrete steps and sat down hard, sobbing heavily. 'She is dead. I am sure she is dead. Allah, what can I do?'

I looked across at the photographs. Instantly I could see the problem. They were the images of missing or unidentified people. If a casualty had been brought to Islamabad from the mountains, they were not always accompanied. They might not have even spoken Urdu, the Pakistani language. The name of their village, or town, or hamlet may not have featured on a map. Even if it had, the villagers may have named it differently. This was a refugee crisis in the making as casualties may have been unable to describe from where they had come. It was thus unlikely they would ever return home once they had recovered from their injuries. Children were separated from parents, husbands from wives, brothers from sisters, and friends from friends. The United Nations High Commissioner for Refugees, or UNHCR, had its work cut out to deal with the problem. To me, the lesson was simple. It was better to treat the injured where they lay rather than take them away from their familiar surroundings. If there was ever a case for a Merlin field hospital on the mountainsides of Kashmir, this was it.

I stayed with the sobbing man until he had settled . There was nothing I could do to reunite him with his mother and no way of establishing if she was alive or dead. The man was one of so many separated victims of disaster. The UNHCR had estimated that, worldwide, there were up to forty-million displaced people. The Great Earthquake had contributed more than two million to that number.

Deep in my thoughts, I turned away from PIMS to start the long walk to the guesthouse. As I turned I felt a silent hand on my shoulder. For a brief moment I froze, yet the hand did not feel threatening. I looked to my left to see the smiling face of a middle-aged man, slightly greying. I had never seen him before but he was looking directly at me.

'What can I do for you?' I said.

The man smiled more broadly and then spoke.

'You don't know me, Doctor,' came the words, 'but thank you for helping our people. Pakistan is grateful.' With that, the hand fell from my shoulder and the man went on his way, back into the sombre shadows of PIMS.

'Thank you, too,' I whispered in return, as my unidentified companion slowly disappeared. He did not look back and I doubt he even heard me speak. Yet his words had a profound effect. A simple thank-you, from a character I would never meet again, was all it took to give me renewed vigour. Whatever the difficulties I encountered, at that moment I felt my efforts were worthwhile.

There was no time to lose. The international aid programme was beginning to heat up and different agencies were vying with each other for the best locations, the best communications, the best method of transport and the largest number of patients treated. So far I had managed to treat six casualties and narrowly avoided creating a refugee riot, not a record I was happy to publicise. Meanwhile, the United Kingdom Government had sent two Chinook helicopters, a tiny contribution when considering the size of the disaster, but a huge contribution in terms of political status.

Over a crackly mobile telephone link, I made contact with the NATO helicopter chief in London. He appeared glad to speak, particularly as I was his first voice contact with the field. Until then he had attended interminable London meetings, and had been briefed by individuals who had not visited Kashmir. I explained Panjkot's location, as well as its co-ordinates, to ask if the UK Chinooks could pay it a visit. Even though they would be too heavy to land, the Chinooks could air drop vital supplies, which Merlin could then distribute on the ground.

'No problems,' was his emphatic reply. 'We'd be happy to do that.'

At the guesthouse, the atmosphere had definitely changed. There was a buzz of excitement in the air, even from Dorotea, who had now reappeared. She greeted me almost like a long-lost friend, which surprised me. She too must have realised that we had to up our pace and that a succession of aid meetings was inappropriate. Decisions had to be made, and fast. Action had to be taken. Even Dorotea became caught up in the enthusiasm.

'We must return to Panjkot immediately,' I said to her as we sat quietly in a remote corner of the lounge area. Dorotea had asked for a description of the day. My tales of Manohar and of the photographs of the missing and unidentified hit her hard.

'I agree,' she replied. 'Let's make it happen.'

I barely knew how to react. What is she on, I thought, with such a character change in such a short time?

Yet whatever decisions were made on the ground, nothing could happen without London's blessing. They were the ones who paid. Each evening a telephone conference was held with the London office. This was an important event. Internet access was unreliable and rarely adequate to allow videoconferencing, so mobile telephone was the best method of communication. A mobile would be placed on the floor in the middle of the room, set on maximum volume loudspeaker and the staff would crowd round. Sitting on the floor, we would lean over the tiny device, shout out our views and listen to our instructions. It worked surprisingly well. London would normally give instant decisions. On this occasion, when I asked for their blessing to return to Panjkot, their reply was simple.

'Yes.'

* * *

Chapter 10

Vodka is a Real Man's Drink

Early the next morning, Paquito and I headed towards Islamabad Airport in his increasingly battered minibus.

'Hey!' I had shouted to the Spaniard in the dawn-lit guesthouse car park as I had clambered on board. 'Isn't that another dent I can see?' Immediately in front of one rear wheel was a freshly made hollow in the bodywork.

'Two, actually,' Paquito replied, half grinning and clearly speaking with pride. 'There's one the other side, too. This is Islamabad driving. Back right was a Toyota, back left a cyclist. Before you ask, the cyclist is fine.'

We both laughed loudly. Islamabad's roads were well known to be a challenge for the hardiest and most experienced driver. One moment the thoroughfares would be empty, the next filled with exhaust-spewing open-topped vans overcrowded with passengers. It was not unusual to see locals hanging onto the outside of a van while standing on the bumpers. Lanes were marked but rarely used while rear-view mirrors seemed for decoration rather than function. Indicators were a joke. During my short time in Islamabad I could not recall seeing one used. Horns, however, were a widely employed method of communication. Hand signals, too, of course. These were largely abusive.

'The most important thing,' explained Paquito, 'is not to stop. If you do they hem you in and you will stay there all day. This is warfare not driving.'

Our high spirits were created by one thing - the final message from London at the very end of the previous evening's conference call. The disembodied voice from the tiny mobile had simply said, 'The team will arrive tomorrow morning.'

The voice had gone dead at that moment, so I had no idea of the team's exact timings. Yet that did not matter. Fully in my mind, and throughout the night, I had visions of the mass of casualties waiting at the Panjkot landing site. We needed to return there, and fast. It seemed a safe bet to arrange an afternoon helicopter sortie so that we could be in the mountains by nightfall. Paquito meanwhile had been hard at work obtaining tents and equipment. He appeared to have bought half of Islamabad. Our journey to the airport was to prepare the equipment for loading and to check we were ready to go. I was blissfully happy. At last the project was reaching a momentum that would be impossible to stop.

At least I thought that would be so, until we arrived at Islamabad Airport.

It hit me the moment we arrived at the airport's cargo area. Through the thick open-mesh twelve-foot fencing surround, I could see two large piles of boxes and bundles lying on the tarmac to one side of a battered aircraft hangar. One pile was tidily arranged, each box and bundle perfectly packed and aligned, the other was haphazard chaos.

Paquito pointed through the fencing at the well-ordered pile. 'Us,' he said proudly, pointing to his chest. Then he indicated the other, 'Another organisation's.'

I nodded. Before us was evidence of a huge problem in disaster relief. At such times, large sums of money and volumes of equipment are donated. Yet there is no saying its condition when it appears, or whether the equipment will arrive at all. The other organisation's equipment was largely unusable, yet had probably cost a fortune in time, money and effort. Merlin's equipment was ready to roll. The difference? Paquito.

Paquito smiled wryly. At least he did so until he tried to open the high open-mesh gates leading to the cargo area. He could not. They had been chained tight shut, a large padlock and thick, rusty chain dangling threateningly. The way was barred.

I glanced at my watch. After much negotiation with Rafael over a crackly mobile at midnight, I had arranged for the Mi-8 to return to Panjkot at two o'clock that afternoon. It was now eight o'clock; we had six hours. Yet the supplies we needed were the other side of the barred twelve-foot fence. They were lying innocently, almost shouting, 'I am ready! How about you?'

I looked around. There was no sign of life. I shouted through cupped hands, 'Hello-o-o-o!'

No response. I shook the gates noisily, the chained padlock and fence clanking and clamouring with enough noise to mobilise an army. Not a whisper, not a movement. There was no one to be seen; just Paquito and I on one side of an impassable fence, our equipment on the other.

There then followed three very frustrating hours. It should have been simple to find someone to open a padlock for you in a disaster zone, but it was not.

We visited the office of a grandly titled individual, the Senior Vigilance Officer. Tall, thin, athletic, dressed in Western style rather than *shalwar qameez*, he was charming. Yet he did not possess the same sense of urgency as Paquito and me. After a lengthy welcome, so customary in hospitable Pakistan, plus an accompanying sweet tea, I explained that we required access to our equipment and would he be so kind as to unlock the gate?

'No problems,' he replied. 'We must find the guard. He has the key.' With a flick of his head, he turned to the uniformed security officer to his left and barked an order in Urdu. The officer started to turn, as if to follow the instruction, hesitated, then turned back and spoke quietly to his chief, again in Urdu. I could not understand a word. However, I could read the chief's expression. It was one of disbelief. The two men talked, incomprehensibly to me, for several minutes. Then the Senior Vigilance Officer spoke in English.

'This is embarrassing, Doctor,' he said, his eyes looking at his desk rather than me.

'How?'

'The guard with the keys went home last night. Something to do with his wife. No one has seen him since and he has taken the keys.'

'A spare set?'

'No. They were lost several weeks back. I am sorry but we must find the guard.'

How I wanted to challenge the Senior Vigilance Officer at that point. To say how it defied belief, in a land immersed in conflict and terrorist troubles, that an airfield could remain unguarded all night and that one man's domestic troubles could bring an aid programme to its knees. Yet I restrained myself. In disaster-riven Pakistan this was the way it was.

'No problem,' I lied. 'When do you think that will be?'

The Senior Vigilance Officer did not answer but made a rapid brushing motion of his hand towards his junior. The uniformed security officer, with a subservient nod, instantly sped off to track down his colleague.

Our conversation continued. The Senior Vigilance Officer enjoyed talking. Throughout I could feel near panic in my chest. I would surreptitiously look at my watch as we talked. Eight-thirty passed, then nine; nine-thirty and then ten. Endless tea came and went as my bladder became more distended. We talked of the Kashmir conflict, and of the forthcoming visit by the English cricket team. We talked of the airfield being closed for a visit by the Turkish Prime Minister. We talked of so many things, none of which related to aid provision to the mountains of Kashmir. Still in my mind were the images. Images of Manohar, of Captain Mungavin controlling the crowds, and of the man by the PIMS board for the missing and unidentified. These were a desperate people in desperate trouble. We needed to be in Panjkot today. Not tomorrow or the next day, but today, today, and today.

It was as both bladder and tolerance were about to burst that I heard the gentle knock on the office door. The Senior Vigilance Officer and I turned simultaneously to look towards it.

'Come!' the Senior Vigilance Officer shouted.

The door opened. There stood the uniformed security officer with a smile on his face. In his hand dangled a large set of keys, which he shook towards me with a slight tinkle. 'I have them, sirs,' he said. I looked again at my watch. It was almost eleven o'clock. That gave three hours to assemble equipment, find a medical team and have them en route to the mountains. That was nothing short of impossible.

Yet somehow we did it. Thirty minutes after we left the Senior Vigilance Officer, the open mesh gates were unlocked and Paquito and his team were busily assembling, packing and piling huge quantities of equipment for loading onto the Mi-8 that afternoon. Meanwhile I returned to the guesthouse, by taxi rather than Paquito's minibus. The small black Suzuki cab, with its cream-coloured roof, was far more dented than the minibus. The driver never indicated once, used his horn incessantly, and shouted abuse to anyone and everyone we passed. He also greatly overcharged me when we arrived. My mistake, I thought, for failing to agree a price before departure.

The guesthouse was fully active. People were everywhere. A group of Malaysian troops had moved in and Dorotea had already left for Sweden. Whether she had been asked to leave, or had simply decided to go, I never did establish. I felt sorry for her, as she had been the squarest peg in the roundest hole. A heart of gold but not cut out for disasters.

In the guesthouse's back garden, sitting calmly around a wooden table and drinking tea, was the five-person medical team, comprising four men and one woman. They had arrived from London only a few hours before, while I had been with the Senior Vigilance Officer. I could instantly see they would be suited to a disaster programme. Of the five new arrivals, two were ex-military and one an ex-policewoman. Previous military service is a great asset for a disaster aid worker as Service personnel generally have a positive approach to life. Nothing is too difficult. They are used to discomfort and can handle themselves well during the long periods of waiting, interspersed by brief moments of activity, which are a feature of both disaster relief and conflict.

Quickly, I briefed them on what I knew, that the full hospital had not yet arrived but we would have enough equipment to offer initial treatment. I warned them of the massive workload awaiting them in Panjkot and gave a quick run through of the use of a satellite telephone and global positioning system, or GPS. For the ex-military individuals there was no need to rehearse putting up a tent. For them this would be reflex.

'When do we leave?' the ex-policewoman queried. This was Frances, the only female in the group.

What a fool I am, I thought. I had been so immersed in the minutiae of equipment and workload, I had forgotten to tell them perhaps the most vital item of all.

'Sorry,' I replied apologetically, looking at my watch. One-fifteen. 'Finish your tea. Let's go.'

Not one of them appeared perturbed. In fact one of the ex-soldiers, as he rose instantly to his feet, said, 'Why so slow?'

I did have one concern. It was not something I discussed during the briefing as we were now at a point where there was no going back. The problem was that the medical team was fully specialist. There was a plastic surgeon, Cameron, and his specialist nurse, Frances, the ex-policewoman. Plastic surgeons deal with skin and muscle loss, crushed limbs and faces, common problems after an earthquake. There was also a consultant anaesthetist. These were highly qualified professionals who spent their lives in properly equipped operating theatres.

However, my own visit to Panjkot had shown that the bulk of the major injured had died during the thirteen days it had taken aid to reach Panjkot. There was now no need for plastic surgery. The requirement now was for basic medical care; minor injuries, dressings, simple wound suture, conditions that would not normally require a top-flight specialist. The situation had changed. This is a feature of all disaster relief programmes, anywhere in the world. What is needed one day may not be needed the next.

The specialist team immediately offered to downscale their activities. Instead of performing skin flaps and grafts under the glare of an operating light, Cameron agreed to be in charge of dressings. Meanwhile Frances volunteered to run the pharmacy, and the anaesthetist appointed himself head medic in the outpatient clinic. Such attributes are key for any aid worker. You may think you are going to a country to provide one level of service. By the time you reach there you can be sure the requirements will have changed. You must accept that. Indeed, you may be the globe's most famous professor but if someone asks you to dig a latrine you should not complain. Take the shovel, smile, and get on with it.

We arrived at the airport with minutes to spare. The Mi-8 was positioned neatly beside the runway, all Paquito's boxes and bundles in place in the cargo compartment. Standing beside the still open tailgate were the two Russians. Although it had barely been twenty-four hours since we last met, we greeted each other like long-lost friends. As with war, disasters are intense occasions. Much happens in a short time, and friendships are forged.

'Dr Richard,' smiled the pilot as he hugged me in a firm Russian embrace. 'It is good. Yes? We are together again.'

'Yes. It is good'. Much as I admired the pilot, I quickly slipped myself out from his strong hug.

The hugging complete, I indicated to the team that they should take their seats and then stepped into the Mi-8 myself. The vodka bottle still lay there in its now established corner of the cargo compartment. It may not have become a friend but it had certainly become a mascot. As we sat, one of the local Pakistani packers stepped on board and made to pick up the bottle and throw it towards a large rubbish skip. I intervened immediately, removed the bottle gently from his hand and laid it down once more in its rightful place.

The packer looked at me as though I should have been locked away. The Russian pilot, now seated in the cockpit, turned around to see my action.

'Hey, you a good Russian!' he shouted, giving a firm thumbs-up sign. 'Vodka is a real man's drink!' With that he turned back to his controls and slowly, ever so slowly, juddering and complaining, the Mi-8 struggled upwards to the sky.

* * *

Chapter 11

The Body in the Woods

As the Russian pilot brought the Mi–8 carefully into Panjkot that afternoon it was clear Captain Mungavin had been at work. An orderly line of casualties lay on makeshift stretchers to one side of the landing site. These were the patients awaiting surgery once our tented hospital was in place. Any we could not handle, we would evacuate to PIMS. The moment the engines of the Mi–8 could be heard from the ground, I could see tiny figures far beneath me scurry towards the landing site, too. These were the walking wounded, who had clearly been waiting for us to reappear. The crowd slowly began to assemble once more. Meanwhile two soldiers stood either side of the landing site holding large military flags, both in welcome and to give the pilot an estimate of wind direction and speed. This was a very different Panjkot to the one I had seen the previous day.

Akram was first off the helicopter, pointing out to the medical team the locations he had found for the tents. There were only five hours until nightfall, so we would have to work fast to put up at least one tent for team accommodation before dark. Rapidly, several soldiers helped unload the Mi–8. Within ten minutes the cargo compartment was empty and its contents perfectly piled nearby. Three soldiers, each armed with a Heckler and Koch G3 assault rifle stood guard over our equipment. I had heard that many international agencies had lost equipment from burglary. I could see a number of individuals in the growing crowd glance, and perhaps estimate whether they could remove some equipment without us noticing. Captain Mungavin was clearly aware of this.

Once unloaded, and with an emphatic thumbs-up from the Russian pilot, the Mi–8 was away, heading down the Panjkot Valley to Islamabad once more. I could see the disappointment on the stretcher patients' faces. How they wished they could be on board the helicopter and headed to safety, too. I glanced across at Akram and caught his eye.

'Can you tell them we will treat them here?' I asked, pointing towards the line of stretchers. Akram nodded and walked across to the injured. I saw him kneel down beside one stretcher, gently take the patient's hand and begin to talk. Akram was a kind man, one of the best. I could see the patients took to him instantly.

'How long will you be staying?' asked Captain Mungavin as we stood in the post-helicopter silence on the edge of the landing site.

'One day only for me. I have other locations to set up. The team will be here for several weeks.'

Captain Mungavin nodded. 'When will you be ready for work?' he asked.

Together we looked at the site chosen for the hospital. It was about 100 metres downhill from the landing site, on a flat terraced area that had been especially cleared by the Army. Already I could see the medical team erecting a large, cream-coloured canvas tent. This would be the staff accommodation. I smiled. Back home the medical team members would have been used to others preparing their accommodation for them. Here, high in the Kashmiri mountains, no one stood on ceremony. If there was a job to be done it was all hands on deck. The ability to treat a casualty is only one of the skills required of a medical aid worker. The ability to look after yourself is key.

'I doubt tomorrow will be early enough,' commented Captain Mungavin. 'Look over there.'

I looked to our left. A long line of patients, probably more than 200, was slowly walking towards the hospital area. Some patients were being carried by others, some were limping and hobbling, while others were wearing makeshift slings and bandages. A number had clearly been blinded, and were holding on to the shoulder of a colleague in front. It was like a scene from World War I.

The anaesthetist had spotted the problem already and had started work. I saw him make a seat from a large medical box, position himself in one corner of the field, and use that as his impromptu clinic. He had a teenager beside him, most likely acting as interpreter. One by one the patients came to him. It was slow work, and he could not offer much treatment until the tents were erected and the medicines unloaded, but at least it was a start.

'I will put a guard on your camp tonight,' said Captain Mungavin. 'Tell your people not to stray from that field.'

'Why?'

'We shot a snow leopard last night. There is another on the loose that we have been unable to trace.'

That was not something I wanted to hear. The snow leopard is a carnivorous animal that leads a solitary life and can kill animals three times its size. It can leap up to fourteen metres and kills, usually through an ambush, by a bite to the neck. Snow leopards are crepuscular, being active at dawn and dusk, just when the human guard is down. I did not want to meet a snow leopard in Panjkot.

I nodded my thanks. A guard would be welcome. Snow leopards had certainly not formed part of my pre-mission briefing to the team in the guesthouse's garden.

'I have something else for you, too,' continued Captain Mungavin. 'Please follow. We're going to those woods.' I followed Captain Mungavin up the mountainside, glad that I was also a mountaineer. He walked fast and never looked back.

On the way we passed a collection of five collapsed houses. There may have been six, but the destruction was so total that it was impossible to imagine how the properties had looked before the earthquake. To walk through an inhabited earthquake zone is a depressing activity. Panjkot had been flattened. Nothing was spared and lives had been laid bare. Shredded schoolbooks and torn clothing lay scattered around, while stained and disfigured photographs appeared trapped, half buried, deep inside collapsed ruins. The stench of death was thick and cloying, marked and unmarked graves were dotted here and there, some grouped together, others lonely and abandoned. Meanwhile young children wandered aimlessly through the debris, many crying and distraught.

'How will they ever rebuild this?' I shouted at the Captain Mungavin's rear view.

'I doubt they ever will,' he replied, his voice uncharacteristically sympathetic. Then he turned and continued upwards, his pace steady. He did not stumble once, despite the rough, pitted and irregular terrain.

Our ascent continued for a further ten minutes as we weaved our way from one scene of distress to another. Then we were beyond the last of Panjkot's destroyed houses.

Before we entered the woodland, I looked back at the helicopter landing site and the hospital area beneath it. They were now tiny specks far below us. I could see the speck of the anaesthetist holding his impromptu mountainside clinic and the long line of specks awaiting his attention. There was the tiny cream dot of the staff accommodation tent that had now almost reached the vertical thanks to the specks busying around it. From what I could see, the team members were securing the guy ropes, so their task was almost complete. Then, somewhere in the distance I heard the loud thump of a single explosion. I scanned the mountainsides but could see no puff of smoke or fresh rock fall.

'Fighting?' I asked.

'No. The engineers are clearing the road of landslide debris.'

There was only one road up the Neelum Valley and only one to Panjkot. These thoroughfares, some of which were precariously perched on the very edge of the mountainside, a perilous thousand-foot drop below, were now completely obstructed by rock fall. The quickest way of clearing them was with high explosive.

'It'll take several days, maybe weeks, for the engineers to reach Panjkot,' added Captain Mungavin. 'We will depend totally on helicopters until then.' Then he stepped carefully into the woods.

Once in the thick fir-tree cover the temperature dropped quickly. The bright blue sky was now replaced by the darkened, damp gloom of a forest and its distant musty smell. Everything cracked underfoot. I stepped carefully, watching where I put my feet.

'Snakes?' I asked, in a half-whisper. Then I laughed to myself. I was talking as if a snake might hear.

'Himalayan Pit Vipers,' came the reply, 'but not at this time of year. Winter is almost here, which is when they hibernate, and they are lazy snakes anyway. I lost two soldiers last year from Pit Viper bites. Lower down you can see an occasional Levantine Viper. They can kill, too.'

I still did not know what to expect, as Captain Mungavin had not explained why I was to follow him. Yet as I took a few more steps into the woods, I realised there had been no need. The smell was my clue, that overpowering, nauseating, revolting odour that only long past death can create. Thirty more metres and we were there, Captain Mungavin standing beside the body, pointing to it as if it were some prize.

'This is what I need you to see,' he said, continuing to point and seemingly unaffected by the stench. 'My men found the body this morning. I want to know when he died and how. Can you help?'

It was a pitiful sight. The man, for that was what he once was, lay spread-eagled face down on the ground, his body grotesquely swollen, fingers bloated, fingernails engrained with dirt. He was fully clothed in stained white *shalwar qameez* trousers and torn woollen jacket. His muddy, slip-on black leather-look shoes were still on his feet and a well-worn *pakol* lay abandoned to one side. Tentatively I turned the body half over, enough to see its face. The lips, too, were swollen while the eyes were missing. Either pecked clean by birds or eaten by animals, I thought. Either way, the eye sockets were almost spotless. The man looked in his forties, maybe younger, but the distortion of death made age estimation hard. He was of local appearance, as best I could tell. Harder still was to say when death occurred, and how.

'Why do you need to know?' I asked.

'Because if there is evidence of enemy action, we need to be prepared. If this is a murder, we must find the culprit.'

I nodded my understanding. Yet the imprecise science of predicting time and mode of death can test even the most experienced pathologist. It was clear, from the corpse's swelling and putrefaction that death had been at least several days earlier. When a person dies many changes take place with their body. Stiffening, or rigor mortis sets in quickly as does cooling of the corpse. Rigor mortis is normally complete after about twelve hours but then the body starts to become flaccid once more. The body that lay on the ground before me was now limp, or largely so.

The experts will assess time of death by taking rectal temperatures but these are generally only useful in the first twenty-four hours. It is difficult also to say much from the attitude of a body or how it is found. If, say, someone moves a body after death by dragging on its arms, rigor mortis will set in with the arms above the head. Putrefaction also occurs, where the body rots under the action of bacteria and its own internal chemicals. This is what causes the swelling and the smell.

For the next twenty minutes I studied the body carefully. I could see no evidence of external injury and guessed the man had been dead roughly a week. It could have been longer, because of the cooling effect of the woods. Left out in the clear sunshine of the mountainside, the body would have rotted much faster. There were no knife or gunshot wounds and no sign of being mauled by a large animal. I looked carefully at the back of the skull to see if there was any evidence of execution. I had seen that frequently during the Bosnian War in the mid-1990s. There, the giveaway sign was the single wound to the back of the skull, sometimes the forehead, surrounded by a rim of dark blue staining. This was where the pistol or revolver had been placed against the victim's head before the trigger had been pulled. Here there was no evidence of that at all. I could not tell if a snake had bitten him, as the body was too deformed to show any puncture marks made by fangs.

'I cannot be sure,' I said eventually, thankful that Captain Mungavin had remained quiet and allowed me to examine the corpse. 'But there is no evidence of foul play. It might be snake bite but the only way of being sure is to have a pathologist perform a full autopsy in a proper facility.'

'And when do you think he died?'

'It's a guess, but within the last week. I do not think he died during the earthquake. I hesitated briefly, before saying, 'There is one thing.'

'What?' I had Captain Mungavin's full attention.

'His pockets are empty. I cannot find any trace of identification on him.'

'Strange.'

'Very. This man was either robbed of everything or did not want to be identified. We are near the border here. Could he be an agent?'

'Maybe,' replied Captain Mungavin thoughtfully, his right hand playing with his chin. 'I must report this to Islamabad.' With that he turned and headed down the mountainside, retracing our steps. I never did find out the true explanation for the body in the woods.

The team had done well. By the time I had returned to the terraced field, not only was the staff accommodation tent in place but a latrine had been dug and a further tent was being erected beside the anaesthetist. Despite his hard work, the line of casualties awaiting treatment appeared to grow longer rather than shorter. The message was clearly out that the medics had arrived.

Yet I could see morale was also high. There was laughing and joking between team members, particularly the ex-military and Frances the ex-policewoman, who were in their element in the Kashmir mountains. It seemed the more uncomfortable they were, the happier they became.

By nightfall, we had a total of four tents in place, a cooking area and an underpowered generator that barely had sufficient output to power a single electric light bulb. The queue for the anaesthetist's clinic was no shorter, even though he had already treated at least fifty of the minor injured. In the gloaming I could see the shadows of the next day's patients settling down for the night in blankets, or under plastic sheeting, waiting for the dawn.

It was after midnight that I made it to my sleeping bag, positioned in one far corner of the staff accommodation tent. I lay directly on the ground, albeit separated from it by one of Paquito's groundsheets.

Instantly I was asleep, but only until three o'clock that morning.

It was the sound of animals in distress that woke me - dogs yelping and jackals doing the same. There was a cacophony of noise. Every animal that lived in the wilds of Kashmir seemed to be screaming in terror. Then, suddenly, they stopped. They were almost in perfect time; one minute chaos, the next total silence. Silence until no more than five seconds later when I felt the earth strike me hard in the middle of my back; so hard that I was winded. I rolled onto my side immediately, my face a picture of pain in the dark. The aftershock had been sudden, unannounced and violent. There had been none of the swaying that warns of an earthquake, none of the feeling of instability. Just a vicious, unexpected attack from a foe over whom I had no control. The Kashmir earthquake that year created 147 aftershocks within twenty-four hours of the first tremor; twenty-eight of those were stronger than the original on the 8th October. Statistics would subsequently show 978 aftershocks of Richter 4.0 or above by the 27th October.

Following the aftershock there was, again, total silence but only for five seconds at most. Then I heard the rattling of rock and the rush of dirt as multiple landslides cascaded down the mountainsides around me. I had no escape. I lay in my sleeping bag in the dark, waiting to be buried alive. I felt so tiny, so ineffective. The power of the planet is massive while mankind is incredibly puny. When Nature decides to have a go, there is nothing you can do.

I was lucky that night. Despite the multiple landslides, the terraced field was spared. Akram had done his homework when selecting a safe location.

In the early morning, as soon as dawn allowed me to see the mountains, I looked out of the tent. My eyes were stinging furiously from the insecticide impregnated deeply into Paquito's tarpaulin. On the far side of the valley I could see a fresh landslide, and several more on mountainsides in the distance. There were none in our local area. We were lucky.

The response of the animals had been remarkable. The cacophony of noise immediately before the aftershock could only be explained by one thing. Animals can sense these events. The last thing I had been considering was an aftershock. The dogs, jackals and other living creatures thought differently.

I was not the first to notice animals' ability to predict disaster. The ancient Greeks discovered it almost 2,500 years earlier before an earthquake destroyed the city of Helike. Rats, snakes and weasels deserted the place days before the event. In more recent times, immediately before the 2004 tsunami, there had been many eyewitness accounts of elephants screaming and heading for high ground, dogs refusing to go outdoors, and zoo animals rushing into their shelters. In 2005, the animals of Panjkot had shown that same sixth sense.

That morning, as the Mi-8 thump-thumped slowly up the valley towards the Panjkot landing site, I felt sad, as I knew this would be the last time I would see the place. My job there was done, although further down the valley there was plenty more to do. The Panjkot medics were functioning well, the patients were in position and I could see the team would be busy for several weeks to come. The anaesthetist's clinic was now well established, while the plastic surgeon and Frances were busily applying dressings and stitching minor wounds.

I waited, watching the battered white fuselage of the helicopter grow gradually larger as it drew near. Yet, over the top of the thump-thump of the Mi-8 I could hear another, deeper noise. It was a sound that made the whole mountainside shake. I recognised it immediately as there is no mistaking a Chinook. It was there, high in the sky, way above my head and way above the Mi-8, too. I fumbled in my pocket for the small monocular and held it to my eye, focussing on the ungainly, rectangular shape of the dark green, military helicopter and looking hard for the sign. Yes! It was there! A wave of pride burst through me as I leapt to my feet, flinging my arms in the air and ignoring the confused looks from Captain Mungavin, his soldiers and the many waiting patients.

'Look! Look!' I cried. 'It's them!' I pointed at the Chinook. Everyone's eyes followed my own.

Then the bundles appeared as the airdrop began. Tents, food, medicines tumbled from the sky. The villagers, those who could, ran half stumbling towards the drop zone, a safe wide area about 300 metres uphill.

'It's them!' I cried once more, still pointing. The small Union Jack emblazoned on the Chinook had said all. For me, as well as for the survivors of Panjkot, this was a very important moment, so much so that I actually cried –something I rarely do. Tears of relief, happiness, and emotion streamed down my face. The NATO helicopter chief in London, he had not let me down.

* * *

JAVA 2006

Chapter 12

Multiple Disasters

Lava flows and earthquakes wait for no one, as Java in 2006 showed. The world had responded and I was part of that response. I had to be there fast as the casualties mounted.

Java is a long way from England yet inspires huge emotions in me when I say the name. They are emotions of wonder, not horror. Java is a mystical sort of place, where strange things happen but where everyone lives happily in the end. I am part of that generation which sat spellbound by Kowalski's 1969 blockbuster, *Krakatoa: East of Java*. Krakatoa Island was actually west of Java but the idea that Indonesia, Java in particular, was filled with adventure and drama, romance and challenge, never truly escaped me and remained right into adult life.

So, when on Tuesday 30th May, I sat in the Economy Class of Singapore Airlines flight 319, en route to one of many Indonesian disasters, I was strangely happy. Despite the human misery that would no doubt unfold, for the first time in my life I would see the land of my dreams.

Indonesia does nothing by halves. Its timeline of disasters is horrendous. Barely a year goes by without several earthquakes, volcanic eruptions and tsunamis. My involvement had been triggered by an earthquake on the 27th May, 5.9 on the Richter scale, with an epicentre near the city of Yogyakarta in central Java. The UK Government had offered four million pounds and I was on my way.

Not to be outdone, the nearby volcano, Mount Merapi, had erupted once more on exactly the same day. The name 'Merapi' is a contraction of two Indonesian words, *meru* (mountain) and *api* (fire), leading to 'Mountain of Fire'. The boffins had warned that an earthquake plus an eruption meant the eruption might become worse. There were already plenty dead and plenty homeless.

But there was more. To add to Merapi and an earthquake, there had been an outbreak of bird 'flu, or H5N1. This was not a good thing to contract as it carried a seventy-seven per cent chance of death. Twenty-six of Indonesia's thirty-three provinces had been affected and the entire globe was on alert for a pandemic.

And then there was terrorism to add to the local woes. Indonesia had been the focus of regular attacks, including a triple suicide bombing in Bali seven months earlier that had killed twenty people and injured 129. Travel warnings had already been issued by a number of governments, particularly for the Easter period. The major at-risk nationalities were Australia, the United States and, of course, Britain. That meant me.

Politicians do create problems for aid workers, particularly the terrorism they seem to have encouraged. I sometimes wonder if they know. When statesmen wage war on foreign lands for reasons that seem unclear, I wish they would consider lowly folk like me. Politicians have the privilege of flying in and flying out without being exposed to life at grass-root level. They will probably have armoured vehicles, their movements will be kept under wraps and they may be surrounded at all times by eight-foot monsters carrying heavy-duty weapons. For an aid worker these facilities do not exist. We enter foreign lands unprotected, fully exposed and unarmed. We survive by virtue of our native wit, an occasional prayer, and plenty of good fortune.

The May 2006 Java earthquake was small in intensity terms. Richter 5.9 is no big deal. However, it was shallow, being no more than one kilometre underground, so that many of the more rickety buildings found near the Indonesian coast did not stand a chance. The sub-district of Bantul had been particularly badly affected. The earthquake had also occurred at 5.55 am local time, so many folk were still in their houses. You do not want to be indoors during an earthquake.

To put depth into perspective, about ninety per cent of tremors occur at depths of less than 100 kilometres. Anything less than seventy kilometres is called 'shallow focus', anything over 300 kilometres is 'deep focus'. Between the two is 'intermediate focus'. The Java earthquake, on this occasion, was undeniably shallow focus.

Java lies on the boundary of the Australian and Eurasian tectonic plates, forms part of the so-called Ring of Fire, and is a major at-risk zone for extreme geological activity. On this occasion, added to the primary tremor itself, there had been 752 aftershocks within forty-eight hours. The end-result had been nearly 6,000 deaths, more than 36,000 injured, 135,000 damaged properties and 1.5 million homeless. The injured were my job.

The 2004 Boxing Day tsunami was fresh in everyone's mind. That event had killed a quarter of a million people in fourteen countries, so many of Java's roads were jammed with locals fleeing the coast for fear of another tidal wave. However scenic Java might be, however civilised and well-organised, however accustomed to natural hazards, this was a major disaster. Funds were flooding in from around the world and the UK was one of the biggest donors.

Since the Boxing Day tsunami, the UK had been active in the Indonesian province of Aceh, so had aid workers on the ground who were able to act almost immediately. My job was to support them and to create a specialist trauma facility. Sounds easy? Let me talk you through what happened.

From Singapore it was onwards to Jakarta, again by Singapore Airlines. This time I was at the back in seat 47A, my six-foot frame squashed into a dwarf-like space. Yet there was something unreal about the journey. I had left my home country, dead set to help the injured and the needy, but in Jakarta there was no sign of trouble. I was accommodated splendidly in a private house in the suburbs of the capital, alongside other aid relief staff. We ate well, our conversations centring around the principles of aid work, the difficulties of securing funds and the usual in-house politics that have plagued aid organisations since time began. I felt guilty and impatient. I had come to help, not to dine and talk. The folk around me were well dressed and well spoken, clearly excellent ambassadors for the cause of medical relief. Yet I was fidgety, restless, worried, and concerned. I needed to be right next to the disaster.

My destination was to be Yogyakarta, as near to the epicentre as one could fly. It was a large Indonesian cultural city and was once the capital of the land, albeit for only four years during the Indonesian National Revolution. Only 276 miles from Jakarta, it was a short aerial hop. Short it may have been in travel terms but long emotionally. The problem was the airline, not the route, the final words of the London office ringing loudly in my ears.

Only twenty-four hours earlier I had attended Merlin's London offices for my pre-mission briefing. Were my travel jabs up to date? No. How could I establish if I would need a visa? God knows, the Indonesian Embassy was closed. Where were those spare socks? Long since disappeared. What about tomorrow's fully booked operating list? Cancel it. So it went on, from one nightmarish reorganisation to another. No wonder, I thought, that medics found it so difficult to offer their services to disaster zones. The rejigging of a fully functional practice was mind-boggling.

Yet the London office had been a haven of common sense and tranquillity. The staff there moved effortlessly between the various desks and appeared totally unflappable. Meanwhile items of equipment had appeared as if by magic to weigh down an already load-conscious relief worker. Water bottles, food, surgical instruments, sleeping bag, satellite telephones, rechargers, and documents by the dozen.

'No problem,' the logistician had said. 'Here's a larger holdall for you.' Travelling light was not an option.

Merlin had given me their normal security brief, which essentially said I was crazy to consider leaving England. I had then started to hurry from the office to catch my flight.

It was as I had neared the office's main exit doors that the words chased me down the corridor. 'Whatever you do, don't fly AdamAir,' shouted the deep, male voice.

I had waved casually over my shoulder as I had been in haste. AdamAir? It had meant nothing to me as I hurtled towards London's Heathrow Airport. I had plenty of other problems to solve.

Now in Jakarta, the pressure was on to reach the earthquake zone as soon as possible. It was now five days after the tremor and I was still surrounded by the comfort and wealth of a modern, undamaged capital city. Meanwhile, the Jakarta Post of that day headlined 'Displaced fend for themselves to survive'. The local population was reported as becoming increasingly impatient by what they saw as the long overdue arrival of relief. For me I had to reach Yogyakarta by any means available. There was no way of avoiding AdamAir flight KI122.

Barely three months earlier an AdamAir flight had become lost, landing at an airfield more than 480 kilometres from its intended destination. The airline's record was appalling, accusations being made of multiple breaches of safety regulations. It was even said that pilots had been bribed to fly unsafe aircraft. No wonder it had been possible to find seats at the last moment, I thought, as I joined the largely non-existent check-in queue. To either side was line upon line of passengers waiting patiently for other airlines. Way down one end of the check-in hall I saw two Indonesian youths stare and then point directly at me. Finally, they convulsed in laughter. No surprises that my baggage was among the first to be checked in but to a largely empty airplane. The other airlines were fully booked, indeed overbooked, with waiting lists that went on for pages.

For a brief moment I wanted to run away, abandon my task and leave Java to its own solutions. Then training and humanity took over. There were casualties out there, plenty of them. So far the world had not done much. What the hell, I thought as boarding was announced. AdamAir it had to be.

* * *

Chapter 13

The Makeshift Hospital

I should be more mature but clearly I am not. There I was, the ex-SAS soldier with plentiful combat experience, sitting rigidly in my AdamAir seat, facing directly forwards for the entire length of the very short flight. I probably forgot to blink. In my mind, every creak, every bump, every tiny change in engine tone, spelled imminent disaster. Sweat poured down my trunk, soaking my shirt, and my hands were clammy, cold and slimy. I could not speak. Anyway, in my terror, I would not have known what to say to the passenger beside me. He was Indonesian, incapable of speaking a word of English, but was totally and utterly relaxed.

It did not help that through the aircraft window I could see a haze of volcanic ash and an erupting Mt Merapi in the distance. But this did not appear to perturb the pilot.

Despite the ash, the jet engines kept turning happily until the bumpy, lurching landing on the cracked and pitted runway of Yogyakarta Airport. The runway had been closed for a brief period after the earthquake on safety grounds but had now reopened. I sensed rather than heard the sighs of relief from within the half empty aircraft when our wheels touched Mother Earth.

As I walked down the aircraft steps, my courage now re-established and my emotions in better control I immediately smelt that unmistakable odour of sulphur. Whenever the Earth's core connects with the atmosphere above, a smell of rotten eggs is the result. This can sometimes reach toxic levels and has been known to kill folk. On this occasion, the rotten eggs were in the atmospheric background, not dangerous, a simple indicator that all was not well with Merapi.

As usual my battered, black North Face bag was last off the belt, so I was last to depart an almost empty baggage hall. Two local aid workers who had arrived in Java the day before met me at Arrivals. Squeezed into a tiny and battered Nissan, together we headed towards the suburbs of the city.

'It's chaos,' one said. 'Down by the coast there has been extensive damage. They say the casualty estimates are way under the reality.'

'Probably Government propaganda,' said the other. 'They don't want to worry the survivors.'

I looked out of the car window as we drove. Despite the jam-packed streets, I could not see much damage. There were certainly no bodies piled on the pavements, no destroyed bridges, and few cracked walls. Despite the mobilisation of half the globe's aid machine I saw little evidence of trouble. A vague smell of sulphur, a tiny crack in the baggage hall's ceiling, and a few missing polystyrene tiles had been the lot. This looked nothing like a disaster. Had I really travelled all this way for this?

I sensed that the response to Java might have been overkill. There was a mass guilt-trip created by the world's inadequate response to the Kashmir earthquake the previous year and the Boxing Day tsunami the year before that. Time would no doubt tell.

Twenty minutes later the car drew up at an abandoned healthcare facility on the outskirts of the city. It was a bungalow type of arrangement, a large communal treatment area surrounded by primitive staff accommodation, storerooms and administrative offices. Again, and unusually for a disaster zone, there was electricity and some running water.

After rapidly dumping my luggage at the accommodation I was off and away, driving towards the epicentre, to see what Yogyakarta had to offer.

When I arrive in a disaster zone the first question I ask myself is, 'Where am I best located to do my bit?' The choice of location depends on many things but it certainly needs to be near the action and within easy access of patients. It should not be hidden away. It also needs to be proportional in size to the amount of equipment available. If all you have are a few sticking plasters you can easily work from the side of a road. With more sophisticated equipment you need a building, of sorts, in which to work. I had almost nothing, other than my hands, experience, a recovering sense of humour after my AdamAir flight, and a North Face bag part filled with surgical instruments.

Bantul, some twenty kilometres south of the city and near the coast, had been the most heavily affected area, so it made sense to head south. I immediately excluded one location en route as unsuitable because it had more than seventy chicken coops nearby, not a good choice in the middle of a bird 'flu alert. I stopped at several other health facilities on the way to Bantul. Some were fully-fledged hospitals run by local Javanese; others were more simple health centres. At each location the response was the same. 'We are fine. We don't need your help. We can manage.'

I was puzzled. These responses flew in the face of the urgent need for assistance being put out by the world's media. Yet I could also understand. A fully-fledged disaster relief programme is as near to a military invasion as it comes. Many different agencies are involved; more than 500 is not unknown. They come from throughout the world, speak many different tongues, and set up shop in a foreign land as if they own the place. Governments, and the people, can feel they have lost control.

Meanwhile the Javanese had responded to help their own kind. The roads were bursting with local vehicles laden with aid. Small pick-ups with mattresses hanging dangerously over the sides; overladen roof-racked buses spewing thick, black diesel exhaust; three-up on motorcycles, both passengers clutching grimly to pots, pans and the occasional kettle. All were headed to the epicentre and that meant Bantul.

As I drove, dead centre of the chaotic roads stood young men waving boxes at each passing vehicle.

'Put into this box what you can!' they would shout. The local aid machine had swung into action by itself independent of any global or Government input. People, when left to their own devices, do respond, irrespective of what their political masters might decree. Indeed, I sometimes wonder whether politicians are any use at all in disaster relief. The May 2006 Indonesian earthquake was an excellent example of this. The locals seemed to be managing perfectly well on their own.

Feeling unloved, unwelcome and surplus to requirements, I soon entered Bantul. In my mind I was already planning to return home as there seemed so little for me to do.

Yet in Bantul the situation was different. Around me lay the debris of a manifestly vicious earthquake. Still there was the occasional survivor looking shocked, unstable and confused, wandering through the ruins of their life. Road signs hung at a drunken angle, lamp posts were bent, telephone lines dangled dangerously, roads were cracked. At a small crossroads, almost precisely at the epicentre itself, I saw a gathering of people, with injuries, waiting patiently for what looked like treatment in a large marquee-like tent. I stopped, exited the car, and walked across to the tent. It was a hive of medical activity.

The tent was well laid out. At one end was a large table, behind which sat a girl in a well-used white coat, perhaps in her mid-twenties, dishing out pills, capsules and syrups from a number of cabinets behind her. This appeared to be a makeshift pharmacy. On the ground to the girl's front, and extending the length and breadth of the massive tent, were ten large Persian carpets acting as floor covering. Bamboo matting filled any gaps between the carpets. Scattered around in a disorderly fashion, were several upright wooden chairs. On each chair sat a patient, while in between the chairs and lying on the ground, were dozens of injured casualties. Some were only slightly injured; others were in major trouble.

Each casualty, and any accompanying friend or relative, sat or lay patiently waiting for their turn in the queue. The logic of the queuing system escaped me, as there was nothing linear about the arrangement at all. However, there was clearly a priority system somewhere, understood by everyone other than me, so that each injured person was seen in turn. No one was forgotten. Beside each chair, attending studiously to their casualty, was a white-coated individual doing what they could. There was suturing of wounds, dressings being applied, splints readjusted and plasters changed. The atmosphere was one of calm professionalism. I went up to the girl behind the pharmacy table and spoke.

'Hello!' I said, with as much jollity as sleeplessness and jetlag would allow. 'I'm a doctor from England. Can you tell me who is in charge?'

The girl looked at me with an air of sympathy. 'In charge?' she replied in flawless English. 'What do you mean? We are all equal here.'

'Well who is the most senior doctor? I would like to introduce myself.'

'There are no doctors. We are medical students. None of us has qualified yet.'

Instantly I felt humbled. These young medical students, not one over the age of twenty-five years, had shown the way. Within hours of the earthquake they had brought together as much tentage and medicine as they could and had set up shop right at the epicentre. They were so close to the action that they could have been in Hell itself. Aware of their priorities each had dropped their studies in Yogyakarta and had moved to Bantul instantly.

'Where are your supervisors?' I asked.

'They would not come.'

I could not comprehend how an academic supervisor could allow students under their care to deal alone with the horrendous injuries created by an earthquake. That could not be in the best interests of either patient or student. I had no explanation.

I decided to stay. Waving farewell to my driver, who promised to collect me some hours later, I set to work. The appreciation on the medical students' faces was clear although the workload was immense. In came broken wrists and broken hips, dislocated shoulders and cracked skulls, nerve injuries to the arms and displaced knees. There were crushed feet and half-amputated fingers by the dozen, as well as broken teeth, damaged eyes, chest injuries and paraplegics. The students' hospital was a haven of safety but it was not a place for upmarket treatment. Its aim was to patch and mend. It was a tent where sterile technique was impossible and water was nowhere to be found. The equipment, too, was fast becoming exhausted. All I could do was ensure that a patient's condition was stabilised, so they would survive their journey to the nearest undamaged hospital. There were not too many of those.

All the while I was working, there were plenty of opportunities to teach the medical students, who lapped up this opportunity like a cat takes to milk. Most doctors will never attend a disaster in their professional lifetime, so training in how to deal with them is hard to find. The students' hospital in Bantul was a unique opportunity, so as I worked I also taught. The students absorbed the information like sponges, turning it into practice immediately. I showed them how to put on plasters, and take them off, how to relocate dislocated shoulders without an X-Ray to help, how to stabilise a broken neck so as not to pith the patient and how to suture the tattiest of wounds. By the time my transport arrived several hours later, I was exhausted, falling asleep instantly as the driver weaved his way through the traffic of the suburbs of Yogyakarta.

*   *   *

Chapter 14

Politicians Do Not Like Me

There is little time for rest in disaster relief. Much as I wished to remain with my head lolling side-to-side and my eyes tight shut in the back of the dilapidated Nissan, sleep was not an option. With a screech of balding tyres and an explosive spray of dust, my driver came to an abrupt halt outside Yogyakarta's Provincial Health Office. It was here that the cluster meetings were held, the opportunity for aid agencies to meet, to liaise and to minimise duplication.

An imposing official from the World Health Organisation chaired the meeting. I think he was from India. A number of Indonesian health bigwigs were also present. The bigwigs sat behind a long, brown, mica-topped table at one end of the broad, rectangular room. The workers, that was me and others like me, were sitting theatre style in uncomfortable chairs to their front.

The place was filled to the brim. There were Americans and Canadians, Finns and Swedes, French and Germans, Russians and Poles. Many nations were represented. Uniforms were everywhere, some drab, some bright and some military. Old friendships were being reforged, while new faces were introduced to veterans. However, there was one thing we all had in common. Everyone looked serious.

Suddenly, there was a thump on the mica table from a paperweight wielded by an Indonesian bigwig. Silence instantly gripped the room. I looked and I listened. For a brief moment there was nothing. No movement and no noise. Then, unexpectedly, the silence was broken.

'Happy Birthday to you, Happy Birthday to you!'

Someone, a dominating male voice, was singing. I could barely believe what I was hearing. I looked towards the aisle to my left to see a WHO official wheeling a birthday cake on a trolley towards the front of the room. One of the bigwigs was having a birthday.

'Who is this joker?' said a Frenchman to my right. 'We are in the middle of a major disaster and the country has been brought to its knees. This guy is celebrating a birthday while the population bleeds.'

I nodded. The joker's entry was as inappropriate as it seemed. Apart from disapproving whispers to each other, everyone remained silent.

The joker then proceeded to chair the cluster meeting. At least, he was meant to chair it. The end result was him telling us what he thought of the aid effort. He clearly felt as if he had total control. What the joker did not realise, and was unable to hear, were the various comments made by his audience. The Indonesian bigwig behind the mica-topped table remained silent, as did his WHO colleague. But a middle-aged American who sat directly behind me, and wearing the beige photographer's waistcoat so commonly displayed by relief agencies, leaned forward and tapped me on my left shoulder.

'Hey,' he whispered into my ear with a deep Southern drawl, 'do you have any idea what this guy is talking about? Do you have the remotest view of what is going on?'

I smiled, shaking my head in mock despair. 'Not a clue,' I whispered in reply.

To my front were two Japanese aid workers, brightly clad in red and blue uniforms. I could not hear what they were saying but their body language was evident. They, too, were confused and frustrated. Everywhere I could see shoulders shrug, palms turned upwards in exasperation, while pencils were placed firmly onto closed notebooks. All around I could hear the low hubbub of a dissatisfied audience. Two French aid workers even rose to their feet and left the room, deep in rapid and frustrated discussion.

I could see the meeting was going nowhere and there was still much work to do. I could sense from those around me that I was not alone in my views. So I rose to my feet, arm thrust firmly upwards in schoolboy fashion. It brought the joker's monologue to an instant halt.

'Questions?' he asked, looking directly at me. 'Are there any questions?'

So I began.

'I have a question,' I said. 'I am a surgeon from England. We were told you are in desperate need of surgeons. Apart from some very welcoming medical students, every facility I visit tells me there is no need for my services. Why?' Around me I could see heads nod.

'That has happened to us as well,' came a Scandinavian voice from somewhere behind me.

Then many other voices joined in. Several members of the audience were now on their feet.

'And us.'

'And us.'

'And us.'

The low hubbub had now become a noisy tide of dissatisfaction. The joker could see and hear that he was rapidly losing control. He raised both arms in the air and, obediently, we fell silent. I sat down, aware that I was now a marked man. I had sought to challenge the authority of both the WHO and of the Indonesian bigwigs. Outspoken discontent was not allowed.

'We clearly need a meeting to discuss this further,' said the joker.

I sighed. A meeting is management's way of creating thinking time and of defusing difficult situations. For the joker, faced with a large audience of frustrated aid agencies, I had created a difficult situation.

For a brief moment I wanted to rise to my feet once more and challenge the officials further. To leave that meeting without a specific tasking would lead to no tasking at all. Yet I could tell that to challenge the joker again would lead nowhere other than to turn frustrated managers into lifelong enemies. So I nodded obediently and agreed to attend a meeting later that evening. I also accepted gracefully when a bigwig suggested I should coordinate the event.

Unsurprisingly perhaps, the meeting was a further lesson in aid politics. Fifteen agencies attended, each with a similar story. They had visited local hospitals and had been told there was no need for their services. The hospitals could manage. The joker never reappeared, either alone or with the birthday cake, while one of his colleagues attended in his stead. The meeting lurched from one unsatisfactory agenda item to the next and, by the end, none of the fifteen agencies was any the wiser. No taskings had been allocated and none was expected. The fifteen agencies left as frustrated as they had arrived.

'Why is it like this?' I asked, once I had returned to the base. We were a small group of four, gathered together in the shadows of our base facility. 'All these people have come to help but nobody wants them.'

'It is always the same,' came the wise-sounding reply from a Russian colleague. 'The bigwigs never know what is needed.'

My mind flashed back to the year before and the incredible inefficiencies after the Kashmir earthquake. There had been the seemingly endless discussions, the vested interests and the power-hungry administrators aiming to make their mark. To the mountain people of Kashmir this would have seemed ridiculous. I was sure the people of Java felt the same.

I did not sleep well that night, in part because my bed was the hard, tiled floor next to my Russian colleague. By virtue of being in Java twelve hours before me he had the privilege of making the first choice of sleeping surface. To him the kitchen table was the perfect bed. That left me the floor. Throughout the night my thoughts went everywhere. The unsupervised medical students, the closed doors wherever I went, the politics of disaster relief, and the dozens of frustrated agencies around me, each with the same thoughts. For me, one question dominated. Was there really a role in Java for me at all?

By dawn I had reached no conclusion, other than feeling unslept, unkempt and not a little depressed. I had travelled a long way, had left behind a thriving practice and, so far, had achieved little other than anger and frustration. It was time to change tack.

* * *

Chapter 15

Surgical Disasters

Although the students' hospital was a brilliant idea and responsible for more lives saved than many, it was not somewhere I could operate. Surgeons need operating theatres to function so I had to find somewhere different. I was saddened to move on, particularly as the medical students had benefited so much from my visit. I hoped they would understand if I did not appear that morning. Instead I went to Maramina Hospital, an established hospital in Yogyakarta with a mixture of state and private funding.

Maramina had a long track record of caring for the needy, both within its walls and in the community. It was a remarkable place – huge, imposing and clean. When I passed through its large front doors I felt I was in a truly professional hospital. A few walls carried cracks, with some scattered rubble on the floor but Maramina had seen earthquakes previously and was largely undamaged. I could also see that it was staffed by folk who placed a patient's interests first.

As with other hospitals in Yogyakarta, Maramina had become immersed in the massive relief programme, visiting teams from around the world knocking on its doors to offer assistance. Normally with beds for 370 patients, Maramina was now home to 800. The nursing staff were exhausted, as were the doctors, relatives taking up residence beside their hospitalised loved ones so that they could help with basic care. This brought the ward population to well over 1,000. Maramina was good but with such huge numbers was on the verge of chaos.

My idea to visit had come from a conversation I overheard between two aid workers at the farcical cluster meeting. I had also heard Maramina's name from a colleague with Médecins sans Frontières. So, that morning, and despite a sleepless night, I resolved to seek out Maramina's General Manager and to offer what help I could. If I waited for guidance from the joker, I would be waiting a very long time.

Lack of sleep could not hide the spring to my step that day. I thought it might have been a surge of optimism but soon realised it was the coffee. Back home I am a decaffeinated man. I drink gallons of the stuff. Unfortunately, in the wake of the earthquake there was a serious water crisis, so it was difficult to trust water from the tap and the bottled version was in short supply. Around the corner from the base was a local roadside stall. Its bright colours meant I could not miss the place. As the stallholder boiled his water it was also likely to be safe. The stall's major trade was proper coffee, not the stuff I normally drink. To the stallholder, decaffeinated was a dirty word. The coffee-making ceremony, for that was what it was, took a good five minutes. The boiling of the water in the carbon-covered kettle, the choice of coffee flavour, the savouring of aroma depending on choice, followed by rapid stirring and ladlefuls of sugar came together to produce an incredible drink. One sip and I felt a jet afterburner in each buttock. I spoke fast, thought fast, sweated, felt sick, and had a tremor. Yet I had limitless energy.

It was in such a state that I sat before Dr Sujatmi, the General Manager of Maramina Hospital, to plead my case. At the start, our conversation was strained. I was not the first overseas surgeon to have sat before Dr Sujatmi. She was a highly successful woman in a male-dominated world. She also poured more coffee, real Indonesian black liquid with energy in every drop.

'We already have teams from throughout the world,' she said. 'What do you have that they do not?'

I could feel another door about to shut in my face, particularly as the question was so hard to answer. After all, what did I have that was different? Perhaps not much, I thought. Yet was I ready to leave empty handed once more? What was it about this country that made it so difficult to offer services in the aftermath of a disaster?

'They don't have me,' I replied, allowing my ego to emerge.

'That's true. So tell me why you are special.'

So I did. Yet even by the end of my lengthy explanation I did not think she was convinced. I was simply not special enough. Whether it was her desire to see me leave her office, or whether she felt I showed a glimmer of potential, I do not know. However, Dr Sujatmi eventually agreed. She asked me to visit the operating theatres, to talk with the staff and see where I might usefully assist. I could barely stand without shaking at that point, so high were my blood caffeine levels. I walked out of her office backwards, bowing slightly, as if taking leave of royalty. Yet my spirits were high. At last I had a surgeon's work to offer.

Maramina Hospital was a busy place. Ambulances pulled up to its imposing front entrance one after the other. Yet more injured were unloaded and carried through the maze of hospital corridors to the wards or operating theatres. The wards themselves were filled almost shoulder to shoulder with patients. In most hospitals the beds are placed down each sidewall of a ward. In Maramina there was an extra row down the middle, and beside most patients sat a relative or friend. The place was filled to busting. Extra wards had also been opened up, so a large open space that had once been used for physiotherapy was now filled with bedridden injured. Maramina had responded and it looked to be doing well. Appearances however, can sometimes be deceptive.

During less troubled times, a patient who is scheduled for surgery will probably be admitted to hospital a few hours before the operation, sometimes even a whole day earlier. This allows important safety checks to be made. Like being sure the side is correct, making certain a patient is well enough for the operation, catching up on any missing investigations and ensuring everyone understands fully what is involved. Normally, if a patient is to undergo surgery on an arm or leg, a large indelible arrow or cross is drawn on the limb beforehand so that siding mistakes cannot be made. Only then, when everything is ready, is the patient allowed into the operating theatre.

In a disaster, however, the rules change. Patients, instead of arriving in ones and twos will arrive in their one and two hundreds. Disasters are like mass casualty incidents that go on for days. It is hard for anywhere to cope. There may be too few beds on a ward to cater for patients both before and after surgery. Patients on one ward before operation can thus appear on another afterwards. There may be insufficient medical staff for the number of patients involved as medical staff can become earthquake victims, too. It is all hands to the pumps during a disaster.

Casualties with broken bones can appear on wards that normally treat patients with eye conditions. Gynaecology staff might be expected to look after psychiatric cases while surgeons who would normally specialise in knee operations will suddenly be asked to deliver a baby. That is the way of things with a disaster. In fact, patients may not come onto a ward at all before surgery. There may be so many casualties that a patient may be sent directly to the operating theatre from the street and bypass the ward altogether. The surgeon who undertakes the operation will simply be the first surgeon who has a spare slot on his operating list for that day. He, or increasingly she these days, might be from anywhere in the world and can also be exhausted, irritable, and hungry. Everyone takes risks in disasters, both the patients and those who care for them.

My first visit to the operating theatres of Maramina Hospital that day highlighted some of the critical problems that disaster surgery can create. The three operating theatres were working at fever pitch, a European team in the first, African in the second and Indian in the third.

In the corner of the European operating theatre, Theatre 1, surgery was well underway. In the far corner, clipped to a lightbox, was an X-Ray of a chest and shoulders. Beside the light box, taped to the theatre's tiled wall, were two sheets of A4 paper stapled end to end. On the paper was typed line upon line of names and operations. This was the day's workload, what is called an operating list. I counted at least seventeen different procedures. Judging from the tick marks beside the names, the patient on the table before me was only number four. Under normal conditions, few operating theatres would undertake as many as seventeen operations in one day. Four or five would be normal. The European team was in the middle of a massive workload and was clearly exhausted. They greeted me as I walked in, although because they were fully sterile, we clearly could not shake hands.

'What sort of surgery do you do?' asked the senior European surgeon.

'Bones and joints,' I replied.

'Thank Heaven for that,' came the reply. 'We're having a problem with this shoulder here.' With the tips of his surgical forceps, the surgeon indicated the open wound before him. I could see the white glistening surface of the ball of the right shoulder shining at me from the bottom of the large surgical gash. The whole of the surgical field was brightly lit by the powerful overhead operating light.

'This guy has broken his shoulder socket,' the surgeon continued, indicating the X-Ray on the lightbox. 'He's about 25 years old.'

I walked the few steps to the X-Ray to take a closer look. The shoulder socket had been largely obliterated, most likely from crushing by falling debris. This was a major injury by any standards.

'Why is that a problem?' I asked. 'The fracture is clear to see on the X-Ray.'

'That's the issue. We've opened the shoulder joint but cannot find the fracture.'

I came closer to the surgeon and looked over his shoulder at the open wound. Then I glanced at the X-Ray, then back at the wound. Slowly the realisation dawned. Surely not? Godammit! My heart sank. I was witnessing a surgical disaster.

'You're operating on the wrong shoulder,' I said.

'No, I'm not.'

'You are, I'm afraid. Look, the X-Ray department has mis-sided the X-Ray film. The large letter 'R' at the bottom right of the film does not mean the right shoulder but the right side of the film. They mark their X-Rays differently over here.'

The surgeon then fell silent. All I could hear was the rhythmic breathing of the patient, carefully controlled by the anaesthetist at the head of the operating table. Then the surgeon spoke. Realisation had dawned.

'Shit, shit, shit! You're right.'

I was certainly right. I did not want to tell the surgeon that I had seen the problem before, many years ago when working in central India. At that time I had been involved in the operation directly, although as the assistant rather than the main operator. It is a rare occurrence but one of the many reasons why a surgeon should always see a patient before surgery. For this Javanese casualty, he had come straight to the operating theatre, bypassing the wards, without being properly consented and marked. Because of the huge influx of casualties, the surgeon had not been able to talk with him before surgery, such was the pressure of work. This was a recipe for error and an error had been made.

The end-result was fine, as the first shoulder wound was stitched up, the patient turned, and the other shoulder opened. The shattered shoulder socket was then identified and repaired. Yet after surgery someone had to explain to the casualty why he had broken only one shoulder but had two large scars as a consequence.

Once surgery on the correct shoulder was properly underway, I made my excuses to the European surgeon, walked out through the operating theatre's swing double doors and into Theatre 2 next door. Here, surgery was also in progress, a hip operation being performed by an African surgeon and his European assistant. The operation was easier than that for the broken shoulder socket. It was a simple broken upper thighbone that needed metal plates and screws to secure it.

Although the surgeons were performing the correct operation, it was how they were doing it that horrified me. The surgeon's sleeves were not tucked into his gloves, masks were akimbo and sweat was dripping from the assistant's forehead into the wound itself. Any one of these manoeuvres was asking for trouble as it increased the risk of infection enormously. Quietly I slipped out of the operating theatre as I found it hard to hold my tongue.

I thought that would be an end to it but it was not to be. I walked out of Theatre 2 into the theatre reception area to find another patient awaiting surgery. On this occasion the problem was a broken left lower thighbone, just above the knee. I glanced at the X-Ray films that accompanied the patient. They were marked with a very large 'L', but on the right hand side of the X-Ray. Here again was the potential for another catastrophic wrong-sided operation unless everyone took care.

Meanwhile, there was much mumbled discussion taking place between the theatre staff in the final operating theatre I visited, Theatre 3. A patient with a broken spine had been accidentally paralysed because the anaesthetist had sat them up too abruptly to administer an epidural injection. No one had thought to X-Ray the patient's spine before surgery, so they had missed the unstable fracture of the vertebra. The moment the patient was sat up in preparation for the epidural, the broken vertebra had shifted and the sharp fracture fragments had severed the patient's spinal cord. The end result had been complete paralysis below the waist.

By the end of my short visit to the operating theatres of Maramina Hospital, I was horrified and alarmed. There were too many patients and too few surgeons. What surgeons there were had become exhausted and mistakes were being made. In the space of forty-five minutes I had witnessed two major surgical disasters, clear evidence of poor surgical technique, and a near miss.

There are many reasons why such things happen. None is a valid excuse. However, the surgeons came from different parts of the world where they were accustomed to different standards of practice. Some would write comprehensive operating notes, while some would write sketchy ones. Some might give precise instructions about how their patients should be handled after surgery while others would say almost nothing. After their operation, patients would go back to a ward where their operating surgeon might never see them again. Anyway, what was the point of seeing them when neither party could speak the other's language? It was possible also that neither party could read the other's writing, thereby making detailed instructions of no value to the reader.

In disaster zones there are hundreds of other mini-disasters lurking round every corner. I had seen just a few of them. I saw instantly what I had to do. My primary task would be to improve the standards of safety for the patients arriving from the epicentre. Somehow, and rapidly, the standards of surgery and its aftercare had to improve.

I returned immediately to Dr Sujatmi's office and explained my worries to her. She was horrified. Instantly she realised that to have so many surgical errors under one roof would be a public relations disaster. She gave me full authority to put things right. Over the next few days I toured the hospital with my little black book, one of my trademarks for those who know me. You want to stay out of my book if you can. I talked, I recorded, I took photographs, I examined wounds, I operated, and telephoned my UK colleagues for advice. As best I could, I left no stone unturned.

Three days later I had finished and within a week the situation had begun to improve. Patients would only receive an operation if their surgeon had seen them beforehand. It made no difference how many casualties arrived that day. A big black arrow would always be drawn on a patient before surgery so there was no danger, ever again, of wrong side surgery being performed.

Yet my time in Maramina Hospital showed me that not all treatments and not all surgeons are equal. Disaster surgery is best left to highly trained experts, those who have done it before. All patients, from wherever they come, deserve the very best doctors can offer. That starts with basic surgical safety.

* * *

HAITI 2010

Chapter 16

The Call

In January 2010, I had barely heard of Haiti. It was somewhere far away, full of poor unfortunates I would never meet. To me, Haiti was an occasional place for the rich and famous to take their seaside holidays. It was somewhere I would never see, had no wish to see and would struggle to find instantly on a map.

'Bugger it!' I muttered that cold winter's morning as I fell nearly headlong over the pile of clothes scattered on the bedroom floor. The alarm had woken me seconds before. It was the early hours of January 13th, still dark outside and I had slept appallingly. I was not in the best of moods. The day was scheduled to be chaos with at least a dozen surgeons visiting the hospital to see me operate. I groped out in the darkness to turn on the radio and then headed for the bathroom, about six steps away. My London flat was tiny. As I splashed the ice-cold water onto my face I felt the energy begin to slowly course through me. In the distant background I could hear a crackly BBC. An earthquake in Haiti, it said. Casualties were said to be limited, but news was sparse.

I carried on washing. Earthquake? Not interested. Life had moved on since Java and Kashmir. I had done my bit then and had plenty of other things to do now.

'That is them and this is me,' I thought. I had no wish to be involved.

That morning there were more important things in my life. Shirts late back from the laundry, a filthy flat that needed cleaning, a broken dishwasher and a coffee machine that had died a premature death. Yet I am ashamed when I think of it now. How pathetic I was. How unreasonable. How simplistic. How selfish. What, oh what, was going through my mind? On a remote island 4,500 miles away, horror had descended on good and decent people. All I could think of in London were my tiny, insignificant, miniscule worries by comparison. I look back now and realise how my life then had become so much out of proportion.

By lunchtime that day it was clear that Haiti was a major problem. The body count had reached several thousand and I knew there would be more to come. My eyes kept glancing towards the small television in the badly painted staff coffee room, that place of sanctuary where surgeons hide from the world between operations. Yet there was no hiding for me. No hiding from the visiting surgeons and their incessant questions and no hiding from the earthquake. The news reports were coming in fast.

One visitor did take me briefly to one side, flicking his head towards the television.

'You going?' he asked.

'I doubt it,' I replied and then our conversation returned to surgery.

It was the six o'clock news that evening that did it. By then the body count was in the tens of thousands and headed higher. The British Government had already passed comment, as many of its own nationals had also disappeared in the few seconds it takes an earthquake to wreak its havoc. Back in my flat, exhausted from an operating list that had seemingly gone on forever, I flicked aimlessly forward and back through the television's many channels. They all carried the same reports. Haiti.

Something clicked inside me as I watched. I had felt it so many times before. Perhaps it is just that I am a doctor. It is the same instinct I have when a stranger falls to the ground in front of me, or a drunk collapses, or an elderly lady simply cries for help. You have to move, you have to act, you cannot ignore it. Turning the other way is simply not an option.

Haiti was going to be a big one. The aid agencies of the world would have to mobilise fast. I was on my feet instantly, a surge of adrenaline abolishing my exhaustion in less time that it takes to blink. Within seconds I was at my computer and the one-line email had gone. 'If you need an orthopaedic surgeon for Haiti, I can leave tomorrow,' it read. I so badly wanted a reply.

The next morning I awoke even earlier than usual. My problems were the same; the mislaid shirts, the dirty flat, the non-functional dishwasher and coffee machine, were still there just as before. Yet somehow the day felt different. My whole focus had changed. I now saw these tiny problems as just that. Minor irritations, which if they were never solved until the end of time, would remain insignificant. Trousers half on, shirt draped across one shoulder, one sock on and the other off, I flicked on my computer with one hand while trying vainly to brush my teeth with the other. My email Inbox was filled to its brim. With one forefinger I slowly traced the message headings down the screen, certain that I would find an answer to my emailed offer of assistance.

I spoke quietly to myself as I read the headings.

'Research paper? No. Surgical equipment? No. Lecture invitation? No. Society dinner? No. General Medical Council? No. Come on, come on, come on! Where is it?' My forefinger now came off its steady descent and flicked this way and that, up, down, left and right. 'Where is the damn thing?' I shouted, although there was no one who could hear my plea.

Yet despite my frantic pointing and ill-considered shout, there had been no reply to my email. The one message I wished to receive was not there. No one, it appeared, wanted me in Haiti.

The problem is, the moment you volunteer for disaster relief, it is difficult to think of anything else. You keep your telephone on maximum ring, you check emails every five minutes and you leave messages wherever you go. 'If so-and-so telephones, let me know immediately,' you say to anyone who is happy to listen. Yet the call always comes when you least expect it, when you are sure the disaster has passed you by. Why is it, you think, that those who organise disaster relief do not have the same sense of urgency as you? Well of course they do. It just does not feel that way when you are waiting for the call. Mentally you are on your way already. Physically you are not.

That day I was scheduled to spend ten hours in my clinic, seeing patients who might need surgery alongside those who had already been through my hands. It was hard to focus, particularly as 24-hour news was blaring from the television in the patients' waiting room. I could hear every word. It was Haiti, Haiti, Haiti, every minute of the day. Yet always in my mind was the question, repeating itself continually. 'Why haven't they rung? Why haven't they rung?'

Mid-morning coffee came and went – not a whisper. Lunchtime arrived but still no news. By then, despite my secret hopes, I was sure Haiti was not for me, so I made plans to attend a surgical meeting in Manchester the following day. The moment the internet had verified my credit card details and money had changed hands, my mobile rang, its screen identifying the number. It was Merlin. The call! The female voice at the other end sounded frantic. This time it was not the ever-relaxed

Suzie. The voice, tense, quavering and tight, was struggling hard to find medical staff.

'This is the big one, Richard,' she said. 'Are you OK to go?'

'No problems,' I said. 'When?'

'Now,' came the reply.

In disaster relief, now means now. There is no time for pondering, no time for reflection, no time for doubt. When called upon, you go. As the mobile descended from my ear, I turned to my secretary. I barely had to say a word.

'Haiti?' she inquired.

'Haiti,' I replied. 'Cancel everything until I return.'

With that I walked out of the clinic and headed across London to receive my briefing, leaving a trail of confused patients in my wake and an assistant whose workload had just doubled. My secretary's job was to smooth the situation, to reschedule and rebook and, naturally, to apologise.

I am what Merlin calls a Surgical Team Leader, not a title I find particularly attractive. It smacks of healthcare management speak. In fact, I do not lead at all. I prefer the title 'fixer' because that is what I do. The fixer's job, my job, is to be in at the start and put together whatever is needed for the larger medical teams that follow. I had done that for Kashmir, although had been many days delayed, and had tried that for Java but had failed. This time, I resolved, it would be different.

Merlin's office was astonishingly relaxed. No raised voices, no hurried steps, no slamming of telephones. The dozen or so staff appeared truly focussed despite the total environmental chaos on the other side of the world. As I entered at one end of the huge, warehouse-like office, desks littered haphazardly around, a few casual eyes looked in my direction and then returned to their task. Screens flickered, computer mice moved, printers spewed out long lists of equipment, while a small television screen flashed up video images of the disaster.

At the far end of the office I could see a vast black duffel bag being packed by two enthusiastic logisticians. Even from a distance it looked impossible to lift. I walked towards them, weaving my way between the scattered desks. To my left, sitting behind a scratched mahogany table, piled high with crumpled paper press releases, an attractive face looked up and smiled as I passed. This was the communications desk. Behind it sat Melanie.

'We have some interviews for you,' she said, rising slowly to her feet and waving casually to me as I approached. I nodded and headed for the duffel bag, Melanie in hot pursuit.

The issue with all disasters is to predict what you will need before you actually need it. This is made particularly difficult because every disaster is different. There is little point, for example, in turning up to an earthquake with a rubber dinghy. There is every point if you are stuck in a Pakistani flood. Logisticians spend weeks planning these things, the end result being lists, lists and more lists. If a prize were to be awarded for the most indigestible reading on the planet it would surely go to an aid equipment spreadsheet. These are invariably thrust into my hand as I walk out the door headed towards an emergency. By then my mind is firmly on other things. How do I get there? What are the risks? How do I eat, drink or even sleep? The last minute is never a time to pass comment on a 2,000–item spreadsheet.

So as I approached the duffel bag and one of the logisticians turned to greet me, his right hand extended in welcome, I was not surprised to see the thick document folder wedged tightly under his armpit. I knew what was coming.

'Hi Richard!' he smiled. 'Wonderful you can do this. Would you have a moment to look through these spreadsheets?' The document folder was immediately transferred from his armpit to my hand. I did not complain.

I asked to see what was going into the duffel bag, which had also been decorated with several aid stickers. 'Urgent Medical Supplies', 'Disaster Relief', 'Emergency Aid' shone brightly from its sides. Big white stickers that declared real intent. I leaned down to press the corner of one sticker more firmly to the bag's surface. For a moment I let my hand hesitate over the sticker's words. So this was it, I thought. I am on my way.

One by one the carefully packed items were removed from the vast holdall, which was certainly as heavy as it looked. It was so laden I could barely lift the thing and its roller wheels made little difference.

The two logisticians produced each item in turn from an apparently bottomless pit.

'Tent,' said one, carefully placing the tightly packed bundle to one side on the floor.

'Mosquito net,' said the other, as a smaller package emerged and took its place alongside the tent.

'Water purification tablets.'

'Meals ready to eat.'

Slowly the duffel bag emptied and the pile on the floor grew. The items had clearly been carefully thought out and were designed to allow an operative to survive in a hostile environment without resupply for several days. There was, however, one item I could not explain.

'What's this?' I queried, kneeling down beside the logisticians. I held up the thin, brown cardboard box, which gave a gentle metallic rattle when I shook it.

'An amputation saw,' came the reply. 'We thought you might need one.'

'I see,' I muttered hesitantly, after several seconds delay. My lack of enthusiasm was obvious.

What is it about earthquakes and amputations? It appears to be a standard topic discussed with all aid workers in the aftermath of disaster, earthquakes in particular. 'How many amputations will you be doing?' is frequently the first question the media will ask and is seen by some as a measure of aid success. The more limbs you remove the more effective you have been. Yet why? I am the guy who has to do it and I would never use amputation as a measure of success. My job is to preserve limbs if I can, not remove them. Amputating is the last thing I consider and something I try hard to avoid.

'I won't be needing this,' I said gently and laid the thin cardboard box to one side. Slowly I rose to my feet, thanked the logisticians, and walked back to the communications desk.

The media are a mixed blessing at times like this. I was besieged by interview requests – Merlin's communications team, Melanie in particular, had been working hard. One poor chap called from a distant American radio channel and launched into the how–many–amputations–question, but could clearly sense my eyeballs roll as I answered.

'What do you think you will see?' he added, changing immediate tack.

'Lots of dead and wounded,' I replied.

'And what are you hoping to achieve?'

'A secure environment. We must save as many injured as we can.'

I grimaced as I spoke. As the words emerged, I knew I was saying the wrong thing. I had introduced the concept of security and that was daft. The journalist immediately latched onto it and I now had to wriggle my way out. Haiti was well known to be a security nightmare, both environmentally and geologically.

Standing beside me at the communications desk, Melanie pointed towards the State Department security brief, fresh from the United States. 'There are no safe areas in Haiti', it said. 'There is persistent danger of violent crime...kidnapping, death threats, murders, drug-related shoot-outs, armed robberies, home break-ins and car-jacking are common...' The earthquake was the least of my worries. Immediately, I hung up on the journalist. It was time to start work.

As I walked from the hangar-like office towards my waiting minicab, struggling with the titanic duffel bag whose stickers were now on luminescent display, I had only one thought, repeating itself continually in my head. 'What have I done?' it said.

I was headed to a country of which I had barely heard to treat an unimaginable number of casualties in an environment that did not take kindly to strangers. I glanced down to my right hand, which was firmly gripping a small, box-like portable video camera, a gift from a major news channel. It was the final item Melanie had given me as I walked out of the office door. 'Film everything and anything and send it to us,' she had instructed. These journalists. They never miss a trick.

*   *   *

I opened the door to my London flat hesitantly. It was impossible to be quiet as the duffel bag racketed noisily up the concrete steps. Faces peered around curtain corners, front doors opened a crack. Once indoors I turned on the radio, to maximum volume. News bulletins flooded in. There were more horror stories of Haiti, more criticism of the fledgling aid programme for taking so long to swing into action, more comment offered by people confined to soft armchairs in comfortable homes. I cursed them all. You just try this, I thought. Just try it. Turn your life upside down in the space of seconds, cease all income-generating activity, turn your back on everyone and everything you know, travel with worthless life insurance to a disaster zone, then you might understand.

I darted everywhere, packing further essentials I might need. The ten-ton duffel bag grew larger still. My endorphins were racing. Meanwhile, my mobile rang perpetually and the doorbell likewise. One media interview after another flooded in, almost all with the same question – how many amputations? I avoided the question if I could.

My mobile rang once more. I had lost count how many times. It was Merlin.

'Your flight is booked,' said the voice. 'Take-off in four hours from Gatwick. OK?'

'OK,' I replied, looking at my watch. Four hours! There was barely enough time.

'And proof of life?' queried the voice. 'We need that before you go.'

Proof of life; the questions you leave behind that can be asked in the event of kidnap. After all, how do negotiators know if a hostage is alive or dead? Answering a unique question is one way out of that. Allowing the kidnappers to chop off your finger and send it in an envelope may be another, although I would not recommend it.

'That'll be done,' I replied curtly. 'I'll email proof of life across.'

The Gatwick Express was filled to bursting, seemingly with the world headed for their winter in the sun. Haiti was already front-page news. Newspaper headlines littered the carriage, shouting in a dozen languages. 'Time Running Out For Victims,' screamed one. 'Thousands of Bodies Pile Up in the Streets of Port-au-Prince,' yelled another.

There were no direct civilian flights to Haiti and the main runway in Port-au-Prince, the Haitian capital, was closed to anything other than occasional humanitarian aircraft. My route was from London to Madrid, Madrid to the Dominican Republic and there my ticket ran out. I would need initiative and good fortune to enter Haiti. I joined the lengthy check-in queue and could see my struggles with the ten-ton duffel bag were attracting curious glances from my fellow passengers.

'Mummy, where's that man going?' asked the little boy to my left. He pointed, adding, 'That man there with the big bag and the stubbly chin.'

I smiled as I felt my face. The boy was right. I had forgotten to shave. I was looking less the professional surgeon by the minute.

My first stop, Madrid Barajas Airport, was mayhem and clearly acting as a hub for international aid headed west. The jet which took me from there to the Dominican Republic was huge, every seat filled with travellers headed for Haiti. They were from throughout the world - Europe, Japan, China, Philippines, Australia, Africa, India, and countries with names that take a week to pronounce. The sense of anticipation was enormous.

I sat beside Arnaud, a logistician from MSF. Although new to each other, we fast became friends.

'What is that?' asked Arnaud, incredulity in his French-accented voice, as he pointed towards the pile of spreadsheets I had brought from

London. The long flight to Santo Domingo had seemed a perfect opportunity to see what they contained.

'You tell me,' I laughed, sliding the pile towards him. 'Light reading from London.'

Arnaud picked up the pile of spreadsheets in both hands, then threw his arms upwards to simulate scattering of the papers far and wide.

'You know what I think?' he asked, more as a statement than a question, as the spreadsheet pile returned to his tabletop. 'These will make perfect firewood in Haiti.'

I had to agree.

For the remainder of the trip to Santo Domingo, Arnaud and I swopped one disaster story for another. He easily outdid me. We both noticed that the jet was mainly filled with media personnel; there were very few aid workers. Such is the difference between our two professions. The disaster medic can only function when supported by equipment. All the knowledge in the world will not drain an abscess. The equipment is a large tail, which has to catch up with the body before any truly useful work can be done. That makes the medic very slow. Meanwhile the journalist can move fast and, these days, may act in a self-contained capacity – filming, recording, editing, and transmitting, all in one. The notebooks were already out on that flight to Santo Domingo. The stories were appearing fast.

The arrivals area of Las Americas Airport was filled with humanity. There were people everywhere, eyeing up each new arrival in the minutest detail. It was 9 pm, dark, and very hot. I weaved my way through the crowd that surrounded me, ignoring the hawkers who were trying hard to tempt new arrivals into their taxis. I had no idea where to go anyway. I must have looked confused as very soon an American, perhaps in his mid-twenties, approached me.

'You headed for Haiti?' he inquired. I nodded.

'Be careful,' the American advised in a voice that would have made a gangster proud. 'They're throwing bodies in the road to make you stop. Then they take everything you have.'

'Thank you for letting me know,' I replied, steadying my voice and trying to sound the unflappable Englishman, yet probably failing to do so. The American smiled, nodded wisely and wandered away to frighten another new arrival.

Yet he had highlighted a common problem in the wake of catastrophe.

Disasters breed many activities, not all of them honest. However well meaning your intention, the moment you step from that aircraft, or boat, or train and enter a disaster zone, you must be on your guard. You stay that way until you return. Assume everyone is guilty until proved innocent. It is the best way to stay in one piece.

Slowly I watched the crowd disperse as each new arrival was met and escorted to a waiting taxi; each new arrival except me. I looked over, under and through the thinning sea of humanity for a familiar face. I saw no one – no smile, no wave, and no fluttering sign to draw my attention. London's reassurance that I would be met at the airport had not materialised. At least I thought that was the case until the crowd thinned to two – me at one end of the Arrivals Hall and a balding, middle-aged local at the other. He was leaning against a concrete pillar, hands in his pockets, casually surveying the area. Several times he glanced in my direction but each time looked away.

'Hello-o-o!' I cried, waving one arm frantically while trying to control the duffel bag with the other. I saw the hands come out of their pockets, the balding head jut forward and the casual lean against the pillar become a vertical stance. Slowly the stranger walked towards me, his pace increasing as he came near.

'You Dr Reechard?' he queried in a Dominican-cum-Spanish tone.

I nodded, realising the problem. The squinting, added to the thick glasses that almost embraced the stranger's scalp, were the giveaway. His eyesight was appalling. I would have been nothing but a blur from the far side of the Arrivals Hall. Even near to me his eyes were tightly puckered.

'Hello doctor,' he said. 'I take you to your hotel?'

Having been filled with terror in London about all things Haitian and Dominican, added to the American in the Arrivals Hall, I saw a kidnapper, murderer and rapist around every corner en route to the hotel. My driver's English was as good as my Spanish, so we staggered through each conversation in Spanglish, a mixture of the two.

The journey was uneventful, apart from one police roadblock where the taxi was searched for illegal contraband. After a brief inspection of the overloaded car boot, the two dozy, armed and slightly intoxicated policemen sent the taxi on its way. That was not before they had much amusement competing with each other as to who could lift the ten-ton duffel bag one handed. They both failed. Another reason for not taking an amputation saw in your personal luggage to a disaster zone, I thought.

Try explaining that to a drunk Dominican policeman on a dark night in Spanglish.

At the hotel, which was wedged inconveniently between a decibel-busting nightclub and a shopping precinct, I met the other members of the UK team. We formed a small, five-man group. We had never met before, yet such is the pressure of disaster relief that we instantly bonded.

Full credit must go to London for inserting us into Haiti at all. Many agencies were to be entirely disappointed. I sensed trouble the moment we arrived at Santo Domingo's secondary airport, La Isabela. At the front entrance stood a German search and rescue team, each member dressed in a sparkling, well-pressed uniform that put my tatty jeans and T-shirt to shame. Yet the Germans were clearly having problems finding suitable transport to take them into Haiti. News was coming in that Haitian airspace had been closed by the US military and that the only logical entry point would be by road. My heart sank. That would be a further day wasted and time was limited. Not only would casualties be dying in their hordes as a consequence of this delay but hot on my heels was a full field hospital, flying out from UK. I needed to find a suitable location for this and had less than seventy-two hours to do so.

Whenever I ask my colleague how he did it, even now he goes quiet, so I do not know whether it was bribery, bullying, death threats, or simply his charm and tact that did the trick. I suspect it was the latter. However, while the Germans hopped from foot to foot in frustration, my colleague emerged from a chipped and battered airport office to say that we should check in our equipment immediately and would be leaving for Port-au-Prince in Haiti within thirty minutes.

There was also documentation to complete. Even disaster relief teams need visas, whatever the degree of urgency. Wherever I have been in the world, whatever the occasion, one way of hindering your entry into a far-flung land is to arrive with incomplete paperwork. Immigration officials hate it. The planet was in ashes a short distance away, but to the immigration officials of La Isabela Airport that day, the documentation had to be perfect.

There were fourteen passengers in the turboprop that had been tasked to make the unpredictable journey into Haiti, flown by two Dominican pilots. Only half the passengers were medical, the others were journalists. Equipment was everywhere, squashed into each tiny corner and under every seat. The ten-ton duffel bag was still intact and occupied a position of honour immediately behind the pilot. Many of its sticky labels had disappeared and a large abrasion ran down one side but it was still the largest bag by a considerable margin.

Sitting in the front passenger seat I had a ringside view of the pilots as they pushed knobs, flicked switches and spoke to each other in a language I could not understand. They too were excited, happy to do their bit for what was a desperate situation. The engines revved furiously, the turboprop shaking like a dysfunctional massage chair, unsecured items falling wherever they were to be found in the passenger cabin. I am unsure whether the object of this revving is to test the aircraft frame for structural problems before takeoff or simply to gather a good head of speed. Either way, the turboprop reached the start of the runway intact, the engines revved still further, reaching almost fever pitch. We were away. My eyes were tight shut, something for me that is normal. I was actually praying. You see, I hate takeoffs.

'Here I go,' I whispered to myself. 'Haiti here I come.'

At least I would have been had the aircraft taken off but it did not. The frantic shaking suddenly ceased, as if the engines had failed. I opened my eyes slowly as the noise died away, recoiling slightly to find a pilot's face only inches from my own. He was staring right into me, anger in his eyes. This was real anger, the sort that drives men to violence. He gripped my left shoulder as he spoke, as if to emphasise the words that were to come.

'Doctor,' he said, 'they have bloody cancelled us.'

Then, releasing his firm grip on my shoulder, he looked towards the other passengers and added, 'I am sorry, but Port-au-Prince has said we cannot land today. An American politician is visiting and all Haitian airspace has been closed to civilian traffic as a security measure.'

I could barely believe what I was hearing. The aid effort was already being widely criticised for delays. Yet there I was, poised to go, barely thirty minutes from the disaster zone, being denied entry on account of a visiting politician. Surely not? But yes, it appeared, surely so.

My walk back to the terminal building seemed to take an age. I had lost the spring to my step, a spring that had been evident when I first boarded the turboprop. The pilot had said it would be unlikely we would enter Haiti that day but he would try again tomorrow. Tomorrow was clearly unacceptable. As I returned to the departure area, hands in pockets, head held low, my shoulders rounded and feet scuffing the ground, I saw one of the German search and rescue team look in my direction. A tall, fair, Teutonic type, he winked. It was not a friendly wink. It simply said, 'I told you so.'

I had no desire to start an international incident so held my tongue. However, the German's glance did highlight one thing – there is much competition between agencies and countries when it comes to the provision of aid.

There then followed a seemingly endless wait, or at least it felt that way. I drank multiple coffees in the departure area, made numerous frustrated telephone calls to colleagues back home and waited...and waited...and waited. Any of us would have walked, crawled, indeed sold off our livelihoods to reach Haiti. The Germans had by now disappeared to negotiate an alternative route into the country. Probably by road, I thought. That would take an age, assuming they could avoid the dead-body roadblocks to which the American had referred. I gave a knowing nod to the winker as he passed, much to his annoyance.

'England 1, Germany 1,' I whispered to myself. And then he was gone.

We were alone, our small team of five, sat quietly at a dilapidated airport table, empty bottles of water and cracked plastic coffee cups mounting up steadily on its dirty grey surface. You could almost hear the gloom.

Then, unexpectedly, the smiles reappeared as our pilot emerged as if from nowhere. 'Come!' he said, 'we must board now!' Tomorrow had suddenly become today.

Within minutes, I was squashed once more into the tiny turboprop, which now had only twelve passengers. Two journalists, frustrated by the abandoned takeoff, had chartered a small helicopter at huge expense and were leaving for Haiti just as we boarded the overladen turboprop for the second time. Then came the familiar rattles and shakes, the eyes tight shut, the prayers, the scratch marks in the upholstery, the tumbling equipment and we were up, bumping our way through the darkening clouds towards Haiti.

*   *   *

Chapter 17

The General

It is difficult to tell the extent of earthquake damage from high in the air, particularly if you are untrained. Go lower and all is laid bare. What was striking for Haiti was that some locations were completely destroyed while others remained untouched. Port-au-Prince showed this perfectly. This was no act of God but more an act of construction expertise at the time of building.

Puffs of white smoke, perhaps dust, rose like mini-tornadoes throughout the city, evidence of the continuing collapse of buildings or the fires the earthquake had created. This was desolation and destruction – extreme, total and distressing. From above, I could see that many roads were totally free of traffic while others were at gridlock. Meanwhile military helicopters were flying everywhere. The tiny white dots of United Nations armoured cars could be seen dashing through the city, its soldiers in a futile effort to assert a degree of control. Haiti was a war zone, a disaster zone, and a global centre for gang conflict. It was as socially deprived as it could get.

I had only to look at the figures to realise my own good fortune. Barely one in every 10,000 Haitians had access to a qualified physician before the earthquake, let alone afterwards. Up to eighty per cent of the adult population was unemployed, fifty per cent practised voodoo and ninety per cent of all the HIV cases in the Caribbean could be found in Haiti. Haiti was struggling badly even before the earthquake arrived.

The turboprop landed easily and, as the engines died, within seconds the cabin door was opened. We, the passengers, were rapidly herded onto the runway of Port-au-Prince's International Airport. This was not an occasion to expect airport transport to appear and deliver passengers to the cracked, partly subsided terminal, which lay 400 metres away. Along one side of the rectangular terminal building was a snaking queue of Haitians trying to leave the country. They seemed to be waiting so patiently. There was no screaming and no shoving. They simply stood still. Meanwhile, huge cargo planes from throughout the world landed every two to three minutes and taxied past, their wings passing directly overhead as I waited on a grassy area to one side of the single runway. We formed a line and unloaded the turboprop bag-by-bag, box-by-box, making individual equipment piles for our respective teams. I saw the journalists set to work immediately with their satellite telephones. This was an opportunity for them which was too good to miss.

We had arrived. As with most disasters we had nowhere to go, no one to meet us, nowhere to sleep, drink, eat, or pee; no transport, appalling communications, limited shelter and the environment was a security nightmare. None of us had any idea if, when or how we would return home. Everything I possessed was in the ten-ton duffel bag with a much smaller daypack on my back. That is the life of a fixer. The job? Create something out of nothing, ignore all personal discomfort and prepare the way for those who follow. Haiti was going to be a massive challenge.

Thirty minutes later, a small forklift truck appeared driven by a silent Haitian and towing a large, orange, open trailer behind it. This was the result of intensive negotiations between our pilots and the surviving airport cargo staff. I helped fill the trailer to the brim with equipment and walked towards the terminal building, watching our treasured load bounce and lurch uncontrollably across the dry, grassy surface which ran alongside the runway. The forklift driver did not look behind him once.

As I approached the terminal building I began to see the facial detail of the many Haitians waiting alongside it. These were a frightened people, unsurprisingly. Strong yes, but most definitely frightened. Children clutched tightly to a parent's trousers, or skirt, or blouse. Babies cried, mothers breast-fed, wrinkled elderly lay on the ground in a tight, foetal ball. A multitude of eyes stared at the equipment as we approached, the white plastic water containers standing out clearly and bouncing like dice on the very top of the trailered pile. I broke into a jog to catch up with the trailer and tried futilely to squash the water containers out of sight. In this environment people would kill for water.

The forklift came to a halt immediately outside the terminal. The driver climbed from his small cab, still without any glance in our direction, and disappeared into the building. Meanwhile I rapidly packed the water containers into our individual rucksacks although by then everyone could see what we had. Within minutes, at least two of the containers had disappeared. I never saw who took them. Water was in very short supply and the weather was hot. The water containers represented our total, personal ration. Without them we, too, would be in trouble.

The vanishing water emphasised a critical feature of disaster relief, the same feature that had been highlighted by the American at Las Americas Airport. The moment you arrive in a disaster zone, the population is in survival mode. You, the new arrival, must have your wits about you. There is no acclimatisation, no time for rest, recovery and familiarisation. You are on duty, your senses fully alert, the moment you arrive. Your life, and the lives of your colleagues, will depend on it.

* * *

A bored immigration officer sat awkwardly at a plastic table – an improvised immigration counter – and looked briefly at my documentation. My passport was stamped with fading ink and I was through into the innermost part of the damaged terminal building. It was not somewhere I wished to dally. Huge cracks were everywhere, both in the ceiling and the walls, doors had been ripped from their hinges, bare electric cables dangled haphazardly and puddles of water were dotted around. An American television crew was waiting in an unlit corridor as I tried to manhandle the pile of equipment past them. A young reporter, clutching a large furry microphone, blocked the way.

'What took you so long to get here?' he asked.

'Now that is one hell of a welcome,' I replied, wondering whether I dared risk creating an incident by striking him down where he stood. But with cameraman and producer, there were three of them and one of me. I was destined to lose. For a brief moment I pondered further. Then I added, 'Anyway, how many lives have *you* saved with that camera?'

The reporter was immediately dumbstruck, looked at his feet, and remained motionless until I had gone past. I smiled to myself.

If I had felt the queue alongside the terminal building was large, I was mistaken. It was tiny compared with what greeted me on the far side once I emerged into Port-au-Prince proper. People were everywhere. Scrabbling, shoving, pushing, pulling, everyone was trying to escape.

'How many times have I done this?' I thought. I seemed so frequently to be headed towards trouble when others were headed away. I was one of five entering a country while five thousand were trying to leave. The Haitians evidently knew something we did not.

Keeping the ten-ton duffel bag as close as I could I weaved my way through the unsettled crowd. To one side I could see a white minivan, stationary but with engine running. It was MSF, fortuitously at the airport for an equipment collection, who had come to our rescue. They had agreed to take us to the nearby United Nations base where we would be reasonably secure.

'*Vite! Vite!* Quickly Dr Richard!' I heard the driver cry. I jumped into the back of the minivan and sprawled in between my colleagues. Instantly the driver was off, weaving his way through the traffic, while I secured the rear doors as we moved.

*   *   *

I did not feel welcome at the UN base. The place was clearly struggling. Agencies from throughout the world had started to arrive but the establishment seemed unable to handle the increased numbers. Sadly, the UN itself had lost more than 100 of its staff in the earthquake, individuals who had known each other well during more peaceful times. The sense of sadness, at times inertia, was overwhelming, much of it created by this loss.

In the early days of a disaster relief programme there are no offices and desks to which new arrivals can report and ask for instructions. This is not a package holiday with a tour guide to greet you. The few individuals who may be tasked to provide information are as hampered as the rest by lack of communication, lack of information and lack of the basic essentials of life. By the time such things do appear, an aid programme has grown so large that it is bigger than any one office can control. It is every man for himself in the early days of disaster relief, an observation that applies both to survivors and those who seek to help them.

The UN base was at least secure and allowed a location from which to operate or to find alternative accommodation. Key to success in a disaster zone is how long you intend to stay. Major disasters are besieged by many hundreds of groups from all over the world, often hastily assembled, who hurtle to catastrophes with a truckload of water, or a few medical kits, perhaps some lifting apparatus, but who may only be on site for a few days. Any help is clearly valuable but continuity is all. To say to local people that you are there for the long haul is a major asset in almost all negotiations. How long I intended to stay was the first question I was asked by many Haitians throughout my time in the disaster zone.

Way down one end of the UN base we found a small, open, rocky yet grassy area. Normally home to an occasional scorpion, rat, or abandoned dog this, to us, was a perfect campsite. Or, at least it would have been had the tents been simple to erect. What should have been a smooth-running, professional performance by well-seasoned travellers and outdoor experts became a hysterical exercise in inefficiency. I was particularly ashamed as I should have known better. The combination of an earlier military life and frequent mountaineering has forced me to spend many, many nights under canvas. Erecting a tent should, for me, have been reflex. But it was not.

London had sent four tents for five people. Each tent was a different colour, size, shape and design, and each was erected differently. This was a recipe for disaster. We mixed up poles, pegs, flysheets and guy ropes. Fibreglass supports went in one tent sleeve and out the wrong way, pole elastics were unintentionally snapped, while flysheets were attached back to front. It was only when I fully assembled my own tent-shaped bag of dirty washing that I realised I had pitched it on a coil of old, rusty barbed wire. A normally ten-minute exercise took us the best part of an hour. Our frustration, our exhaustion, and perhaps the emotion of Haiti, made us burst into uncontrollable laughter repeatedly during this futile exercise. It seemed wrong to laugh so openly when surrounded by so much misery although laughter on this occasion was a welcome release.

The end result was a discreet, comfortable and secure location away from the ever-prying eyes of disaster victims and other aid agencies. We could talk privately without fear of being overheard. So we swopped tales, exchanged family stories, and described our ambitions for the future. A tent is also one of the safest places to be in an earthquake. The most that can crush you is a back-to-front flysheet.

* * *

The problem of operating from a UN base was that I was cocooned from the realities of life outside. I could almost pretend the disaster did not exist. I knew I had to be out there, among the survivors, the injured, and the dead. They were the reason I had come. They were the ones who needed me. I needed to start somewhere – but where?

There was another problem, too. The UN was short of surgeons for its own field hospital on the base. The hospital comprised two aircraft hangars positioned end to end. One had become the ward and was filled with low beds, more than 200 in total. In each bed lay an earthquake casualty. The other hangar was an improvised operating theatre. Meanwhile several shipping containers were positioned immediately beside the ward hangar. These were for body parts. The containers would rapidly fill and need to be renewed.

The surgery hangar was a lesson in improvisation as I learned very rapidly when I became involved with an amputation. Unfortunately, I do mean an amputation, the operation that I would cross continents to avoid. Yet on this occasion there was no alternative. The patient, a man in his mid-twenties, had almost escaped from his collapsing house during the earthquake. However, a concrete block had caught and crushed his leg when he had almost made it to the road outside. He had lain in the open for ten hours, screaming, trapped and unable to move.

'They walked past me, doctor,' he said, his eyes a picture of disbelief. 'They walked past me and didn't stop.'

'Who?' I asked.

'All the people. Even my friends did not help.'

As with so many things Haitian, this was a tragic story. A tale of the selfish struggle for survival that takes place after a disaster. The young man had eventually been released by a UN patrol, but by then his left leg was crushed, distorted and irrecoverable below the knee. I looked at the toes. They were blue and cold. There were no pulses to feel, while bone, muscles and tendons lay macerated and crushed above the ankle. The skin was also dead, pale, mottled and contaminated by the grit and dirt of the disaster. Left as it was the leg would become infected. This would in turn kill the patient in double quick time. For the sake of his life, for the sake of his future, amputation was the only option. So amputation it was.

The operating table was truly a table, borrowed from the UN restaurant. Meanwhile the operating room was only a compartmented section of the hangar. There were two restaurant tables in this one compartment, a surgical team at each one, working day and night until exhaustion took its toll. Then the next team would start work. Surgeons from Miami undertook the bulk of the surgery and did well. The Haitians were lucky to have them. But even the Miami teams could not do everything.

The amputation was quick and easy, the leg coming off just below the knee with the young Haitian asleep under a general anaesthetic. The process took little more than fifteen minutes. With the amputated leg wrapped in a towel and headed to the shipping container for disposal, it took little time to neatly close the skin of the amputation stump. The patient was back in his bed in no time at all. Then it was time for the next operation, and the next and the next. So it went on for twenty-four hours continually.

With so much work to do on the UN base itself, I was tempted to stay where I was. Yet however bad the ward hangar looked, I knew there would be much worse outside. There were still victims to be rescued. There were still areas that had not even been visited. Staying safe and secure behind the high walls of the UN base had attractions but it was not why I had come. The problem was where to go and where to set up a UK field hospital. Having seen inside the UN facility, I knew I could do better.

The answer was to come from the so-called cluster meeting, held within two hours of our arrival. Clusters are daily meetings hosted by either the UN or World Health Organisation, at which agencies with common objectives can meet. Clusters come in many shapes and sizes. The one that interested me was the health cluster, a small affair, with no more than a dozen organisations represented. The aim of cluster meetings is to ensure that five separate agencies do not turn up at the same location and offer the same service at the same time. It also allows you to make friends, and you do need friends on these occasions. Indeed you cannot function without them.

The early days of disaster relief are similar to a gigantic cocktail party. Wherever you go, you stop, you greet, and you talk to folk from other agencies. 'Why are you here?' you ask, 'What will you be doing? Where will you be going? How long will you stay?' Wherever I went on that UN base, I did exactly that. I stopped, I talked, I shook hands, I smiled, I even photographed on occasion. Then I moved on. My aim was to develop a network of individuals and agencies as fast as I could. I would need them all by the end. And they would need me.

Key items in a disaster zone are a notebook and pencil. Into the notebook I write every name, telephone number and email address I encounter until I have created as large a network of contacts as I can. I do this in double quick time, as I never know when I will need that specialist in rehabilitation, or water supply, or transport, or mapping, or security. As with the rest of life, disaster relief is as much about who you know as what you know.

A charming WHO official, who struggled to provide any decent information, chaired that first cluster meeting. The shortcomings were clear for all to see. The official had no idea of casualty estimates, nor of their locations and almost no knowledge of what aid was present in Port-au-Prince at all.

'Hospital ships will arrive shortly,' she stated.

'When?' came the doubting question from a voice in her small audience. There were about twelve of us present in total.

'Soon,' came the reply. 'And a field hospital, too.'

'When?'

'Soon,' came the reply.

'And when is soon?' boomed the question from a tall Swiss seated to my front.

The official shrugged. It was a helpless movement. She looked around for support but there was none.

'Soon is when it comes,' she bravely replied. 'That is as much as I can say.'

So much is promised in disaster relief but much less physically arrives. I could sense the restlessness of the various aid workers present.

'This is worthless,' the Swiss declared. 'How can we do anything based on this information? Where are we to go?'

As he spoke, and as I watched the WHO official shift awkwardly from one foot to the other, a tall, black individual, stethoscope draped around his neck, pushed his way gently into the small remaining space to my left. Almost instantly he began to speak, his voice deep and dominating. It drew everyone's attention, particularly my own.

'I am Matthew Jantot,' he said. 'I am a surgeon. I work outside Port-au-Prince in a village called Mantobet. We need trauma specialists desperately. We have the facility but we do not have the manpower. We need help and we need it now.'

The WHO official stepped backwards in surprise. Such a direct approach is unusual at cluster meetings, where there is a tendency for much to be said but little to be done. Yet Matthew Jantot's voice carried passion and urgency. It was clear, to me at least, that he was in genuine need of help. Immediately I raised my hand to draw the attention of the WHO official. She glanced towards me. When I had her gaze I spoke. 'I'll handle this,' I said, and then turned to Matthew Jantot to add, 'and how can Merlin help?'

* * *

In the early hours of the next morning I left for Mantobet in Matthew Jantot's four-by-four. Matthew was a remarkable man. Well-educated and bright-eyed, a Haitian himself, he had a natural passion for his country. During normal times he would work as a surgeon both in the Dominican Republic and Haiti's Mantobet. When the earthquake had struck he had been in the Dominican Republic but had returned to Haiti by road the moment he had heard the news. Matthew was perhaps the first doctor to start work in Haiti after the tremor.

As we drove, he described his problems. I listened carefully, trying not to interrupt.

'We cannot manage,' he said. 'Before the earthquake we would see 400 patients each week. Now we are seeing 4,000. Many of them need surgery.' He fell silent. I waited, but nothing came. Then I saw the tear in his eye and immediately understood.

'How many operating theatres do you have?' I asked.

'Just one,' he replied, trying hard to disguise the choking in his voice. I was with a man at the end of his tether.

'What about the ones you cannot handle?' I asked.

'We send them across the border to the Dominican Republic,' came the hoarse reply.

'How do the patients get to you?'

'By road from our clinic in the centre of Port-au-Prince. An area called Nanjui 24. Some cannot travel that far and have died on the way.' Emotion still clear in his voice, Matthew expertly negotiated the car through a tiny gap between two UN armoured cars and then he fell silent.

* * *

One hour after leaving the UN base, we had arrived at Mantobet's hospital. It was tiny but a real haven of tranquillity. The area was truly scenic – trees, open fields, beautiful lakes - a perfect place for a holiday in more peaceful times. Set beside the main road to the Dominican Republic, the hospital was simple to access for those headed to the border. Any casualty leaving Port-au-Prince would go directly past its front doors. In many respects, I thought, Mantobet would be an ideal place to position a field hospital as the infrastructure was already there. Team security was simply not an issue.

However, the distance from Port-au-Prince was a problem. I had felt that strongly as Matthew had driven me steadily eastwards from the UN base. I had not wished to comment for fear of upsetting my already distressed companion. All the same, it had not taken me long to realise that, for this immediate post-earthquake phase, Mantobet was the wrong place to site a UK field hospital.

Once in Mantobet, the epicentre was a long way distant. When we had first left the UN base the destruction had been horrific. Piles of bodies lined the streets and the stench of death was everywhere. Elderly survivors sat motionless on the ruins of their homes, children ran wildly in all directions screaming for their parents. Fires burned, choking dust filled the air. A bridge even collapsed before us, only seconds before we were due to cross. Port-au-Prince was an ongoing, major tragedy.

Yet as we had driven eastwards, towards Mantobet, the number of destroyed properties had decreased, the cries for help had diminished, the signs draped over piles of irregular debris that declared 'Bodies Inside' had disappeared. However attractive, however scenic, however welcoming Mantobet might have been – and it was – it was not where I needed to be. My location could only be where damage was the greatest, where need was desperate and where the casualty load was as high as high can be.

My visit to Mantobet over we headed back to the UN base in Matthew's four-by-four. I noticed that he was again silent. Matthew was an intelligent man. I was sure he would know what I felt. It was as if he was waiting for me to speak.

I hesitated for a moment, wondering how best to phrase things and then the words came out. 'It's a lovely hospital but not for me right now. Let's have a look at Nanjui 24, the place your casualties come from.' I hesitated again, adding, 'How safe is Nanjui, do you think?'

Matthew glanced briefly in my direction as he gripped the steering wheel, gave a half smile, but did not reply.

* * *

Imagine the most tightly packed, tightly built, ramshackle part of the poorest city on earth. The buildings have been constructed badly, their reinforcement suspect or non-existent. Then put hundreds of thousands of people into those buildings, five or six to a room; mothers, fathers, brothers, sisters, tiny babies and the very old. Then collapse the lot with everyone inside and you have Nanjui 24. It was more of a war zone than a war zone, large irregular concrete blocks littered everywhere, tortuous steel rods protruding from them, roads cracked and deformed, bodies lying in the gutter, a hand or an arm dangling motionless from between concertinaed floors. The smell of death and decay was everywhere. I struggled hard to suppress the nausea that welled up inside me. I needed to appear the controlled disaster surgeon I was meant to be.

Forced into an emotional silence by the horrendous images of human suffering around me, I had little recollection of the route Matthew took to reach Nanjui 24. I did recall gridlocked traffic, most leaving rather than arriving, while bulldozers shifted tons of debris with seeming disregard for any victims still within. I recalled also the screams from inside the pancaked properties, screams created less by an inability to escape than for fear they might be burned alive. Disease was becoming a major problem as the dead bodies rotted. To stop this, some of the ruined properties were doused in petrol and set alight, again without any true search for trapped victims inside.

Ninety minutes after leaving Mantobet, Matthew pulled up alongside one of the many collapsed buildings in Nanjui 24. To one end was an intact fenced area with access only through a large, ten-foot cast iron gate. A Haitian in his mid-twenties stood guard while around him stood many dozens of his countrymen, all trying to gain access to the open area beyond. I exited unsteadily from the car.

'What is this place?' I asked as Matthew guided me towards the rubble and the waiting crowd.

'A school. There are at least thirty children's bodies still inside.'

Matthew helped force our way through the throng at the gate. A few words in his native Creole and we were past, the desperate Haitians parting politely to let us through. A few hands reached out to touch my arms or shoulders as I walked, perhaps wishing to see if I was real. Voices spoke as we slowly made our way through the crowd.

'*Aides-moi!* Help me!'

'*Viens! Viens! On a perdu ma mère!* Come! Come! My mother is lost!'

And from one voice in particular, a firm slap on my back. '*Merci.* Thank you.'

This was distress in the extreme. I found it hard to take. Meanwhile, the space beyond may have been open but it was certainly not empty. Within this fenced area was one of the busiest, thriving clinics I have seen. Casualties lay on the ground all around while others sat patiently on benches positioned alongside the collapsed building. Again the smell of death, again the waves of revulsion, my worst fears being confirmed when I saw a tiny, motionless arm protruding from the rubble to one side of the clinic.

I walked slowly round the clinic area where I could see at least six medical staff hard at work. There was the elderly missionary couple. The husband was applying a small crepe bandage to a gaping and bloody wound on a young man's shinbone. His wife, meanwhile, was wrapping a few pills in a twist of old newspaper, pills that were destined for the crying infant held tightly in the young mother's arms. To the other side of the clinic area were two young men, both American. One was talking earnestly to two teenage males who had just brought in their friend. The friend was lying on the ground beside them, agony etched on his face. I could see the deformed shoulder and guessed, more than likely, that the upper arm bone had been shattered. The second American was busily applying a plaster cast neatly to a patient's wrist. Putting on plaster casts has long been regarded as an art form in medical circles and this American was clearly artistic.

Dominant of all, perhaps, was another American. Tall, blonde and attractive, Eleanor was a physician whom I subsequently learned had left her Philadelphia practice the moment the earthquake had occurred. She had answered the Haiti call. I watched her move effortlessly between patients, examining here, reassuring there, prescribing when needed and applying dressings if required. She exuded an air of calm. Just what was needed in Nanjui 24.

There were also others doing what they could to help. Two nurses were busily suturing a scalp wound, while another was trying to remove a rubble fragment from a patient's eye. The clinic at Nanjui 24 was working hard and working well. Moreover, everything they did was for free.

I walked across to the second American, who was now standing slightly back from his patient in order to admire his handiwork with the plaster cast.

'Looks good!' I declared as I came near to him.

The American turned and smiled broadly. 'Yeah,' he said. 'Not bad for a carpenter.'

'Sorry?'

'Not bad for a carpenter, I said. That's what I normally do.'

'But you're a doctor, too?'

'No, just a carpenter. But then I guess we reconstruct things as well.'

I laughed and we then introduced ourselves. Zak was a carpenter from America's mid-West and he, too, had answered the Haiti call. He realised that reconstruction after an earthquake begins the moment the final tremor has ceased. Somehow, and I never did establish the precise mechanics, Zak had arrived in Nanjui and had offered to help at the clinic. No one had presumed to ask what type of assistance he could provide, so Zak was pointed in the direction of the first major casualty. Before long he had demonstrated a natural flair for applying the perfect plaster cast and had now become Nanjui 24's state-of-the-art plaster technician. He was delighted, the patients were delighted, indeed everyone was delighted. Back home he would have been thrown in jail.

Zak did, of course, highlight a major issue with disaster relief. In the very early days of an emergency response there is often little or no control of the type of individual arriving to offer help. Who has the time to check the credentials of someone who claims to be a doctor or, perhaps, a priest? You can claim to be anything you wish and it is most unlikely you will be found out. Many people do. That is why the major aid agencies are so critical to disaster relief programmes as they undertake all the necessary checks well in advance of a disaster occurring.

Yet despite the care and attention provided by the Nanjui 24 clinic, I could see one major problem. Much treatment was being given but no surgery was being performed. Broken bones could not be fixed, infected wounds could not be cleaned, tendons could not be repaired and skin grafts, the mainstay of disaster surgery, were impossible. The clinic needed to raise its level of care if it was to be truly of use in an earthquake zone. I glanced at my watch briefly, not that the exact time was relevant. However, judging by the text messages from London, the full field hospital would be arriving in little more than twenty-four hours. Maybe, I thought to myself, this school could be a location for it.

But there was another problem - the school itself was a disaster area. The open area, once a playground, would have been perfect for a hospital. Yet the stench said all. The decaying corpses were both an emotional and a health hazard. Already staff and patients were wearing masks to keep the smell at bay. Flies buzzed around and through the rubble, again creating a huge infection risk.

I walked around the outside of the collapsed building to inspect it in more detail, followed by dozens of locals. There, in the gutter, lay a half-incinerated body part. It looked like a hand but the smell was overpowering. I could not escape it. I stopped in my tracks, transfixed by this evidence of further human tragedy. It was truly awful.

As I pondered in my distress whether it would be right to site a field hospital beside the collapsed school in Nanjui 24, I was deep in my thoughts. I was well away, somewhere different, clearly less aware of my surroundings than normal. My guard was down. Suddenly I felt a large hand grasp my right arm. I was instantly back to reality, trying hard to pull away. Yet I could not. The grip was properly firm. I could not have wriggled free had I tried. I turned to see who had grasped me. I was ready, I suppose, to fight. But when I turned, I found myself staring upwards into two very emotionless, brown eyes. Beneath them was an almost square face, a chin as chiselled as they come and a small moustache draped over a pencil-thin upper lip. The Haitian tried to smile but he did not do a very good job.

'You the British doctor?' he said in a husky, slightly high-pitched tone. I nodded.

'Then you don't want this place,' said the Haitian nodding towards the school. 'Come with me. I have something better.'

With that I was frog-marched 200 yards down the road from the school. My Haitian companion said not one further word but I noticed how the locals parted as we passed. Occasionally someone would even bow. No one, absolutely no one, stood in our way. I had just met the General.

*   *   *

Chapter 18

Aftershock

My frog-marching session ended three minutes later when we arrived at some hard tennis courts beside the main road that ran through Nanjui 24 – The Enrique Mercado tennis club. I sniffed the air in a sommelier-like way and then inhaled deeply. There was no smell of death, just pine resin from the many undestroyed trees that surrounded the courts. For a brief moment I could imagine I was back home.

The tennis club was invisible from the road, protected from it by a high wall. It had clearly been a thriving establishment before the earthquake. There were five courts in total, on two levels. Their hard, almost polished green surfaces were still in good repair. On one, the intact tennis net was being used as an impromptu clothes line by the gradually expanding, tented refugee camp I could see through the trees at the far end of the courts. The multicoloured clothing, in many shapes and sizes, was almost decorative, draped in its irregular fashion across the centre of the court. Much of the area was enclosed by a crumbling brick wall, which had suffered during the earthquake. Pale red and broken brick lay scattered over the court surface, interspersed with boulders, gravel, concrete dust and sand. High, albeit buckled, wire fencing completed the surround.

At one point the courts had subsided almost three metres, leaving a gap between their concrete surface and the bottom of the fence. I could see three children's heads peering through the space, their tiny, excited bodies trying to remain still and unnoticed. Yet their habitually restless legs, playfully kicking each other's ankles, combined with their darting, sparkling eyes, gave the game away. I smiled; life goes on after an earthquake, the sea covers over, the survivors survive.

I was far away, my mind wandering from its task, when I heard the General speak.

'What do you think, Doctor?' he half croaked, his voice the archetypal

Godfather. On the far side of the courts, over the General's shoulder, were two muscular young men, both in their late twenties. They were watching our every move. It was a baking hot day and they were wearing long baggy coats. That could only mean one thing – concealed weapons.

'Perfect,' I replied, 'although we will have to keep our eye on that.' I pointed high up to our right where, beyond the upper layer of two tennis courts, I could see the cracked facade of a tall apartment block. The building was still being used, despite the evident dangers, but a hard aftershock would easily bring it down.

In another life, in another world perhaps, I would have sought an engineer's advice about safety. Here, in the aftermath of the world's sixth most destructive tremor since records began, an engineering view was something I did not have. By eye, I reckoned, with a tented field hospital appropriately sited, it would be sufficiently distant from the cracked building to be secure. Health and Safety back home would have had sleepless nights for weeks.

'They say you have a hospital coming,' said the General.

I nodded.

'I'd like to look after that for you, Doctor.'

'That's OK. What can I do for you in exchange?'

Deals are an important part of disaster relief, certainly in Haiti. The key factor is to establish early on what the other party seeks. Is it money? Is it security? Could it be employment? Or, perhaps, is it power? It is unlikely you are being helped for the good of mankind, however noble your own actions have been. Many are involved for gain.

It did not take long to strike a reasonable deal with the General. The basic outline was that I would defer to him for all problems and he would solve them. Power was his thing. To him, it was important that he was seen to be in charge. I was happy with that. Over time the balance of power would most likely change but at the start a field hospital needed protection. I was way outside the UN base, had no security of any sort and needed to start work very soon. Wherever I looked I could see the casualties mounting up.

I liked the General. He was a man's man who was widely respected and who delivered what he promised. I think he liked me. He tolerated my schoolboy French well, and I his stuttering English-cum-Creole-cum-French. Somehow we communicated, sometimes with much hilarity when one or other of us reached his grammatical limit. The General was critical to the success of this project. I was about to insert a full field hospital with its staff of more than twenty unarmed foreigners, into the destroyed centre of a capital city with the highest crime rate in the Western world. There was a higher chance of being killed in Haiti than in the war zones of either Iraq or Afghanistan. This could be a nightmare if handled badly.

What I did not reveal to the General was how worried I was, worried that my promises about a soon-to-arrive field hospital would come to nothing. My promises and his reputation depended on my success.

The problem was that my own success depended on many other people whose actions I could not control; the London office, the surgical team, the equipment supplier, the delivery companies, even the border guards on Haiti's frontiers. I knew that the surgical team was en route as I was in intermittent text message contact with them. Landlines were non-existent and the mobile telephone system provided by the UN was so overloaded that I stood no chance of connecting by voice during normal daylight hours; text messaging was the only way. I had a satellite telephone, too, although this was battery hungry and recharging was almost impossible.

So with the deal struck, I walked back towards the club's main gate, heading for the road. The General walked beside me, no longer gripping my arm.

'When will you start?' he asked as we walked.

For a brief moment I stopped, turned towards him and gave a confident smile. 'Tomorrow,' I replied, looking him in the eye. 'Please keep these courts free for us to use.'

The General nodded his understanding, adding, 'Of course, Doctor,' in his uniquely husky and frightening tone. 'I'll be here at nine o'clock tomorrow morning. My people will start work then.'

He started to turn away and then hesitated briefly. 'One more thing, Doctor.'

'Yes?'

'Over here a man's word is his bond. We have strict penalties for those who fail.'

With that he gave me a firm handshake, turned on his heel and left. I waited where I was until he was almost out of sight. I knew the protocol well. With men like the General, you never show your back. They leave you, you do not leave them. It may have been Haiti, it may have been poor, it may have just experienced a major earthquake but there was no doubting the power surrounding the General. There was also no doubting that if I failed to produce a field hospital within twenty-four hours, I was likely to have a slit throat.

*   *   *

A reserve option had to be the solution. The stakes were simply too high. I needed somewhere else to treat casualties if London let me down.

First stop after the tennis courts was the established Hôpital de la Paix, about fifteen minutes' drive away. Pascal would be my driver. In his pre-earthquake life he had been a student of engineering. He knew Port-au-Prince well, was clearly bright and very keen to help. His personal tragedy had been the death of his brother when the family home had collapsed during the disaster. Pascal had lost everything – money, family, job prospects, clothing, the roof over his head, and his engineering course. Somehow, incredibly, and with impressive fortitude, he had pulled himself together, volunteered to help, and rapidly became a much sought-after driver. Incredibly, he even understood my French. He took me down the hill and past the higgledy-piggledy refugee camp.

The Hôpital de la Paix sounded on paper to be an excellent alternative location for a field hospital. It was known to have two operating theatres, which I could potentially use. Although all the hospitals in the capital had been originally declared unsafe shortly after the earthquake, I had seen an engineer's report at the UN base, which had suggested this was an exaggeration. The Hôpital de la Paix should be usable and a good bet as a first reserve.

I glanced to our right as we drove. A once wide-open space, previously urban parkland, was now filled to capacity by a ramshackle and temporary refugee camp. Some of the survivors had tents, some were sleeping in the open, some under multicoloured polythene sheeting, and some under cardboard. The organisation looked chaotic. I could see injured still lying by the roadside and had to harden my heart when a number held out their hands in supplication as I drove past. Anyway, I had no medical equipment available and could do nothing to assist.

'Just hold on for a little longer,' I said quietly to myself so that Pascal could not hear. 'Then I'll show you what I can do.' My Hippocratic conscience was working overtime.

Unfortunately, it took only a few minutes to establish that the Hôpital de la Paix would be the wrong place for a field hospital. My original

Kashmir. A mountainside near Muzaffarabad had collapsed totally, burying all beneath it.

Kashmir. Our Mi-8 helicopter slowly sinks into the soft earth. We could only stay on the ground a limited time.

Panjkot, Kashmir. The village was completely destroyed.

Panjkot, Kashmir. Death and makeshift graves were everywhere.

Neelum Valley, Kashmir. Massive landslides had blocked almost all the tiny mountain

Kashmir. Refugees battled to board the limited number of tiny evacuation helicopters.

Kashmir. A Chinook helicopter is rapidly unloaded of its critical aid supplies.

Kashmir. Our overcrowded mountain clinic.

Neelum Valley, Kashmir. A collapsed bridge forced local people to sometimes take extreme risks.

Kashmir. Not all aid is in mint condition. A pile of tatty tents (not Merlin's) awaits distribution.

Yogyakarta, Java. There was massive destruction.

Bantul, Java. The medical students' tented hospital.

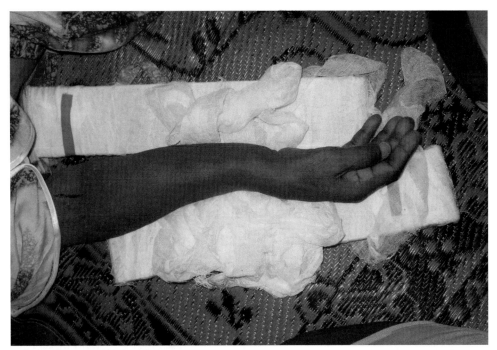

Java. Not all earthquake injuries are blood and gore. A simple broken wrist was the end result here.

Java. I teach medical students how to read an X-ray film in their tented hospital.

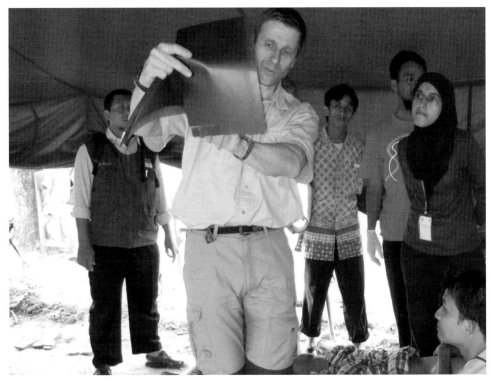

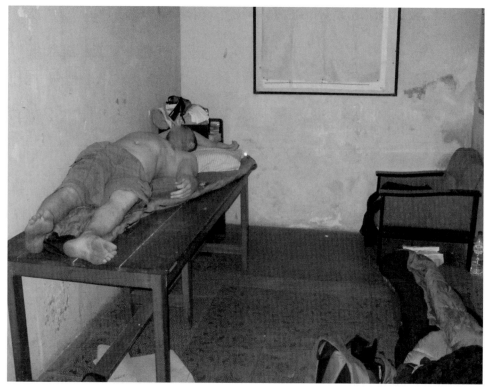

Java. It is rarely luxurious being an aid worker. Our sleeping quarters in Java's Yogyakarta.

Java. Applying a plaster cast to a broken arm.

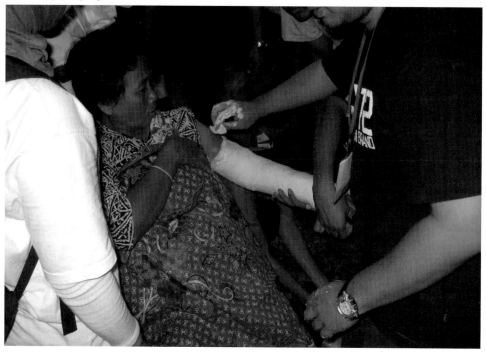

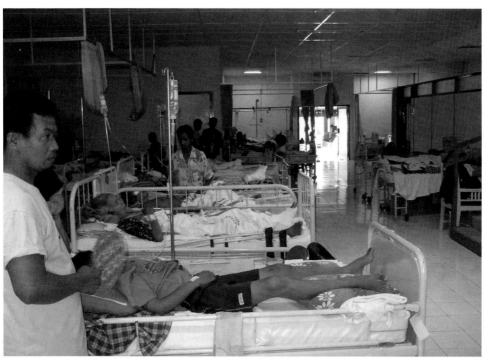

Yogyakarta, Java. An improvised trauma ward after the earthquake. Note the three rows of beds and no nursing staff to care for the patients.

Dominican Republic, en route to Haiti. The media were everywhere.

Port-au-Prince, Haiti. Bodies were simply left on the road for others to remove.

Port-au-Prince, Haiti. A not infrequent finding. Charred human remains found by the roadside. A portion of thighbone (femur) can be seen dead centre.

Haiti. The original destroyed school where I had intended to place a hospital. The stench of dead bodies made working there impossible.

Haiti. The abandoned tennis courts that would soon become home to our hospital.

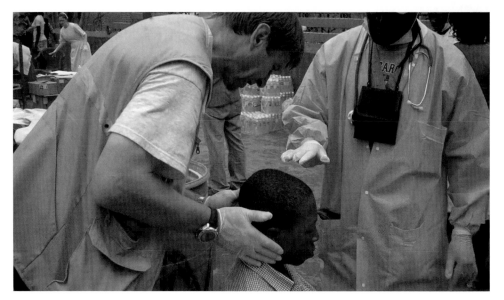

Haiti. I examine a young boy's neck after he had been injured in the earthquake.

Haiti. The tennis court field hospital takes shape.

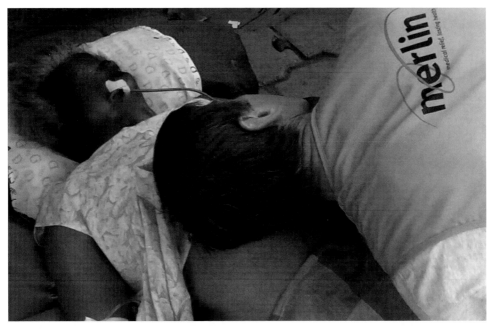

Haiti. Sometimes you just have to improvise. Minus my stethoscope I listen to a patient's abdomen directly by ear. This image has been anonymised.

Haiti. After major disasters, never forget those who escaped injury and death. I talk (and joke) here with survivors.

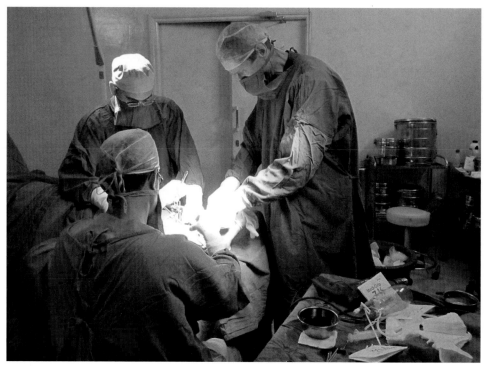

Tataouine, Tunisia. Operating on an injured rebel.

Near Nalut, Libya. Colonel Gaddafi's abandoned armour.

Nalut, Libya. The local hospital, trolleys positioned outside awaiting the next influx of casualties.

North Africa. External fixation of a war-injured ankle. This technique is a critical part of a conflict surgeon's repertoire.

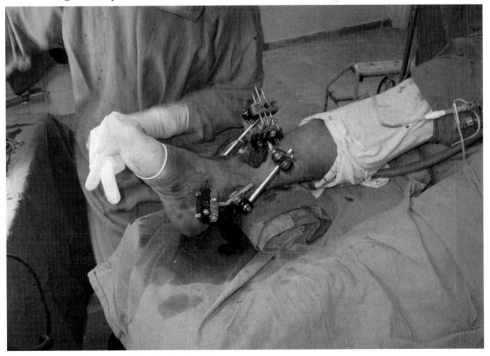

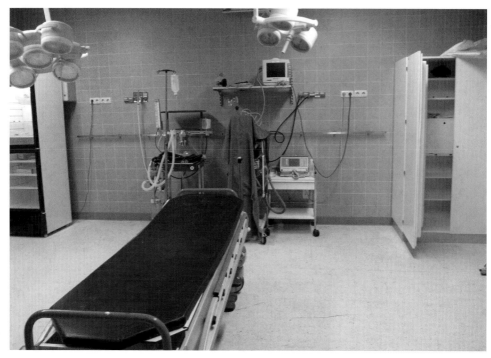

Nalut, Libya. The resuscitation area of Nalut Hospital. Note the largely empty medicine cupboards behind. Some supplies were almost totally exhausted.

Nalut, Libya. A wounded Gaddafi soldier recovers after major emergency surgery.

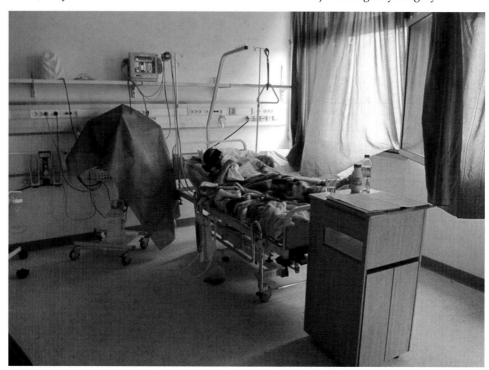

optimism had been significantly misplaced. The car park was laden with aid agencies operating in the open air and largely under appallingly unsterile conditions. I saw several patients being physically held down while their operations were performed without any anaesthetic and at times not particularly well.

Primitive, largely ineffective screens had been erected to deter prying eyes but, even so, there were plenty of folk prying. I forced my way through the throng of patients waiting outside the hospital's front entrance, introduced myself to the staff at the door and was allowed inside. It could have been the Crimean War. Beds and mattresses were everywhere, medical staff from throughout the world doing their best to attend to the many hundreds of patients. The facilities were appalling. I left immediately. There was no way that I wanted a surgical team to work there. There were simply too many agencies present to allow a UK team to operate independently. Proper security would be impossible and the opportunity for longer-term involvement would be lost.

Next stop were the Israeli military, Pascal driving to their location with the confidence of an assured navigator. Never once did I see him consult a map, never once did I see him lost, nor did I see him ask for directions. At the UN base I had learned that the Israeli Army had set up a field hospital and that work was well underway. As perhaps befits their international image, the Israelis had chosen a location very close to the most dangerous part of town, Cité Soleil.

Cité Soleil was regarded as one of the most dangerous places on earth and was top of the list of places not to visit during a lifetime. When the earthquake had destroyed the prison in Port-au-Prince, 5,000 convicts had escaped. The majority went to Cité Soleil.

This reputation did not appear to trouble the Israelis, who were well accustomed to conflict zones. When I arrived, their field hospital had the air of a busy, professional, industrious facility. It was the most perfect of locations – a green, freshly mown, grass playing field with tents expertly pitched and not an item of litter to see. It was difficult to imagine that such a troublesome part of the capital lay only a stone's throw away. No prying eyes, no dogs, no body parts, and none of the noise, chaos and dirt of Nanjui 24. Doctors, either in well-kept uniforms or clean white coats, walked purposefully from tent to tent. Meanwhile patients queued quietly in a tidy line, the watchful eye of several Israeli soldiers being kept over them. Any nonsense from any patient and the offender was simply sent away.

The medical staff looked relaxed and had their own shaded rest area, well stocked with snacks and cold drinks. Remarkably, within eight hours of arrival in Haiti the Israelis had assembled their complete facility and had begun work; they had even delivered a baby. Rapidly, I negotiated with the Commanding Officer the possibility of co-locating a UK field hospital with his own and rapidly the arrangement was agreed. This gave a useful reserve position. My priority, however, was to work in the very heart of Nanjui 24 and to honour my agreement with the General.

Yet as Pascal drove me back to the UN base, horn blaring, swerving this way and that, I began to feel uneasy. London had gone quiet. Things did not feel right and I could not explain why. I looked at my mobile – nothing. No text messages, no missed calls. I looked at the satellite telephone. That, too, was blank. By then I should have heard from the surgical team en route. Yet they were no longer answering my calls and no longer responding to my messages. Where were they? Were they OK? What was happening? Would they arrive at all? I could only pray that they would soon appear. I glanced once more at my watch. Twenty hours left to fulfill my undertaking. I put my hand to my throat and played with my half-formed beard. I had not been able to shave since leaving Santo Domingo. I felt my neck, too. It was intact. I wanted it to stay that way.

*   *   *

Life on the UN base was so different to the real action taking place outside. My tent was as uncomfortable as they come; my own fault of course as the green scrub, which formed our campsite, had a rocky surface, making it impossible to find any comfortable sleeping position at all. That was even after I removed the rusty coil of barbed wire from under my groundsheet. By day the heat made tent life unbearable. I could only ever enter the thing at night.

The choice of location had seemed sensible at the time, largely on the basis of security, but the number of daily flights to and from Port-au-Prince Airport was now increasing rapidly. The once peaceful camping area was directly under the flight path. Sleep was a luxury we did not have.

Meanwhile the UN aid programme was growing fast. White vehicles carrying their blue UN logo were everywhere, long parking lines extending way into the distance. There were few places where new arrivals could sleep, so tents would appear in ridiculous locations; on top of water storage containers, on mini-roundabouts, on roofs, absolutely anywhere. There was also little in the way of sanitation facilities for so many people. To take a shower meant joining a twenty-metre queue even at three o'clock in the morning. I abandoned all hope of having a shower in Haiti and returned to acrobatics I had learned in the Army, which allowed me to fully strip wash under a single outdoor tap, while publicly preserving my modesty.

The toilet facilities were laughable – two filthy sit-downs for the entire visitor population – so it was no surprise when a gastroenteritis outbreak hit the base early in the relief programme. I was exempt this agony, probably because of a total obsession about disinfecting my hands before doing anything at all. Water was in short supply so I always carried a small container of hand disinfectant in my pocket wherever I went. The rules for staying healthy in a disaster zone are very simple. You must develop a total fixation for personal hygiene. Wash or disinfect your hands whenever you can and at every opportunity. If you shake hands, disinfect; if you touch a hard surface, disinfect; if you intend to eat, disinfect; if you go to the toilet, disinfect; in fact if someone even looks at you, disinfect. That way you stand a reasonable chance of the emergency toilet paper staying inside your rucksack.

The UN base was also the only location where it was possible to establish an internet connection with the rest of the world. Communications are critical to relief programmes such as this and the internet is a way of life even for earthquake relief. The best reception was inside the Haiti Aid portakabin, if I was able to enter without being seen. I found it simplest to confidently enter their main door with authority, pretending to be on serious Haiti Aid business – I had none at all – and then secure a seat at one of their four linoleum-surfaced tables. I would then open the lid of my laptop and set to work instantly. Unless they were feeling particularly brave, Haiti Aid would not challenge me. They did once, however, although Nature unexpectedly came to my rescue when I was rumbled.

My accuser was a large lady sitting to my left. She was solid Haiti Aid and proud of it. In a loud voice she was moaning to her colleagues about her various medical woes – the breast lump, the diarrhoea, the haemorrhoids, and the associated depression – clearly seeking their sympathy. As a doctor I was naturally interested although I studiously looked at my laptop's screen and pretended to be working. The moaner's colleagues were manifestly bored with her complaints, which she sensed, so her topic of conversation changed to the disruptive presence of other aid workers within the Haiti Aid portakabin and how they should be outlawed. Slowly she turned towards me, as did several other heads, and I knew what was coming.

'What about that guy over there?' I heard her say. 'Is he with any of you?'

It was as I looked up, as I was just about to smile, that Nature came to my rescue. She could not have timed it more perfectly. It was as if the aftershock had been waiting in the wings for the right moment. It happened then, there, right on cue.

* * *

Chapter 19

A Sleepless Night

If you have experienced an earthquake you may understand. If not, you might have problems.

When an earthquake first strikes it is sometimes difficult to realise what is happening. Things just seem to sway. It is similar to drinking too much alcohol.

Is it your head that is swimming or is the room really moving from side to side? Are you are off balance? What is going on?

Occasionally an earthquake will strike suddenly and out of the blue but there is normally a preliminary warm-up. This can give time to act if you understand what is happening. When I am in a danger area, and if the opportunity exists, I leave a glass half-filled with water within view. If I feel the room sway and the water also starts to wobble, I am in an earthquake. If I feel the room sway and the water is motionless, it is time to either stop drinking or go to bed.

When indoors in an earthquake zone it is good practice to look around your room so that you know what to do in a tremor. You can stay put and hope - not a good idea; shelter under something solid - a reasonable idea; or, dash outside if you have time – an excellent idea. If you are stuck indoors the collector's item of earthquake-safe areas is the bathroom. Bathrooms are a good choice because they are surrounded by plenty of pipe work and do not collapse easily. They do contain much glass, too, so watch out for those fragments as they fly around the room.

If you intend to stay indoors while the heavens descend upon you, think about the so-called Triangle of Life. This is based on the findings of multiple search and rescue teams who have spent their lives dragging bodies from collapsed buildings throughout the world. They found that people who sheltered directly under solid structures such as desks, tables and chairs have learned the hard way that these items are not as strong as they appear. They are squashed hedgehog thin in no time. However, when the rubble does fall, it crushes the desk, or table, or chair, but leaves a tiny space immediately beside the crushed object. This is the Triangle of Life. The theory goes there is a better chance of survival by sheltering beside a sturdy object than directly beneath it.

That day, when the aftershock struck, my reflexes sprang into action from the first warm-up shake. My linoleum table swayed dramatically from side to side forcing me to hold on to my computer to prevent it sliding away. Filing cabinet drawers flew open, books and lever arch files thumped to the floor, while someone's cup of coffee shattered into a thousand pieces. I looked up. Damn it! The main door was too far away so it was under or beside my table I would have to go.

'Oh God! Jesus help me!' It was the moaner.

Across to my left she was already on her feet, hands clasped in simulated prayer. I could see she was terrified. Then she screamed, a penetrating sound that passed through me, right to my innermost core. Taking my computer with me, I slid quietly to the floor to find my own Triangle of Life, the moaner's attention now diverted from publicly exposing me as the imposter I was. I could see her stumble left, right, then left again as she weaved her way to the door, the floor moving beneath her. Her hand fumbled desperately for the door handle, there was a loud click and she was out, as were her colleagues.

I was alone, abandoned to my fate. No one had spared me a second glance. I did not dare join them outside as I knew what would happen if I did. The imposter-hunting would continue. So I stayed where I was, face down beside the table, hands over my head. I thought it unlikely the ceiling contents of a portakabin would inflict much injury if they did collapse. For a brief moment the swaying increased. I lay there, waiting for the inevitable crash, praying that my assessment of the ceiling was correct.

Then the swaying stopped, as quickly as it had begun. I waited in my tiny Triangle of Life for a good two minutes, terrified to move, but nothing happened. It was over. There was that silence that always follows these things, when the dead cannot speak, the injured have yet to feel their pain, and those who have escaped are terrified to move. On this occasion there were no dead or injured, it was just a warning shot. I slowly rose to my feet, looked around at the still empty Haiti Aid portakabin and placed my laptop carefully back on its desk. I was back to work within seconds and remained undisturbed for a further two hours. The moaner never reappeared.

*   *   *

I see the internet as an evil necessity. Since its creation my own workload has risen a thousand-fold. Yet for the Haiti earthquake it was far from evil. The messages of goodwill that flooded in from around the world were remarkable and touching. Friends, from whom I had not heard for ages, made contact to wish me well. People I had never met wrote letters of support. To reply was not always easy. Meanwhile many volunteers put their names forward to assist, more than I can remember for any other disaster. Haiti had struck a chord in the hearts of the world. It had definitely struck a chord in mine.

Much of this global awareness can be put down to the media who had swarmed to Haiti in their thousands. A thirty-second interview in front of a camera on the streets of Port-au-Prince could be on the world's screens within minutes, such is modern media power. For those like me who are in the front line of disaster relief, anything that highlights the plight of the disadvantaged is for the good. Haiti was a job well done by the combined media masses of the world.

However, I did not always have a cosy relationship with the media. The video camera given to me in London by a major news outlet had remained largely unused, so focussed was I on the medical issues. I am also the world's most hopeless photographer. Nevertheless, I did have some footage and had promised to deliver it to their Haitian team. So off I went.

The outlet's location was a once thriving city hotel, now looking deeply suspect as a result of the earthquake. Cracks were in every wall and there was no electricity. Yet compared with a tent at the end of a runway, the hotel was the lap of luxury. It was also a hive of activity.

There is something God-like about media locations when you are an outsider. The closest analogy for a medic is a hospital's intensive care unit. Folk look at you as if you should not be there, that they should not be disturbed and that their work is far more important than anything you could possibly be doing. You rapidly see yourself as the lowest form of human life, indeed subhuman. The news outlet that day was no exception.

'Excuse me,' I whispered to a woman seated behind a desk at a computer screen in one of the darkest parts of the hotel. I had been directed there by a young male receptionist who spoke nothing but Creole and who never looked at me once. He had spent the entire two-minute conversation inspecting the cracked joist above his head, wondering if it was about to collapse.

I presumed I had reached the correct place as the darkened office had a distinctly media feel about it. I also felt very unwelcome, the woman behind the computer ignoring me totally. I tried again.

'Excuse me!' I said, this time a little louder. That deserved a glance, a very disapproving one.

'I'm...I'm...I'm...' I stammered, ready to declare who I was.

The glance had now become a stare. 'Not now. Please not now. Can't you see?'

Unfortunately, I could not see. All I did see was someone being intolerant and rude.

I was on the verge of turning on my heel to leave when two individuals, both men, entered the office noisily. One was tall and one was short. Both were dressed in jeans and T-shirt and I assumed they were newsmen. They were clearly in heated debate.

'What the hell do we do?' asked the short one.

'Dunno,' came the tall reply, reinforced by a pronounced shrugging of his massive shoulders.

'We can't leave her there.'

'I know. She'll be dead if we do.'

Then I said something I knew I would regret. 'Can I help?' I asked.

Instantly, the two men fell silent, both turning to look at me suspiciously. Even the woman behind the computer stopped her frantic typing and inspected me open-mouthed.

The tall one broke the silence. 'You a doctor?'

I nodded.

'That's a stroke of luck. Follow us!'

So I followed, trying hard to keep pace. We went down a multitude of twisting corridors until we emerged at the rear of the hotel into an empty car park. Empty that was except for one car, a taxi that had clearly delivered the elderly lady who was lying on the ground under the shade of a nearby tree.

The taller newsman pointed towards the lady and then turned to me. 'All yours Doc,' he said and left. It was that simple. No request, no introduction, no explanation. Just an 'All yours Doc' and he had gone.

The smaller newsman stayed. 'Sorry,' he said. Even he had been taken aback by his colleague's behaviour. 'Would you mind?' He walked with me over to the patient.

She did not look well. On her right leg was a plaster cast, in her right arm was a drip attached to an empty intravenous bag, in her bladder was a catheter and up her nose, into her stomach, ran a thin and clear plastic tube. The patient was clearly seriously ill. Her breathing was short and shallow and her eyes were closed. I knelt on the ground beside her and gently took her wrist. The pulse was difficult to feel as it was so weak and thready. I carefully lifted each eyelid and watched the pupils react to light. She was alive – at least for the moment.

As I examined the patient I sensed her situation was hopeless. She had been extracted from the rubble of a collapsed building two days earlier and had been taken to an aid agency's location. She had been treated well. The plaster cast on her leg was of excellent quality and had been applied perfectly. Zak, the carpenter at Nanjui 24 would have found it hard to compete.

I looked at the patient's X-Rays and saw the massive fracture to her pelvis. She had bled significantly into her belly, which in turn had paralysed her intestines so that they no longer moved. This is called an ileus. An ileus can cause a massive imbalance of the body's biochemistry. If untreated it can lead to death. That was where this patient was headed, for sure, unless something was rapidly done to help her. It was probably too late already.

The patient highlighted a significant problem in disaster relief. It does not matter how well a casualty may be treated in the early days after a catastrophe, it is the follow-on treatment that counts. The patient had originally been seen by one of the many relief teams scattered around Port-au-Prince. Their equipment had been modern and up-to-date. She had even received an X-Ray, not an item of equipment that all teams had available, or could afford. All of this was good.

The problem was that she had been initially treated and then sent away, with no instructions for follow-on care. Such was the pressure of work, such was the huge number of casualties, that all most teams could do was provide the initial treatment and then leave the patient to their own devices. Yet eventually the patient's drip bag was destined to run out, as it had. There were no nurses to keep her stomach empty by regularly extracting its contents through the tube and there were no laboratory facilities to monitor the body's biochemistry. The end-result was clear. Unless this patient could be admitted to a hospital for continuing care she would die. I estimated she had no more than one day to live.

I had been so immersed in the patient and the inevitability of what was to follow, that I had become completely unaware of my surroundings. It was only when I had finished my examination that I heard the sound of crying to my left. I looked across to see two well-dressed Haitians, a woman in her late-thirties and a man of about the same age. The woman, in a bright yellow blouse and tight brown trousers, was sobbing uncontrollably. The man was trying hard to console her but even he was distressed.

I was sure this was the family and walked the few steps to join them. They rose to their feet as I approached. I indicated that we should sit down and pointed to a thin concrete bench to one edge of the car park. It was quiet, as if the world was our own. There was no traffic outside, no horns, no sirens, no aircraft overhead, no dogs barking, nothing; just the patient's daughter, her husband and me.

I took the daughter's hand in my own and, in the best French I could muster, explained the problem. If her mother did not have proper, supervised medical care she would die imminently. They had to move her, and fast. But where? All the major hospitals in Port-au-Prince had been damaged and were overloaded. The car park of the Hôpital de la Paix had been a good example. The UK field hospital was still…I looked at my watch…eighteen hours away. The patient would be dead by then.

I settled on the UN field hospital or the Israelis and scribbled a hasty note. 'Please admit,' it said. 'This patient requires urgent rehydration and fluid balance.' I added my mobile telephone number, too.

'Now go!' I insisted to the daughter and her husband. 'Go! You have no time to spare!'

Rapidly, gently, we laid the elderly lady on the back seat of the taxi. The daughter sat in the back, too, her mother's head on her lap. The daughter was distraught, tears streaming down her face, as she stroked the forehead of the now unconscious patient. The daughter's husband sat in the front.

Then they were away, the tragic family group, with the mother they clearly loved so dearly. I never did learn her name although I did hear that my estimate of one day's survival was woefully inadequate. The mother died in her daughter's arms even before they reached the UN field hospital. Disasters are terrible, personal tragedies at times like that. As a doctor, you never truly recover from them.

I took one of the local tap-tap cabs back to the UN base. Tap-taps are a type of shared, brightly decorated Haitian taxi. Essentially they are small minibuses with as many locals squeezed into as small a space as possible. Supposedly, they are a cheap and friendly method of travel. Far from it if you are foreigner in the aftermath of an earthquake. I was charged a fortune but did not have the heart to bargain or complain. I was probably the driver's only fare since the earthquake.

I was now becoming worried. Still I had heard nothing from the surgical team that was scheduled to arrive by the morning. That was less than eighteen hours away and I had to honour my commitment to the General. I knew the team had left the UK but for all I knew they could still be mid-Atlantic. I had lost all communication with them. In addition, I was becoming enormously frustrated. Whenever I returned to the UN base there were always meetings to attend; meetings that appeared to go nowhere. There was plenty of talk and very little action. The cluster meetings were now massive, with more than fifty agencies represented. It was impossible to make any decision with so many people present. The fifty agencies at the cluster meeting, however, represented less than ten per cent of the total agencies present in Haiti. The disaster relief programme was massive and still growing.

When I walked onto the rubble-strewn tennis courts of Nanjui 24 the next morning, half-an-hour before my pledged meeting with the General I had heard nothing from the surgical team and not one item of equipment had arrived. It had been a sleepless night. I had texted, emailed, and telephoned London into the very small hours but had made no progress. I had been so concerned, and unable to sleep, that at three o'clock in the morning I went to the ward hangar of the UN hospital to see if I could help. There was much to do. The patients from the previous day had now gone, replaced by 200 new ones, evidence of the continuing flow of casualties from the ruins of Port-au-Prince. There were intravenous drips to reposition, plasters to change and operations to perform. By six o'clock that morning I had been exhausted, walked the short distance to my tent and managed one hour's sleep before the day proper began.

The tennis courts were chaos. Word had clearly spread that the hospital was soon to arrive. The General had been in action. There were dozens of patients needing attention. As I entered, to my right and lying on the ground was a long line of stretcher cases. They had been brought in overnight. I use the word stretcher, but there were, of course, no stretchers. These were patients who were simply unable to walk. They could have had a broken back and been paralysed, or simply had a shattered or absent limb. Whatever the cause, they had relied on others to reach the tennis courts.

These stretcher cases had arrived by an assortment of transports – the back of lorry, a friend's shoulder, or perhaps carried seated on an old wicker chair. Some had even crawled. Few had a single injury and most had multiple injuries. For example, a broken shoulder plus a broken shin bone and a lacerated face; or, a shattered pelvis, a crushed chest and a fractured skull. None had been treated and each looked desperately ill.

I walked slowly along the line of stretcher cases. I could see this was a desperate situation. Any one of the casualties would, in a fully equipped hospital, have taken at least six hours of surgical time to treat. They would have been whisked into a spotlessly clean Emergency Department straight into the hands of a waiting resuscitation team. A drip would have been put in their arm, an intravenous line in their neck, electrodes on their chest to record their heart rhythm and a catheter placed in their bladder. Off they would have then gone to X-Ray or CT. They would have been in the operating theatre under the care of a specialist surgical team within sixty minutes of arrival.

That is London, or New York, or Paris, or Sydney, or many of the other advantaged cities in the world. This was downtown Port-au-Prince, in deepest, darkest Haiti. Dream on, I thought to myself, as I looked at the desperately ill casualties beside me. This was not London or New York or Paris or Sydney. All I could do was my best.

This was taking place to my right. I glanced to my left. At the far end of the tennis courts was a line of eight chairs. On each sat a patient and beside each patient was an aid worker doing what they could. These casualties were not the severely injured; they could at least walk. The aid workers had moved from the collapsed school to escape the stench of decaying corpses and to be near to the hospital when it arrived.

The staff were busying ceaselessly – first this patient, then that, hold a hand here, wipe a brow there, apply a dressing where they could, stitch a wound when possible.

'Doctor, doctor! Over here! Please look at this one!' they would shout.

Dr Eleanor, the Philadelphia physician, would respond, moving from one chair to the next and advising what to do. 'Stitch this...clean that...elevate the arm...try this antibiotic,' she would say. She was seemingly unflappable and clearly highly respected.

The surgeon inside me wanted to roll up his sleeves and set to work, despite the lack of an operating theatre. Meanwhile the fixer inside me could see the destroyed fencing that needed repair, the rubble that required clearing, the lack of water supply, the unpredictable transport and the disastrous communications. All these items, and plenty more, needed attention.

As I looked around wondering how best to start, realising how much still needed to be done, my mobile issued a resounding ping. A text message had arrived. Fumbling in my pocket I produced the device and flicked on the screen. I saw the sender immediately. London! Fantastic! It was certainly about time. Full of optimism I read the message. It was short and to the point. As I read, a wave of despair flowed over me.

'Unexpected problems. Delays encountered. Team MIGHT arrive today. No hospital yet. Will be in touch.'

In the distance I could see the General approaching, surrounded by four muscular assistants. He was well dressed while they were tattier in appearance and clearly armed. From the other side of the tennis courts the General raised his hand in welcome as he strode towards me. I could see his smile and realised he was expecting good news. What the hell could I say now? I swallowed hard. I had ten seconds to decide.

* * *

Chapter 20

The Psychologist

It did not take long for the General to say what he thought. He read my face perfectly and his anger was palpable.

'This is not good,' he said. Again the firm grip on my arm as I was led into a lonely corner of the tennis courts. The four assistants kept their distance. 'This is Haiti, Doctor,' the General added. 'We do not do things this way.'

'I'm sorry,' I replied. 'London is handling this. They say the team will be here soon but the hospital may be later.'

'Look around you.' The General made a wide sweep with his arm. 'These are my people. They look to me for help. I look after them. What will they say?' The grip on my arm tightened further.

At such times I am grateful to be the age I am. I am not ancient, in my eyes at least, but I am not young. In Port-au-Prince two attributes were influential. One was power. The General had that. The other was age and that was my forte. I am handicapped by not having grey hair. But wrinkles? I have a pile of those. Wrinkles, in some cultures, are associated with wisdom and trustworthiness so to have the occasional wrinkle on a disaster relief team has its advantages. It certainly paid its way in Haiti.

'We can easily use the time before they come,' I replied.

'How?'

'To prepare and sort the patients. That will take time. We want the team to start work the moment they arrive.'

I explained how the approaching surgical team was travelling many thousands of miles to reach Haiti, that it contained some of the best specialists in the business, and that we could set to work now anyway, by identifying patients who would be suitable for surgery when the team arrived.

I could see the suggestion pleased the General as it allowed him to maintain credibility and assert some control.

'OK, Doctor. That'll work for the moment,' he agreed.

Turning, he made another sweeping movement with his arm, beckoning to the far side of the tennis courts. In the distance, I saw a dark, muscular fellow of medium height instantly respond. Until then I had not noticed him helping with the seated casualties but he had clearly been keeping an eye on the General throughout.

'Meet Benjamin,' said the General as the man approached. 'He works for me. He is a good man.'

Dressed in perfectly clean operating blues, Benjamin arrived, smiled briefly, shook my hand without a word and then turned to his master. His head tilted slightly to one side, his eyes respectfully lowered towards the ground as he listened to the General's instructions. The tight grip on my own arm had now transferred to Benjamin's left shoulder.

'Today,' came the hoarse, Godfather-like voice, 'we are going to gather the patients together so that there is work ready for the team when it arrives. Their arrival has been delayed but operations will start tomorrow.' His eyes flicked towards me as he spoke. He did not need to explain. They were hard eyes, merciless and pitiless. 'You are on final warning, Doctor,' they implied.

For a brief moment I wanted to interrupt, to explain to the General that operations might not start the next day, that the hospital could at that moment have been anywhere. I had no idea if it would make it to Port-au-Prince on time, if at all. We could be looking at lines of untreated stretcher cases the next day as well, just as we were then. Yet it would have been futile. The General did not want to hear such words. He wanted to portray that the hospital was his idea and under his control. I did not like it, and was very sure London would not like it, but in the security abyss called Haiti strange relationships and bedfellows were critical.

Benjamin nodded slowly, his eyes rising slightly to look somewhere near the General's mid-chest. He still did not look at me. 'Yes, boss,' he said. 'I'll make certain that happens.' Then he turned and briskly walked back to his work.

'Remember,' said the General once Benjamin was on his way. 'We need that hospital. All problems through me. OK?'

'OK,' I nodded, and then watched the General return to his four assistants on the far side of the courts, their long baggy coats still so out of place in the baking hot sunshine. I stayed motionless until they had gone watching them in heated discussion as they walked, the General clearly in control.

Deep in thought, and very worried, I walked over to the line of desperate stretcher cases to see in more detail what degree of work they represented. How could London do this? Whatever their reasons for delay, I was the guy on the ground that carried the blame. Blame for something over which I had no influence. Did London truly understand? I doubted it.

There were about thirty patients in total. Some had clearly received treatment elsewhere although the majority had not. The scene was pitiful – deformed limbs, unstitched wounds, a gangrenous hand, an open skull fracture still leaking clear cerebrospinal fluid, a hip lying dislocated, a young girl paralysed from the waist down. These were but a few. The fact that so many remained alive was astonishing; their inner strength was phenomenal. Even so, it was clear that some of them would not survive much longer. It was very hot, with little shade, no food and the tiniest ration of water.

What water there was at Nanjui 24 lay heaped in a haphazard pile to one side of the tennis courts, a short distance from the stretcher casualties. It had been delivered by a German charity as many dozens of half-litre plastic bottles. I glanced across at the pile; I was parched and totally starving. It would have been so easy to reach out, grab a bottle and down the contents in one gulp. How I wanted to do that! Yet my conscience would not allow it.

Eating and drinking had become something of a luxury in Port-au-Prince. My normal three meals a day was now down to barely one. Even that was an American self-heating meal-ready-to-eat, or MRE, which would barely have fed someone half my size. Yet eating and drinking in full view of earthquake survivors is about as unfair as it gets. They need to see you living in the same conditions as them, suffering with them, enduring risk with them and that you understand everything they feel. You lead by example. If they cannot drink, neither can you. If they cannot eat, you starve too. And if the water has been delivered for their use only, then you go without. It is tough luck and as simple as that. Behind the scenes you ensure you are fully prepared, as a dehydrated, emaciated aid worker is no use to an earthquake victim. To me, the public view is not to grant myself any special treatment at all.

So I ignored the mound of bottled water, feeling my cracked and swollen tongue stick painfully to the roof of my mouth, and knelt down beside one of the patients at the very far end of the stretcher case line. She was about 16 years old, her upper arm fractured and deformed, her breathing rapid and shallow. Beside her sat a middle-aged woman, her head hanging low, her hands over her eyes as she tried hard to control the tears. Her head was covered by a floral scarf, so covered that I could barely see her face.

'What's happened?' I asked.

The middle-aged woman looked up. I gazed straight into her bloodshot eyes.

'Mannie, Doctor,' she replied. 'This is Mannie, my daughter. Her father was killed but we managed to take her from the rubble last night. What's wrong, Doctor? She does not look well.'

I reached across to feel the young girl's neck. There was the faintest pulse, beating rapidly. Her skin felt cold, there was little blood flow to the fingers and her lips were turning blue. As with the elderly lady in the hotel car park, I lifted the eyelid to see the pupils react to light. Mannie was alive, for now. However, she had clearly lost so much blood that she was now in deep shock and deteriorating fast. She needed expert care immediately.

As if he had read my thoughts, leaning over me was Benjamin. I had not heard him approach.

'Not good,' he stated.

'She's in trouble. Have you a central line and an infusion?'

For a moment Benjamin hesitated, then he spoke. 'Give me fifteen minutes and I'll be back.'

A central line is a special form of cannula that goes into the veins of the neck rather than the arm. It is particularly useful when patients are in shock, as was the case with Mannie. Shock collapses the smaller blood vessels so that it is much harder to insert a needle into them. Passing a thin plastic cannula into a neck vein is a way around this problem and was what I sought for Mannie.

To this day I have no idea where Benjamin found the central line and infusion. The missionaries working on the seated casualties at the other end of the tennis courts certainly did not have such technical items. However, in less than the fifteen minutes he had promised, Benjamin reappeared with the brightest of grins on his face. He waved the sterile packets in the air as he strode purposefully towards me.

'Not bad, eh?' he declared, handing the packets to me. 'In Port-au-Prince you can find anything.'

'As long as you are the General,' I thought to myself, smiling. I suspected the Hôpital de la Paix was now missing a central line and infusion as that was the nearest place likely to have had such items in stock. Whatever its source, the apparatus worked wonders. It took me about ten minutes to insert the cannula into Mannie's neck vein and to start the infusion flowing. She was so comatose that I did not even use local anaesthetic to freeze the skin before passing the cannula into her neck. Within ten minutes of the infusion beginning to flow, Mannie's eyelids began to flutter, her rate of breathing slowed and her skin began to warm. I realised the infusion would not cure Mannie but it might hold the situation a little longer. Long enough, I hoped, for the team and hospital to arrive.

While I watched Mannie slowly improve I had time to think. The stretcher casualties worried me as they relied completely on the team and hospital arriving soon. In the absence of a UK hospital, I was tempted to send the stretcher casualties elsewhere, perhaps to the Dominican Republic, perhaps to the Israelis or the UN. However, many of the casualties were simply too sick to move and were unlikely to survive a transfer. Some were bound to die in transit, just like the elderly lady at the hotel. Additionally, there was total gridlock on many of the capital's major thoroughfares, a dwindling petrol supply, and armed gangs were wandering the streets. On the tennis courts we had the General's protection. Out there? I looked at the high wall that barred the way to the streets outside. Out there anything could happen.

As if to highlight the dangers, thirty metres away I saw two young boys enter one of the smaller gates to the tennis courts with a bloodstained, off-white cloth bundle. They were carrying it between them and were struggling to avoid dropping it. Then, just inside the entrance, they stopped, looked quickly and furtively around them and gently placed the bundle on the ground. They put it down almost respectfully. Then, I saw them unwrap the bundle and slowly removing the bloodstained cloth. What appeared was horrifying and about as disgusting as it can be. It was a leg, an entire human leg from mid thigh to foot. Once unwrapped, the two young boys rapidly shouldered the bloodstained cloth and dashed out of the gate into the streets beyond. I saw one playfully punch the other on the shoulder as they ran. To them, depositing body parts had become a game.

There were still many dead bodies on the streets of Port-au-Prince. Beyond the walls of the tennis courts the thick and unbearable stench of death filled the air. The courts, thanks to the trees which surrounded them, were a small haven of tranquillity and largely odour-free. For a population trying to rebuild its existence, yet which did not have the means to dispose of bodies properly, all they could do was pile them in the streets. Body parts were sometimes left near medical facilities, as the shipping containers at the UN base had shown. The tennis courts, despite there being no hospital present, had clearly already become seen as medical.

Not all bodies and body parts were earthquake related in Haiti. Earlier that day I had already seen a cadaver, minus both arms and legs, lying threateningly positioned in the middle of a major crossroads. The traffic had been carefully steering around it so as not to crush the remaining torso. What the man, at least I think it was a man, had done wrong was anyone's guess. Vigilantism was alive and well in Port-au-Prince. If limbs were not removed before or after lynching, an alternative was to burn the victim to death by setting alight to rubber tyres placed around the neck. There were plenty of ghastly ways to die in Haiti.

I had also increasingly picked up talk of kidnappings of aid workers and hijackings of aid vehicles well before they had reached their intended destination. Even before the earthquake there were 100 murders every month in Port-au-Prince and at least five kidnappings every week. To travel through Port-au-Prince was a dangerous process. Yet another reason why casualties, once they had arrived at the tennis courts, were best treated there than moved elsewhere in the capital.

Quietly, I cursed London again. I felt abandoned and ignored. There was little information coming through to me and the casualties were mounting up. Communication is critical to relief programmes like this as the workers at the front line are exposed to dangers that the folk back home are spared. In London there was no need to keep one ear open for the sound of a mounting riot, one eye on a passing Haitian's waist belt to see what weapon they carried, or listen for the unmistakable sound of a UN armoured car screeching to a halt nearby, the precursor of real trouble. Nor did London have to explain itself to the General.

A key part of staying intact during disaster or conflict is to identify problems before they appear and to give them as wide a berth as possible. The fact that I was a volunteer gave me no special privileges and no enhanced protection. To a Haitian gang member I was from overseas and a fair target, however noble my intentions might have been. Furthermore,

I represented my own Government's actions almost by proxy. If some character in Westminster stood up and said it was time to withdraw all aid to Haiti, as an Englishman at the front line of disaster relief, I would carry the can. The same could be said for aid workers in Afghanistan or Iraq, Africa or Central America, for that matter anywhere on the planet. Aid workers can be thrust into the political firing line from no fault of their own.

Although I felt despondent, I smiled at Mannie's mother as she watched the colour flow into her daughter's cheeks. She smiled back, her lips mouthing a silent '*Merci*. Thank you,' as I rose slowly to my feet. I did not have the heart to tell her that the central line and infusion were only temporary measures. They would keep Mannie alive for a few hours at most. I had bought her time, not survival.

Hungry and very thirsty, I walked towards the seated casualties at the other end of the tennis courts, where I could see Benjamin and the missionary aid workers hard at work. I was deep in thought, desperately worried by the stretcher cases and trusting that I had made the right decision on their behalf.

Benjamin, who seemed to have a sixth sense, turned towards me as I approached. Beside him, I saw the middle-aged man, a large World War I size dressing expertly applied to the left side of his forehead. The man was carrying a small child, a girl, who was probably about two years' old. Strangely, I thought, the little girl was well dressed. A clean, pressed, small white dress with tiny, multicoloured polka dots, smart white socks, and sandals which, although old, had been polished within an inch of their lives. She was quietly asleep and oblivious to her surroundings.

Benjamin took one step towards me and then spoke softly into my ear. 'Doctor,' he began, 'We have a problem.' He half extended his left arm, palm forwards, to indicate the man and the little girl. I glanced towards them and then back to Benjamin, inclining my head slightly as indication that he should continue.

Benjamin nodded. 'This little girl,' he said, 'is this man's daughter. Her mother was crushed to death in the earthquake, or at least he thinks she was. They have not yet recovered the body.'

'Could she still be alive?' I asked.

'That is unlikely. But it is not about the mother. It is about the little girl that the father has come.'

I looked more closely at the sleeping child. The girl was so obviously uninjured and must have had a lucky escape. 'She looks like the Sleeping Beauty to me,' I said, smiling at the father. He grinned broadly back.

'He wants you to adopt her,' said Benjamin in a tone that made him sound as if this was an everyday statement.

'Adopt? Me? Why?'

'He cannot look after her. Her mother is dead, their house is destroyed, so they have nowhere to live and he has lost his work. He has no money and all his relatives have been killed. There is no one to bring up his daughter.' Benjamin was counting out the tragedies on his fingers, as if he was counting money. He looked directly into my eyes as he continued. 'He wishes to give her to you, Dr Richard. Take her to England. He has travelled a long way to ask this.'

What could I say? Could I truly arrive in London with an adopted daughter, almost as if I had bought a new pet? Of course not. Haiti had a huge orphan problem before the earthquake; since the disaster it was even worse. Disasters are frequently filled with do-gooder individuals who aim to whisk a child away to a so-called civilised country. Perhaps the father, perhaps even Benjamin, thought I was that type of guy. No. Children are best kept where they are, in familiar surroundings. If they are to be adopted, then that should be given time; all involved need opportunity to reflect.

Anyway, who was to know whether the young girl's mother might not still be buried alive? Who was to know, actually, whether the beautiful little creation, and she was certainly that, was this man's daughter at all? I had picked up stories of kidnapped children being sold for adoption. There were plenty of stories of relatives selling children without parental consent.

For me, adoption was a non-starter. Anyway, I had much to do and little time remaining. As he lowered his eyes, I could see from Benjamin's expression that he knew how I would respond. Slowly, I went over to the man and smiled. Gently I stroked the back of his little girl's hand. She looked gorgeous, still fast asleep, her tiny head with its curled and silken black hair, nestling peacefully on her father's shoulder. Her white dress, frilled at neck and hem, was immaculately clean. There was not a crease in sight. How, I thought, could she look so clean and tidy when surrounded by so much misery? Perhaps there was someone out there looking after her already? Perhaps I was being set up after all?

'Sorry,' I whispered into her ear, yet loud enough for her father to hear. 'One day you will make your daddy even prouder than he is now. Stay and look after him. You do not need England.' I sensed my words hit home and could see the flickering, now doubtful eyes of the father. For a moment our small group fell silent and utterly still. Then, as if he had just woken up, the father smiled, hugged his daughter tightly, and a small tear appeared in the corner of one eye. 'Thank you Dr Richard,' he whispered, clear emotion in his voice. 'Thank you, thank you.' With that he turned and walked away, carrying the little girl, her tiny head bouncing gently on his shoulder.

'This is one hell of a place to work,' I said to Benjamin as the sleeping child disappeared into the distance. 'Haiti certainly delivers surprises.'

'You don't need to tell me that,' came the reply.

The adoption query still in my mind, I walked the now short distance to the seated casualties to see what work existed there for the surgical team when it arrived. The stretcher casualties would certainly keep them well occupied. I saw instantly that the seated patients would be the same. Dr Eleanor, and those alongside her, had been hard at work.

I walked slowly along the row of seated casualties. There was treatment taking place at each seat, the missionary workers focussed totally on their task and oblivious to the chaos that surrounded them. To one side were two cracked wooden benches, positioned end to end. I counted seventeen patients waiting patiently to be treated. The casualties sat quite still, no talking, their impassive faces staring transfixed to their front as they gazed without emotion into the middle distance. Most had dirty, bloodstained dressings in place on either an arm, or a leg or head. This was the waiting area, protected from the sun by a large, sagging sheet of blue plastic suspended between two trees and the mesh netting that surrounded the tennis courts. Nearby, too, were two further benches, six patients sitting quietly side by side. This was the discharge bench, where patients sat after treatment, waiting to be collected by a relative or friend. On the discharge bench I could see only clean dressings, tidily applied, slings properly fastened, plaster casts smooth and shiny. Most striking were the smiles on the patients' faces. No longer the emotionless stare. They could sense they were on the road to recovery.

Coming from the eighth and final treatment chair I could hear the sound of uncontrollable sobbing. In five long strides I was there. It was a young girl, about 12 years old, wearing a shredded brown dress and only one plastic sandal. Tears poured down her face in great rivulets, her body shaking with emotion as she slumped slightly forwards on her chair. The aid worker alongside her, a young missionary, was beside herself with her failure to bring the girl's sobbing under control.

I knelt on the ground at the girl's feet and took her hand in mine. 'What's the trouble?' I asked, as gently as I could. The girl did not wrench her hand away from mine but held tighter, her chipped, dirty finger nails digging painfully into the back of my hand.

'They've both gone,' she choked. 'My mother and father. I have no one.'

I could barely pick out the girl's words; another orphan whose world had been destroyed in an instant. 'Tell me what happened,' I said.

It was as if I had released a floodgate as the horrifying story flowed out of the girl in fast, stammered sentences. Her head was now upright, her eyes opened wide as she gripped my hand in both of hers. The tale was horrifying.

The girl, an only child, had lived with her parents in the same ground floor flat since she had been born. There had only been two small rooms, sleeping in one, living in the other and a shared, tiny bathroom. When the earthquake struck she had felt the first tremor and heard her mother scream. Her father had instantly bellowed, 'Get out quickly!'

As she had run for the door, the girl looked behind to see her father try desperately to pull his wife to her feet. Yet her mother seemed slow, much too slow. The rubble had fallen at that point, massive chunks of ceiling masonry exploding all around. The girl had seen her father first wrap himself around her mother to protect her, then stand up and futilely try to catch the falling rubble. Finally, he had leaned his back hard against the wall, again in a hopeless attempt to prevent it collapsing. Everything her father tried had failed, the girl's final view being his agonised face as the floors above came crashing down one by one – then he had disappeared.

When she had completed her tale, the girl fell silent. Her desperate grip of my hands relaxed, the tears stopped and she leaned back exhausted against the rickety chair. The young missionary looked on in horror. I, too, was dumbstruck. What could I possibly say? Inadequately I rose to my feet and gave the girl's hands a gentle squeeze in mine. I wanted to hug her, to tell her that time would help heal, to stroke her forehead in reassurance, but such close contact with a patient was forbidden in this society. I moved on, whispering to the young missionary as I passed, 'Do what you can.' I should have done more.

The examples of horror and heroism revealed by the earthquake were at times truly astounding. Not only the girl's story of her father, who had died trying to save her mother, but the husband who amputated his wife's leg so she could escape the falling rubble, or the girl who listened to each of her school friends die, one by one, as the slowly subsiding building gradually pressed the life from their tiny bodies. There was the boy who had gone back into a building to rescue his grandmother, only to fall victim to an unexpected aftershock. By the time I had seen all the casualties lined up on the tennis courts that day, by the time I had listened to their terrifying stories, I was humbled. Anything I could do would be a tiny drop in the ocean for these people. I looked around me at the hours of surgical work lined up, each casualty waiting patiently for the hospital I had promised. 'Godammit!' I thought. Where the hell was the hospital? We needed it right now, not tomorrow, not any other day. We needed it at work immediately.

My prayers were partly, but not entirely answered that night when the team arrived, seven strong, having endured the voyage from Hell. Their journey had taken them through Spain to the northern Dominican Republic, then to Santo Domingo and finally by road to Port-au-Prince. They had found accommodation in a central city hotel; not in comfortable rooms but in tents scattered around the swimming pool. No one wished to be indoors as many of the building's walls looked deeply suspect. It would not take much to collapse them. Aftershocks can sometimes be more dramatic than the original event.

I met with the team within minutes of their arrival, each individual pale and exhausted after their long journey. Despite this, they were a very welcome sight. None realised what had taken place before they arrived, nor that my neck was still on the line with the General.

Stress, exhaustion and disasters can bring out the best and worst in people. Within the team there were many interpersonal relationships at play, particularly between medics and administrators. I could have cut the atmosphere with a knife. For the medics, they wanted to be straight into the fray. To them, every second sitting around a hotel swimming pool was wasted. The administrators were different. No less exhausted, they were deep in discussion about meetings, relationships with other aid organisations and a host of matters that did not appear to relate to the treatment of patients.

As a medic, I sided with my own kind. You would not expect otherwise. I shifted restlessly from foot to foot, my mind full of images of the long line of stretcher casualties waiting at the tennis courts, a line that was becoming longer by the minute. I needed the team's help immediately.

I was delighted to see one of the new arrivals, Mike, whom I had met in Kashmir. Mike was just what Merlin needed in Haiti, even if they did not yet realise it. Appropriately outspoken, Mike had a clear view of what was right and what was wrong. He certainly did not tolerate fools gladly. Life was black and white if you were Mike. He was always available, satellite telephone attached to his belt, mobile permanently charged, and was as happy sleeping on a chipped concrete floor in a war zone as he was in a five-star hotel in a Western capital.

In the early days of an aid project such as Haiti there is a vital role for people like Mike. Individuals who will take rapid decisions and who will tread on toes if needed. Mike made decisions. Many aid workers did not. It is this conflict between personalities at the start of a relief programme that leads to so many problems in the field.

'How was the journey?' I asked, more as an icebreaker for two friends who have not seen each other for some time.

Mike rolled his eyes. 'Don't ask,' he said, glancing towards the administrators. They were still deep in discussion, their backs to the medics.

I laughed briefly. I had not expected Mike to say anything else and he did not need to explain.

'Welcome to Haiti everyone!' I declared, 'Briefing time. Listen to what you will be doing.'

Each team member drew up a plastic poolside chair and we sat in a ragged circle. I sensed disapproval from the administrators but ignored their glances. There was no time to lose. Onto the concrete surface at our feet I spread the only map I had been able to find of Port-au-Prince, a tourist plan from Hertz. It was good enough. Orientation when you first arrive in a disaster location is essential. It makes new arrivals feel they belong and that they are no longer strangers.

I showed the team where we were, where key locations were to be found such as the UN base and airport, places to avoid such as Cité Soleil, and where we were headed, Nanjui 24. The team members were restless, each itching to start work. The administrators did not appear interested in the briefing, which puzzled me. Already I could sense a gulf develop between medics and administrators, a gulf that had to be bridged.

Questions came at me from every direction. Is it secure? Can we wash? Where do we eat? What about our valuables? How do I send a message home? Where is the nearest internet? I did my best to answer each query, realising that some team members had never visited a disaster zone before and had not seen a security abyss like Haiti. Ten minutes later - the administrators still talking intently and deaf to everything I had said - I was finished. It was time for the grand finale of my welcome brief.

'There is one big problem,' I announced. Any murmurs from the team members ceased immediately. I had every bit of their attention.

Mike raised his one eyebrow, listening for what was to come. 'Go on,' he said.

'I am here, you are here, the patients are here. But the hospital is nowhere to be found.'

'Shit,' said Mike. He could not have phrased it better.

* * *

That night, after the briefing, I received two text messages. Both were disappointing. The first was from Dr Eleanor.

'The strain has got to me. I am going home today,' it read.

I was saddened to read her words as, in the short time I had seen her at work, I had been impressed. She had won the hearts of both the missionaries and the patients. There was something relaxing about her. Outwardly it appeared she would be impossible to upset. Yet that was not the case.

Dr Eleanor highlighted a problem with aid work that is often ignored. Post-traumatic stress is not only the domain of the disaster victim or soldier. Aid workers can have it, too. When you are busy, when risk is at its highest, there is little time to reflect. You work almost on autopilot, containing your emotions in a huge protective bubble. How else can you handle 300 bodies piled in a street, disfiguring facial burns in tiny children, or the click of a pistol's safety catch as you walk round a corner at night? It is when the dangers have gone that I feel it most. When I am back home, 5,000 miles from the action. When a broken dishwasher and a dead coffee machine appear to be major problems. That is when the nightmare returns.

The second text message was even more disappointing than the one from Dr Eleanor. It was from London.

'Hospital untraceable. Known to have left UK. Present location unknown. Will be in touch.'

Will be in touch? Was that all they could say? I had glanced at my watch. 3 am. I had until 10 am to honour my commitment to the General.

*   *   *

Early the next morning, as I walked onto the tennis courts, this time with the team beside me, the place was filled to bursting. The General had clearly taken me at my word and Benjamin had been hard at work. The row of stretcher casualties was twice as long as it had been the day before and the missionaries were busying with the seated wounded. Yet the place felt emptier because of the lack of Dr Eleanor.

As I introduced the team members to Benjamin one by one, I glanced towards the stretcher casualties repeatedly. Something did not feel right. Something was missing. Benjamin picked up my concern immediately. Gently he took my arm and led me a few paces away to a quieter area of the courts.

'She's gone,' he said.

'I know,' I replied. 'Dr Eleanor texted me last night.'

'Not Dr Eleanor. Mannie. She went last night.'

I turned to look at the line of stretcher casualties once again. I could see the gap now, the gap where Mannie had lain, where I had inserted the young girl's central line and its infusion.

'Where did she go?' I asked. 'The Israelis?'

'No,' Benjamin replied in the faintest of whispers. 'She died, Doctor. We ran out of infusion fluid and she died.'

I did not know what to say. I was appalled and horrified. I thought I had saved her. Why had they not rung me and said? Surely I, or they, could have found more fluid? Perhaps that could have saved Mannie? Perhaps, perhaps, perhaps. Perhaps is frequently said in disaster relief. Certainty is non-existent.

On the far side of the courts I could see the General standing on some high ground looking down on the action. This time there were two overcoated men beside him, not four. I caught his eye or, perhaps, he caught mine. Casually I waved but he did not wave back. I saw him slowly point to his wrist, then to me, then to his throat. That was all. He made no attempt to walk across the courts to greet me. He just stood there, motionless, powerful and intimidating. I glanced at my own watch. 8 am. Two hours was all I had.

Yet when the team members went onto the tennis courts that morning it was a pleasure to see them work. They handled the mass of casualties expertly. The initial process is known as triage, where victims are sorted into those who require surgery and those that do not. Casualties may be spared an operation either because they do not need it or because they are too sick to justify the effort.

It is this last category that is the hardest to handle. Yet why spend hours and a vast amount of surgical resource in trying to prevent certain death? This is where experience comes in. Also the patient who looks the most badly injured is not always the one who is likely to perish. Sometimes a patient can die with no external evidence of anything wrong at all, particularly if there is internal bleeding. It takes a huge amount of skill to triage properly.

It was as I surveyed the frenetic medical activity taking place around me that I felt the gentle tug from behind on my right arm. I turned slowly to find a young Haitian woman, about 28 years old, smiling and looking up at me. She was well dressed in light brown blouse and tight blue jeans, her medium length curled brunette hair glistening cleanly in the sunlight.

'I'd like to help, Doctor,' she said in near perfect English. 'What can I do?'

For a moment I hesitated. After major disasters the survival instinct of those left behind is enormous. All employment opportunities, what few there were, had disappeared as one business after another had vanished into rubble. The local Haitians would constantly ask if I could employ them, so desperate were they for some form of income, however small it might be. I could find any claimed skill on the streets of Port-au-Prince – interpreters, drivers, mechanics, medical assistants, cooks. However, what a local might claim was not necessarily what they were able to do. The public financial response for disaster relief had been good but did I really need to stretch the budget further by employing yet another local?

I looked at the young woman, took a deep breath and began to speak. 'I'm afraid…'

'Please,' she interrupted.

'I'm sorry, but…'

'Please,' she repeated.

'Look,' I said, my voice now quite blunt. 'Thank you for offering but...'

Again the interruption. 'Please, Dr Richard,' she said, her voice now heavy with emotion. 'I must help. I can help. I want to help. I know I can be of use.'

Something clicked inside me. Did I have to be so hard-hearted? Was it so bad that I went even more over budget by employing one more person? I could see passion in the woman's eyes, almost a need. So I sighed, nodded my head gently, and smiled. 'OK,' I said. 'You're hired. Get started over there.' I pointed towards the seated casualties where a number had been left unattended and untreated, such was the pressure of work.

The young woman instantly released my arm and started to run across to the casualty area. 'Thank you,' she shouted over her shoulder. She was smiling now, almost laughing. 'But you forgot one thing.'

'What was that?'

'You did not ask me what I did.'

I smiled. She was right. 'What do you do?' I asked.

'I'm a psychologist,' came the reply.

'A what?'

'A psychologist,' she shouted once more and then her run picked up speed as she headed towards the casualties.

'My God,' I thought. 'A psychologist? I have just employed a psychologist. What conceivable use is that?'

Deep in thought, I walked slowly across the tennis courts towards the General who was still standing imposingly on the high ground above me. I looked again at my watch. I had sixty minutes. I was unsure how to explain it to him but I felt he would want an update.

* * *

Chapter 21

Tents Need Poles

Sometimes I realise mankind is overseen by a power that no one can control. Why the hospital chose that very moment to appear, I do not know. However, it did.

It was the graunching, jerking sound of a lorry reversing that stopped me in my tracks as I headed towards the General. I could see him look up, too. His assistants were instantly alert, their hands held ready on the inside of their baggy coats. There was much revving, hooting and squealing of brakes as the driver negotiated his charge into the narrow forecourt area. Through the half-open back of the lorry I could see the massive pile of medical boxes and bundles of equipment, most covered in a thick layer of grime and dust. The hospital had arrived.

'It has beaten me to it,' I said with a broad grin on my face as I came near to the General. 'I was coming to tell you we can expect the hospital at any moment.' May God forgive me for such flagrant lying, I thought, as I uttered those words.

'It is good to see,' said the General. 'Just in time as well.' He glanced at his watch once more although this time he was smiling. I looked at my own. It had been close. There had been less than one hour to spare.

To look into the back of a lorry at a pile of higgledy-piggledy boxes and to imagine that from that a field hospital will appear is difficult. A field hospital is huge, with multiple tents and more than fifty people to run it.

Unloading the transport took a very long time. Locals and aid workers, all brought together by Benjamin, formed a human chain to unload the boxes and bundles into orderly piles on the tennis courts. With the arrival of several tons of medical materials security became significant. I saw the General nod to his assistants, who in turn signalled to others, who in turn organised others, and within minutes a protective guard was in place. A big feature of using local people to assist was that they took ownership. I was elated. This was a hospital being constructed by the people for the people and I was proud to be in at the start. I could see Haitians dashing here, there, left, right, up, down, organising, arranging, tidying, repairing, and building. Everyone wanted to be involved.

At this stage the most important items were the tents. It was these that would allow surgical operations to start, improve sterility and reduce infections. The team could begin its work away from the prying eyes of the many passers-by who might not all be friendly. However, before any tent was erected, I had to work out where it should be placed. It is not easy to design a field hospital. Every location is different. The principle is that each tent should have an easy way in and an easy way out for patients, whether they are walking or on a stretcher. There should also be a circuit, each tented department leading easily to the next. A field hospital is little less than a mini-village and has to work first time. It is not simple to change the position of a tent once everything is in location as, if you change one, you may have to change them all. In addition to facilities for patients, a field hospital will have an investigation tent, X-Ray, toilets, staff accommodation, sterilisation, somewhere to eat and wash, a water supply, as well as light and heat.

While the hospital was being unloaded, the clinic for the seated casualties continued, the stretcher cases looking on as their eventual treatment was gradually assembled. Notebook and pencil in hand I walked slowly around the tennis courts, sketching multiple diagrams of the various ways the hospital could be fashioned. There was no standard arrangement but whatever I eventually chose had to adhere to the principles of easy access and simplicity. I had the best view of the entire court area from beside the seated casualties so stood there for more than an hour thinking, sketching, erasing and scribbling notes. From my position I could also see and hear the seated clinic in progress. Because I was nearby and there was no Dr Eleanor, the missionaries would sometimes interrupt my sketching and planning to seek my advice. What I had not expected was that my spot by the seated casualties also allowed me to see the psychologist at work.

She was a star. I rapidly learned how wrong I had been. I only had to see her in action to understand how valuable the treatment of emotion and stress can be in the aftermath of a disaster.

As she set to work it was clear that many of the casualties had a strong psychological component to their injuries. There was the young girl with a paralysed left arm who had lain under large concrete blocks for three days before being rescued. She had heard her family die around her, one by one. When I examined her I thought she had probably broken her neck, although I had been unable to take an X–Ray to check if I was right. Yet when the psychologist set to work, simply by talking, nothing more, movement slowly returned to the girl's arm. First fingers, then wrist, then elbow, and finally the shoulder. This was hysterical paralysis, well known but difficult to spot when large numbers of injured are arranged before you. The mind is so traumatised that it loses control of the body.

There was the middle-aged man who was unable to feel both legs, from feet to just below the knee.

'It's like I'm wearing a long pair of thick socks,' he said.

I could prick his legs with a needle and even draw blood. He claimed he could not feel me at all. This had happened as he fled from a collapsing apartment block leaving behind him three generations of his family; all except him had died. Yet I could discover nothing when I examined him, not even the tiniest cut. All I could find was a complete loss of feeling below the knees. When I examined him, I could move his legs normally – they were totally pain free - while the patient smiled broadly at everything I did. I could not explain it. Here was a patient who claimed dramatic symptoms yet my findings and his response simply did not make sense.

'Let me have a look,' the psychologist requested. I was politely but firmly pushed to one side.

Immediately, the psychologist started her magic. I saw her sit down beside the man, hold his hand, look into his eyes, and gently start a conversation. Within minutes the patient was talking as if she was a long-lost friend. I saw her nod, sometimes say a few words, but most of the talking was the patient's.

Within thirty minutes the patient's feeling returned. Within an hour he walked from the tennis courts unaided. His symptoms had all been created by the mind.

Not all casualties in an earthquake zone are created by the earthquake. Life continues alongside all catastrophes. In countries where medical provision is poor, the population will take any opportunity to see a doctor. The fact they may be depriving other more seriously injured nationals from urgent treatment appears to escape them. So on the tennis courts I saw hernias, ingrowing toenails, and flat feet alongside lumps, bumps and moles that needed removing.

'This is not the time,' I would say as I gently sent them on their way, although whether they would ever receive treatment was hard to say in a land that had more gangsters than physicians.

It took me longer than I expected to design the layout of the tents. Not only was I constantly being asked to examine seated casualties but there were so many permutations to the hospital. It was like chess. Each change of position influenced the next.

I muttered repeatedly to myself. On occasion I saw the psychologist looking at me as if I was the one who needed treatment.

'Now,' I would whisper, 'if I place a tent here, then I must place another tent there and yet another in the far corner. Then this goes here, that there, mmm... Oh damn it! That means the patients won't have simple access.'

On it went. Soon my notebook was filled with scribbles and sketches, none of which would have won a Turner prize. There were many feasible alternatives but eventually, after more than two hours, I had an outline of how the end result would look. It was time to set to work and start constructing the field hospital.

The process was delayed when Benjamin came up to me. 'The BBC is here to film this. Do you mind?' he asked.

'No problems,' I replied, confident that all would go well.

The media had done much to highlight the efficiencies and inefficiencies of the aid programme and I was keen to support them. My occasional contacts with London had suggested that a large amount of aid had flooded in as a result of the media bulletins being disseminated globally.

So another media report was not a problem, particularly for the home team, the BBC. I asked Benjamin if he could find three helpers so that I could erect the first tent, fully in the glare of the global spotlight. Within thirty seconds he had found six, each keen to be televised to the world.

Field hospital tents are huge. You can stand in them, walk in them and even play football in some. I chose a smaller tent first. I did not want anything to go wrong in public. The cameras whirred as I removed the protective canvas shell from the first tidily packed tent and slowly unrolled the material. Everyone had stopped to watch, not just the television crew. There was palpable enthusiasm in the air.

It was as the tent unrolled that I felt the first signs of unease. There was something missing, but what? Yet there was no going back. The event was being recorded and, within moments, the planet would know that the UK field hospital was in place. The final part of the tent unrolled, now lying flat on the ground in preparation, and then the reality dawned. It had been noiseless. No clanking, clunking or chinking which is so typical of tents anywhere. I was about to look a first-class idiot. London, somehow, had packed the tents without their poles.

Poles are essential in a tent. Without them I was stuck. Thank Heaven cameras cannot – as yet at least – record thoughts, as what I was thinking was not for public display. I had but one choice.

'These tents,' I announced, 'are the beginning of a major surgical facility in the heart of the earthquake zone.'

To one side I could see the General turn and watch intently. Benjamin, too, had briefly stopped work while both seated and stretchered casualties were watching the proceedings.

I continued. 'Before the tents go up I must see how they will be arranged. First, I must roll out the canvas to work out where the tent should go. It will be harder to move when the poles are in place, so best I do this now.'

By the time I had finished, by the time the television cameras had moved on to their next interview in the capital, I had nearly persuaded myself that packing a tent without its poles was the correct thing to do. However, the moment the BBC had disappeared, I rolled the canvas back up and tidied it away.

My salvation came with the Norwegians and I do not mean the nation. I do mean their tents. At the very bottom of a mound of hospital equipment were two massive tent canvases, four times larger than the one I had already unrolled. Furthermore, they had their poles. Called a Norwegian because of its Scandinavian origin, the tent is double-skinned, windowed and immensely stable. It is excellent at keeping warmth in, or heat out. Ninety minutes later the first tent was in place, a spring had returned to the General's step, as it had to mine, and his assistants were less attentive of my every move. It was a fatal thing to feel in a disaster zone but, for a brief moment, I smelt success.

Slowly the hospital took shape. First the surgery tent, where the operations would be performed and then the ward tent where the patients would recover after their procedure. There would be many more tents to follow. Meanwhile the surgical team was hard at work preparing the patients who would need operations. There was plenty of work to do.

*   *   *

Chapter 22

I Want to Go to America

As the hospital was rapidly assembled, more team members arrived from the UK to staff the facility. I had a near miss on one occasion as a result. I mentioned to one new arrival how the tennis court location had not been my first choice and that the nearby collapsed school had been my original intention.

'Would you like to see the place?' I asked.

'Love to,' came the reply.

So I took the new arrival up there. It was not far away. Together we strolled up the hill towards the collapsed school, no security to accompany us, as if we had not a care in the world. Rapidly we drew away from the fenced protection of the tennis courts, doing exactly what I had advised others not to do. I had allowed us to become exposed and outside the protective umbrella of the General.

The collapsed school looked even more depressing than when I had first seen it. There was no clinic being held in the old playground to give it life. The gate, once guarded, was lying half open, an emaciated dog picking its way through the ruins. The telegraph pole nearby was still tilted at its drunken angle. Meanwhile the smell of rotting corpses hung in the air like a thick cloud so that it felt easier to breath through my mouth, teeth clenched, than through my nose. In the road outside lay a smouldering skeleton. I glanced at the bones and could identify a thighbone, a shinbone, some ribs and part of a pelvis. There was no skull. The bones looked as if they had belonged to a large child, perhaps a teenager. Perhaps one of the pupils at the now collapsed school. It was a tragic sight, so tragic that I missed the steady build-up of the young Haitian crowd around us. First one, then another, then two others, then four, eight, twelve – rapidly the throng assembled and I knew I had made a mistake.

Such things always start innocently, or apparently so. On this occasion it was a local man, perhaps in his late 20s, who was clutching a large display folder. He came straight up to me, a demanding look to his eye, and stood no more than a foot away. 'Where are you from?' he asked.

I looked around me; there was no General and no UN to protect me here. 'Scotland,' I lied, being a full-blooded Englishman.

I have long abandoned any vestige of patriotism in conflict and disaster zones. To openly acknowledge either English or US citizenship is asking for trouble. Once a point of pride to tell the globe I was English, now it is a red flag. I am proud to be a Brit but there are times when it is easier to deny it. This was an example and being Scottish is always a good bet.

'I want to go to America', said the young Haitian, urgency in his voice. 'Look at these.' He thrust the display folder into my hands, forcing me to look at it.

Despite the cracked and time-exhausted plastic display envelopes, I could see the carefully arranged documents within - the photocopy of an expired identification card, the school examination certificates, and the badly typed reference from a previous employer.

'Impressive,' I stated. 'What do you do?'

'He's a drummer,' said a voice from behind me in the crowd as if I should have known.

'A very good drummer,' another voice added. I could see a faded programme at the back of the display folder, evidence of a performance at a Caribbean music festival some years earlier.

'Yes,' said the young Haitian. 'I am a drummer. I have even played alongside Julia Roberts. I want to go to America and play for her again.'

Despite being a modern music and celebrity no-hoper, even I had heard of Julia Roberts. As far as I was aware she was an actress not a singer.

'I do not know Julia Roberts,' I said. 'I don't think I can help.'

'But you must do, Mister,' came the aggressive reply, the young Haitian poking me hard in the chest, hard enough to force me backwards. 'Scotland is part of England, and America and England are good friends.'

'I am a simple doctor in my country,' I replied. 'Simple doctors do not know important people like Julia Roberts.'

As I talked, I gently handed the display folder back to the Haitian, and then I began to slowly turn. I needed to be back at the tennis courts fast. They were the only safe place to be. I could see the new arrival with me was becoming nervous. His eyes darted frantically and his legs began to shake. I gripped his arm and spoke.

'We'll do this slowly. Stay close and don't show them you are frightened.'

'I'm not,' came the bravado reply.

'Bullshit. It stands out a mile.'

Although the tennis courts were only a few hundred yards away, much can happen in such a short distance. Yet as I turned I realised I had no way through. My way back to the courts was barred by a crowd at least twenty deep.

From the back of the crowd came another question, from someone I could not see. 'Then what can I do? What can any of us do?' the voice shouted.

'And me!'

'And me!'

The drummer jabbed me once more, this time on my shoulder. He spoke loudly. 'You see, you have to help us,' he said.

'But I am here as a doctor. That is what I do.'

'We don't need a doctor. We need jobs, we need to eat, we need to live, we need somewhere to sleep and we need money.'

The drummer was right, of course. Already the demands of the disaster were changing. The dead were dead and there was nothing that could now be done for them. Those who had been trapped had mostly been recovered or had died. There would be a few survival stories but these would be a tiny minority. Meanwhile the uninjured, those with quick reflexes and good fortune on their side, had a life to lead. They were the ones who surrounded me now. They wanted a future. They saw me, and the new arrival with me, as their way forward.

'Surely your Government can help?' I asked, as I began to walk slowly down the hill toward the tennis courts.

'The Government!' The drummer laughed. 'Mister, our Government is useless. We have heard nothing from our politicians since the earthquake. We heard little enough before. You must help us.'

As they talked, questioned and shouted, I sensed the throng give way slightly, just enough to make the tiniest pathway through their ranks. I walked slowly onwards, the new arrival immediately behind me, while any hand within range tried to touch me, or jab me, or grab my collar or lapel. With every jab, grope or poke came a demand.

'You must help!'

'I want to go to America, too!'

'Money! Give me money!'

For a moment I hesitated. The slow walk had taken me to the other side of the busy road, immediately opposite the tennis courts. A brief dash would do it, I thought, although whether the two of us would survive the chaos of Haitian driving was anyone's guess. Anyway, the drummer was still firmly clutching my collar, as if he sensed I wanted to hurry away. The crowd had thinned slightly, which was good, but there remained an unspoken threat, a sense of being on an edge where it is impossible to predict how people will behave. So I continued to speak.

'You know that Government of yours? Forget them,' I said. 'You are the future of Haiti, not the grey-haired men in smart suits. You are the buds on a tree. It is from you this country will grow.'

My confident words clearly struck home. I felt the tight grasp on my collar relax, the fire come from the young men's eyes and I saw the smiles emerge. I had their ear and my sense of safety returned. I turned slightly and grasped the shoulder of a young Haitian beside me, adding, 'Now go out there and show them how it is done. Now it is your time, not mine.'

With that, the new arrival and I waved to the crowd and crossed the road to the tennis courts. The crowd waved back. Somehow I had put us in harm's way and had then taken us out. But it had been a close one.

By the time I had returned to the tennis courts, work was well underway. The noisy chug of the generator drowned any possibility of holding a proper conversation. Meanwhile a plastic surgeon was busy closing the leg wound of a young Haitian boy. The anaesthetist stood at the head of the table, an ancient teddy bear lying forlornly on his anaesthetic machine, evidence of his attempts to relax the child before the general anaesthetic had been given. Operating theatre lighting, so critical to decent surgery, was not good, so I could see the head torch worn by the surgeon flash haphazardly as he continually changed his position to ensure a tidy closure of the massive wound.

It was as I saw the plastic surgeon at work, expertly performing his first operation, that the feeling came over me. Similar to a huge wave of depression, it was a realisation that my job was complete. The surgical fixer had done his bit and it was time for him to leave. The confused, somewhat alarmed look on the faces of the surgical team, so prominent when I had first briefed them at the hotel, had now gone. The team had settled into place and was working confidently. None of them was aware what had gone before them. The many problems solved on their behalf, the negotiations made, the risks avoided, and the complex deals struck. There was, however, one vital factor on which successful continuity would depend. It was not far away.

I looked around me. Where were they? There! Up by the seated casualties and still deep in discussion were the two administrators, one senior and in charge while the other was number two. Their backs were turned to the hospital. I walked across.

'Time for me to go,' I said.

The administrators turned with perfect synchronisation. Their faces were impassive.

'When?' the senior asked.

'Right away.'

'Fine,' said the senior. 'See you in UK.' I realised the only thanks I was likely to receive would be from the medics. Administrators generally regard me as a problem.

'There is one thing,' I added.

'Yes?'

'That guy over there.' I turned and pointed to the General, still on his vantage point overlooking the hospital, and now with four assistants around him rather than two.

'What about him?' the senior administrator asked.

'Whatever you do, keep him on side. He'll look after you. No one else will.'

'I don't see the need,' came the reply. 'We're up and running now. Have a good trip home.' With that the administrators turned and continued their discussion. In their view I was history. So I took a short step forward and laid one hand on a shoulder of each. I gripped them firmly and lowered my head between theirs. I spoke quietly but as forcefully as I could.

'Look you two,' I said. 'You may think you are in charge but you are not. Take another look when I've gone. That guy is the General. Everything you see here is down to him. You ignore him at your peril.'

And with that I was gone.

* * *

LIBYA 2011

Chapter 23

The Arrival

April 2011. Squeezed tightly into the back of the ancient Landcruiser, I watched the Libyan desert flash past at what seemed a million miles an hour. It was too dangerous to slow down and assured death if we stopped. Clouds of blast debris broke the distant horizon. This was war Gaddafi-style and I was in it fully, right to the top of my ex-military neck.

'Stupid, stupid, stupid,' I thought. 'What the hell would I do if they caught me?'

You would have had to live in a different universe to miss the chaos that took shape in the Middle East in early 2011. It was the Arab Spring, revolution spreading its way across the Muslim world. No country was spared. Libya was particularly badly affected; pro-Gaddafi on one side, anti-Gaddafi on the other, with NATO circling overhead doing what it believed was right. Into the mix came lifelong tribal rivalries – blood for blood, brother for brother and eye for eye. That is not an argument I will enter, as that is not my job. Anyway, I am about as apolitical as one can be and am the last person to whom you should listen during a current affairs debate.

Most of my work in England is surgery dealing with damaged hips and knees, work which is safe and civilised and fun. Yet during my SAS years, I was more than a doctor. I was a soldier, linguist, signaller and a demolitionist, too. Life has changed since then but that love of danger can still sneak under your skin. Perhaps it was this that found me in the back of the Landcruiser, my Berber driver taking me as fast he dared deep into rebel-held Libya. Gaddafi's forces were within sight and within earshot, while I, the crazy Englishman, was a perfect target.

Yet for a doctor the decision is simple. You go wherever the need is greatest, you dissociate yourself from politics and you treat your patients in order of clinical priority. It matters not from where they come, what colour they are, what crime they may have committed, which religion they follow or what their sexual orientation may be. You treat everyone the same. You deviate from this belief at your peril, indeed, at everyone else's peril, too. My Tunisian contacts, fresh from yet another illegal border crossing, had told me of several seriously injured casualties in the town of Nalut, a remote Berber outpost deep within Libya's Nafusa Mountains. Nalut was where I was headed. Unfortunately, Nalut was where Gaddafi was headed too.

Only days before, I had emerged from a time-expired turboprop into the strong sunlight of Tunisia's Djerba–Zarzis Airport. My tidy surgical practice back home seemed a thousand light years away. The airport was the gateway out of North Africa for many thousands of refugees fleeing from the Libyan crisis. The stories of atrocities taking place in western Libya had been filtering through at an alarming rate, while the tales of heroism by some of the aid agencies defied imagination. I felt humbled and I was also terrified.

Two days before my arrival, MSF, known throughout the world for its skills and courage in the wake of conflict and disaster, had entered a war-ravaged Misrata. They had been at enormous risk. Yet despite this they had, somehow, extracted seventy-two seriously wounded from the war-shredded front line in a boat that some might have condemned. Their aim had been to disembark at the Tunisian coastal town of Sfax but the weather had turned sour and their plans rapidly changed. The casualties, mostly civilians, were unloaded at the nearer Zarzis, a process that took MSF fourteen strenuous hours, under conditions that were as bad as they can be. Drips, catheters, ventilators, life-saving medicines – these all had to be monitored. This was not a film, nor a work of fiction; this was what really happened. And this was the world I was now in. I could only hope that when my turn came, I could do the same.

Waiting for me outside the airport was Madjid, my driver who, I soon learned, was as deeply religious as a Muslim can be. His full and bulky black beard made him appear fifteen years older than his claimed age of twenty-six. Madjid was tall, about my height, and his white forever-pressed shirt, tidy black trousers and permanently polished black shoes were unprepossessing. His brown eyes smiled with him under a full head of well-kept dark hair. I could tell he was a man's man from the moment I saw him.

'*Monsieur Richard?*' he said in rapid Tunisian French, extending his arm for the firmest of handshakes.

I nodded.

'*Bienvenue en Tunisie*. Welcome to Tunisia,' he continued. I was given no time to reply but was directed to the front passenger seat, not the back, my knees forced almost to my chin by the tiny foot well of the brightly polished black Hyundai. Then we were off, jerkily at the start, first crossing the tiny isthmus that joined Djerba Island to Tunisia proper, and then heading south through a desert landscape.

Madjid was an enigma I never truly solved and I half suspected worked for the Tunisian Intelligence Service. I doubted he worked for Gaddafi, although I had been warned by London that I could expect Libyan agents throughout Tunisia. Madjid was more than a driver. He knew everyone and everything. He always had a contact in the tiniest, remotest, loneliest village and there was invariably a so-called cousin or distant relative who could help and advise. Wherever we drove, Madjid would receive repeated calls on his mobile. On each occasion he would stop the car, step out and speak. Not once did he talk within earshot, however hard I struggled to hear. Madjid spoke French, Arabic and English, although never truly admitted to his knowledge of the latter. Yet he clearly understood everything in English that was said. He was bright, with a quick mind – just what was needed at the impromptu police and military roadblocks that would suddenly appear on Tunisia's roads. Madjid would disappear into a building with a heavily armed soldier and emerge moments later shaking hands, smiling, while our car was waved on through. There was more to Madjid than was easily seen, a sort of mystery man who could part the waters when required. I could tell from the beginning that he was gold dust. He had to be kept on side.

The Hotel Odyssée in Zarzis, where Madjid brought the Hyundai to a jerking halt, was a popular four-star tourist establishment. Palm trees, swimming pools, waiters dashing left and right with drink-laden trays, incongruously piped Western music in the background. It all made me feel uneasy when I considered why I was in North Africa. You do not expect such luxury when Hell is burning barely one hour's drive away.

The hotel was the hub of the Tunisian-based international aid effort. It was filled with relief agencies. Every conference room, large or small, housed an office with a smudged inkjet paper sign stuck to its door. It was a Who's Who of disaster relief. Anyone who was anyone was at the Hotel Odyssée.

Despite its convenience – easy food, internet access, comfortable rooms and as much drink as you could handle, if you wanted it – the hotel demonstrated everything bad in disaster relief. The aid agencies lining the Odyssée's corridors were there to serve a population in fear for its life, indeed its very existence. Upwards of 2,000 refugees were crossing the Tunisian border from Libya every day, leaving behind everything they had known, or earned or saved, often over many generations. Now, they were squashed into tiny regimented white tents, or double-bunking with Tunisian families, or fleeing North Africa altogether.

The contrast between the hotel's comforts and the refugees' misery could not have been more extreme. I felt guilty and frustrated from the moment I crossed the hotel's threshold. The bulk of workers in the hotel were not front line aid staff. They were mainly administrators, people unaccustomed to physically delivering the care itself. Most had never seen a gunshot wound and never would. Most had never laid out a corpse, or bargained with black marketeers, or crossed a mined frontier at night to deliver care to those in need. For many, their knowledge of French or Arabic was non-existent, with a consequent inability to communicate with the people they had come to assist. Administrators seem to love meetings. At the Hotel Odyssée there were meetings, meetings, meetings and yet more of the same. Sometimes there were even meetings about meetings. It is so easy to become sucked into this way of things, to believe that the meetings themselves are the aid. Of course they are not. No meeting has ever, since time began, saved the life of a patient.

Yet there is a complex chain of command in international aid relief. The surgeon wants to be at the coalface instantly, dealing with the injured as soon as he can. That is what he is trained to do and that is where he is at his most comfortable. However, even the world's most adaptable and talented surgeon cannot operate without equipment, without anaesthetic, or without at least the most rudimentary of operating surfaces on which to place a patient. Only administrators can provide such items, so in aid relief administrators can rule the roost. However unqualified they may be, however hesitant in making decisions, if an administrator cannot provide essential items then an aid project will almost certainly fail. My instructions from London had been clear. I was to develop a surgical facility to deal with Libyan war wounded. My equipment? I had not yet been given even a single surgical swab. My job on this occasion, as it had been previously in war and disaster zones around the world, was to create something out of nothing.

I was not the only one to show frustration. Madjid showed it too. I had been at the Hotel Odyssée barely eighteen hours and had already attended eleven separate meetings, some away from the hotel and some within its luxurious walls. When outside the hotel, Madjid would normally drive me. There then came meeting number 12, scheduled to take place half-a-mile from the Odyssée. It was late in the afternoon of what had been a hot, dry day. The sky was crystal clear, as was the sea beneath it while in the distance I could hear tiny waves lapping gently against the hotel's sandy beach. At any other time this would have been perfect weather, a tourist's delight. Yet I was tired, irritable, and despite the short distance it felt easier to drive to the meeting. I walked down the hotel's front steps towards the parking area to be greeted by Madjid's broad, bearded smile.

'You OK, Dr Richard?' he inquired as he ushered me into the Hyundai's front passenger seat once more. We spoke in French.

'Don't ask,' I replied. Then Madjid closed the door and we were off, this time without the regular starting lurch that I had come to expect. On this occasion there was something missing. I noticed it immediately. The car's music system would normally blare out Islamic *surya*, Koranic chapters, at maximum volume. This time it was silent. I could see Madjid was deep in thought. He was also driving very slowly. It was as if he wanted to talk.

'What's the problem, Madjid?' I asked. 'What about you? All OK?'

He glanced towards me briefly and then to the road ahead. It was clear. There was not a car in sight. He brought the Hyundai to a gentle halt and turned to look directly at me, grasping my shoulder with his right hand to emphasise his words.

'Meetings and more meetings!' he half-shouted, frustration in his voice. 'What is the purpose of these meetings? You are here to help the Libyan people and all you do is sit in meetings!' He thumped the steering wheel with his left hand in frustration.

'You don't need to tell me that,' I nodded. How could I have disagreed? I felt exactly the same.

'OK,' I continued. 'Take me to Tripoli. Take me there right now.'

For a moment I could see hesitation in Madjid's eyes. 'Was this crazy

Englishman serious?' I could sense him think. He relaxed his almost painful grip on my right shoulder, turned to face the front once more and the road ahead. He breathed in deeply, sucking in air noisily. Then, this time with both hands, he struck the steering wheel again. I could feel the Hyundai shake.

'I am ready Dr Richard! Let us go! Those people need us now!' He glanced towards me once more and then saw my smile. His shoulders slumped and his fiery eyes dimmed. 'You are not serious are you?' he asked. I sensed residual hope in his tone.

'No, Madjid, I am not serious. But I promise you one thing. We will enter Libya soon. I cannot tell you when or how but across that border we will go.'

'You are a good man,' came the reply. Then he leaned forward, touched a button on the car's music system and the maximum-volume *surya* began.

'*Bismillahi ar-rahmani ar-rahim. Bismillahi ar-rahmani ar-rahim...* In the Name of God, the Most Gracious, the Most Merciful...'

For the rest of our short journey Madjid was silent, as was I, both of us deeply immersed in thought.

*   *   *

Chapter 24

Tataouine

I need not have worried, as it was at meeting number 12 that the opportunity appeared. It was a small gathering of health officials, four in total, with me making five. The key individual was Dr Abdullah, a charming, middle-aged representative of the Tunisian Ministry of Health. He had once been a practising doctor but some years earlier had abandoned ship to become an administrator.

My three other companions were from the World Health Organisation, or WHO, and sported their enviable WHO logos on the front of their cotton gilets. The waistcoat-like gilet appears to be standard uniform for the modern-day aid worker. Littered with pockets inside and out, front and back, large and small, it can carry everything from a few pens to an entire washing kit for a week under canvas in the field. Anyone who is anyone wears a gilet. Surreptitiously I puffed out my own to make it appear twice its size.

The meeting started with a computer presentation by Dr Abdullah, in rapid fire French, of events taking shape on the Tunisian-Libyan border and the efforts being made to provide medical support. A number of agencies had already crossed the border to start work in areas to the south of Tripoli, including MSF and the US-based International Medical Corps, or IMC. The picture, however, was not a happy one. It was clear from the figures coming through that a major humanitarian disaster was in progress. Refugees were crossing Libya's multiple borders in their droves; west to Tunisia and Algeria, east to Egypt, south to Niger, Chad and Sudan. Some were also headed across the Mediterranean in flimsy boats to Malta and elsewhere. Not all the refugees were Libyan. Before the crisis, Libya had been home to at least 2.5 million expatriates. There were Egyptians, Pakistanis, Sudanese, Bangladeshis, Filipinos, Nepalese, Palestinians, Chadians, and even a few Brits thrown in. Libya was about as multinational as you can be. However, Tunisia was taking far more than its fair allocation, largely because of the very tight bond they had shared with Libya for many decades. Even in more peaceful times Libyans would cross the border into Tunisia to seek medical care.

After a time the presentation became tedious. I struggled to keep track of Dr Abdullah's French and at one point found myself drifting off to half sleep. Somewhere in the far distance I heard '...urgent need...one surgeon...Tataouine...' and then the Abdullah drone continued. More figures, more maps, more statistics that I found hard to understand. Maths had never been my strong point at school. However for some reason the name Tataouine rang a very strong bell. I glanced to my left at the large map of Tunisia hanging on the wall. Instantly all became clear. That was it! Many years previously I had made plans to cross the Sahara Desert by Landrover and Tataouine had formed part of that route. It was the last port of call before heading for the Sahara. In the event, the crossing was not to be, forbidden by unsympathetic UK bosses in their never-ending chase to meet unattainable health service targets.

By now, Dr Abdullah was well into his stride. I could sense at least another forty-five minutes of computer presentation before any discussions could begin. Death by PowerPoint was in progress. Nevertheless I had seen and heard all that was needed. I rose slowly to my feet, unsuccessfully trying to stay silent as the metal chair legs screeched noisily on the stone floor. My companions turned to look disapprovingly in my direction although to Dr Abdullah's credit his presentation continued without the tiniest hesitation.

'Sorry,' I mouthed. 'Got to go. I'll telephone if I can.' Then I was out and away, striding rapidly down the corridor towards a waiting Madjid and more maximum-volume *surya*.

Once in the Hyundai, but before we set off, it was my opportunity to turn to Madjid. I leaned forward to reduce the volume of the DVD player, which was set at maximum decibels, and then looked at my companion.

'Do you remember Tripoli?' I asked. 'Do you remember what you said to me on the way here?'

Madjid nodded.

'Well we are on our way,' I said. 'I have just the place. Take me to Tataouine!'

'Tataouine? That is the end of the earth, Dr Richard. No one goes there. No one except a few French tourists and Rommel in World War II.'

'Exactly,' I replied. 'So take me there. Let us be the first. I'll explain as we drive.'

For a moment Madjid looked confused. This crazy Englishman was again written on his face. Then realisation hit home, his smile returned and his shoulders drew back. Tataouine! A desert outpost it might be but it was perfectly positioned. Anyone crossing the Libyan western frontier to the south of Tripoli had to pass through the place.

'That's a good idea, Dr Richard,' he replied, grinning broadly through his beard. 'I like it.'

Then we were away, driving rapidly south, Madjid now so happy that he turned his DVD player off completely and started to sing the *surya* by himself. He was as tone deaf as I was mathematically ignorant but I did not have the heart to say so.

In fact, the Tataouine option had in part been created by a chance encounter I had some hours earlier with two other surgeons who had also volunteered for conflict service. They had both appeared briefly at the Hotel Odyssée. Initially I had not recognised them for who they were and had walked directly past without offering even a second glance as they sat uncomfortably in two huge lobby armchairs. Then something had made me hesitate. I do not know what it was, perhaps a sixth sense but for a brief moment our eyes locked. Immediately, the two men rose to their feet and walked the short distance to join me. We had rapidly introduced ourselves and before long were in deep discussion, in a way that only practising doctors can talk. It is astonishing how, in times of conflict and disaster, within minutes of meeting total strangers, you can be firing off stories and confessions as if you were in the company of bosom buddies. Perhaps there is a suspicion that the ever-present danger means that tomorrow may never appear. Best the tales appear now than never to be told at all.

Both surgeons were headed that day to the town of Nalut, a short distance inside Libya's violent border.

'How will you cross the border?' I had asked, aware that the two major frontier crossings at Rass Ajdir to the north, and Dehiba further south, were points of frequent conflict, highly dangerous and often closed. Folk were regularly turned away.

'Smuggling routes,' they had replied. 'Our guide will meet us later today.'

I had smiled. Even warfare produces private enterprise. The moment an official border post closes, frontiers start to leak like a sieve. Europe's illegal immigration is a perfect example. In World War II, the French *passeurs* would guide downed pilots to safety over the Pyrenees along the so-called Chemin de la Liberté. The Tunisian-Libyan frontier was the modern-day equivalent, smugglers forsaking inanimate contraband to carry a human cargo instead; for a significant sum, of course.

Then, almost as quickly as they had appeared, my two surgical colleagues had left and headed for the hotel's main entrance. I could sense justifiable pride in their step. They had left their practices at home behind, had told no one where they were going and had probably received endless grief and zero thanks from their hospital managers. They would receive neither accolade nor medal and certainly no money for putting their lives and careers on the line. They simply believed they were doing the right thing. I was envious, too, as they would be in Libya before me.

Tataouine was normally a small desert town with a population of around 70,000. As our black Hyundai slowed to enter the outskirts of the town, *surya* now blaring from its DVD player again, it was clear that the Libyan conflict was increasing Tataouine's population to almost double as one refugee-laden Landcruiser after another streamed across the nearby frontier. The commonest crossing points were in an area called Umm al-Fahr, to the east of Tataouine, as that allowed reasonable cover for the smugglers. In between sandstone outcrops were interspersed wide areas of flat desert over which a vehicle could drive at more than 100 kilometres per hour.

The whole region had sprung to global fame in 1977 when much of the original *Star Wars* film had been made in Tunisia. Luke Skywalker's home planet had been christened Tatooine. Now Tataouine's streets were busy, its cafés full, its few grocery stores struggling with empty shelves. Young black marketeers would stand in the streets waving wads of Libyan dinar bank notes, trying to exchange their currency for something more worthwhile.

Before the Arab Spring, Libya had been a serious financial player. While the rest of the world had struggled with a financial crisis that began in 2008, in 2010 Libya's economy grew by more than ten per cent. It owned Africa's largest proven oil reserves and had been exporting the black gold for fifty years. Much of it, at least ninety per cent of the country's production, came from the Sirte Basin, slightly down the coast from Tripoli. Sirte, sometimes known as Surt, was where Gaddafi had gone to school. He had been born in a tent twenty miles further south, in a village called Qasr Abu Hadi. Sirte was trying hard to remain a Gaddafi stronghold. Whoever controlled the Sirte Basin was effectively in charge of the Libyan economy. In pre-revolution times, oil had been responsible for more than half of Libya's GDP. No wonder, I thought, that much of the fighting was in the Sirte area and that NATO was trying hard to stay involved. No wonder also that this more southerly region in which I was operating had largely escaped NATO's attention. There was not an oil well to be found.

'Where to, Dr Richard?' asked Madjid while shaking his fist aggressively at a dilapidated taxi that had cut across our path.

'The hospital,' I replied. 'We need to go straight there.'

Madjid nodded and flicked a non-functional indicator to the right as we weaved past a Berber farmer pushing his wooden cart, at least a dozen cyclists, and several young black marketeers standing in the centre of the road selling their illegal wares.

Despite the town being an hour's drive from a major desert conflict, it felt safe. Safety is a difficult thing to quantify in a war zone as such areas are often highly unpredictable. What applies one day may not apply the next. However, sometimes all one can use is gut instinct. You develop that over time but however much experience you might have had in conflict and disaster zones, anyone can make mistakes. I remembered my pre-mission briefing vividly.

'Find somewhere safe and secure,' I had been told. My briefer had little experience of conflict zones herself although did report that she had once been caught in cross fire.

'This is a war,' I had said, while looking over her shoulder at the rain-spattered windows of the central London office. 'How can one make them safe? I can make it as safe as I can but there will always be some danger.'

'That's my worry,' came the reply. 'Perhaps we shouldn't be going there in the first place.'

London's clearly unrealistic expectations were a problem. They wanted guarantees and safety, yet with conflict, guarantees and safety are incompatible bedfellows. It is taking safety to its limit but not beyond, and being happy to work in such an environment, that separates a conflict aid worker from those who offer aid in more organised and peaceful locations. Tataouine was a good start but the next stop would have to be Libya itself. The nearer I was to the point of wounding the better a casualty was likely to fare. The survival rate of war wounded in Afghanistan was now fifty per cent better than in earlier wars, simply because of the proximity of medical care to the fighting.

Tataouine Hospital lay on the far outskirts of the town. You could drive past it without noticing, as it had only two storeys and was hidden behind a high, whitewashed concrete wall. We passed through the high arched entrance, Madjid bringing the Hyundai to a halt immediately outside the building's main front doors.

'I'll wait for you over there,' he said, pointing to a nearby tree that was angled alarmingly but which still provided a large pool of shade in which to park the car.

'Don't wait up,' I smiled as I stepped out into the heat. 'I may be some time.'

*   *   *

Chapter 25

The Mysterious American

My first view of the hospital was that it was hopelessly insecure. Within minutes of my exiting the Hyundai, all it took was one smile and a poorly pronounced '*As-salaam alaykum*' and I was past the sleepy guard on the main doors and into the lengthy hospital corridor beyond.

This surprised me, as Tunisia was far from secure and all the local people knew that. The country had ousted its own leader, President El Abidine Ben Ali less than twelve weeks previously. He had fled to Saudi Arabia. The Prime Minister, Mohamed Ghannouchi, had then also resigned barely six weeks later. Tunisia was in political chaos. Unemployment was high, inflation rocketing and corruption was the order of the day. Meanwhile Gaddafi had put a price on the head of any of his opponents, offering huge financial rewards if they were killed, irrespective of whether they were assassinated within Libya or outside. A Gaddafi opponent in a Tunisian hospital bed was fair game for a Gaddafi supporter.

The corridor was filled with medical staff, all tidily dressed, some strolling, some hurrying, in every direction. Shaking off the cobwebs of my understanding of Arabic script, I followed the hospital signs towards the surgical department. As I walked past one of the main ward doors I heard a scream. A scream so loud that it will remain with me always. A scream so penetrating that it was impossible to misunderstand or escape the agony it declared. It was a young scream, I could tell from its tone. As a doctor, whether or not I was a stranger in this foreign land, I could not ignore it. I reacted immediately. Entering through the open double doors of the ward, I passed by the empty nurses' office just inside its entrance, to see at the far end of the ward a gathering of at least fifteen nursing and medical staff. They were standing in a large group at the foot of a patient's bed. There was much shouting and talking, a few confused heads turning this way and that, while two young nurses struggled to draw up clear injection fluid from an ampoule into a large and threatening syringe. Everyone ignored me.

I could easily see over the heads of the medical throng. The average Tunisian is not tall, particularly those from Tataouine. On the bed mayhem was being played out. The sheets were so crumpled that the blood-stained mattress beneath was widely exposed, two pillows lay almost discarded on the floor, glass fragments from a broken infusion bottle beside them. Spread-eagled obliquely across the bed, from top right to bottom left, was the patient, a boy no more than 16 years old. His left hand gripped the prison-bar headboard so tightly that his knuckles were bleach white. His eyes were wide open in fear, unable to hide the tears that streamed down both cheeks as his head thrashed wildly from side to side. My surgeon's eye picked up immediately the massive deformity of the boy's right thigh, which was angled alarmingly out to one side. The thighbone clearly had been badly broken. I also picked up the movements of the white-coated doctor standing immediately beside the bed. He was holding the boy's hand while leaning over to speak gently into one ear of the thrashing head. I could not hear what was said but could tell that this was true bedside manner in action. The doctor really cared, that much was obvious. For a brief moment I saw the doctor's eyes glance in my direction. They were lifeless eyes, exhausted, huge dark shadows under them. This was a man at the end of his tether trying hard to control the pain of a young patient. The glance was so transient that it barely existed. The doctor then turned back to his charge, gently taking the syringe from one of the nurses, before sliding the needle expertly into one of the boy's elbow veins and watching the painkiller take effect. Probably morphine, I thought, as I watched the patient's eyes slowly close, the tight grip on the headboard loosen and the screaming subside to a whimper.

As the boy settled, so did the assembled medical staff. There is little more distressing than handling a patient in uncontrollable pain. One by one they weaved their way past me until there was just me, the doctor and the patient left behind. The doctor looked up, this time his glance was almost a stare.

'And you are?' he demanded.

'I…I…,' I stuttered.

'I know,' interrupted my newly found colleague, sudden realisation in his face. 'You are that foreigner doctor. The one from England, yes?'

'Well I am from England,' I replied. 'But I do not believe we have met.' I extended my hand in greeting.

'Dr Wassif,' came the abrupt reply, my proffered handshake ignored. 'I am the surgeon here. Zarzis said you were on your way.'

Jungle drums, I thought. Remarkable things. How did they know? How could anyone know I was in Tataouine? I had only decided to go several hours earlier. Dr Wassif sensed my surprise.

'Don't worry,' he said. 'I am not telepathic. The Ministry of Health telephoned to say that I should expect you.'

I smiled. The Ministry of Health - that would have been Dr Abdullah at meeting number 12. He had obviously picked up more than I had realised. My early departure in the middle of his presentation had not stopped him from realising that my sights had been set on Tataouine.

'Come! This will interest you,' said Dr Wassif, friendship now in his tone. 'I have something you should see.' With that he strode past, beckoning that I should follow. Although he was clearly the professional, Dr Wassif was manifestly very tired. His open neck white shirt was as crumpled as a shirt can be, his baggy grey trousers were no better. Meanwhile heavy, black horn-rimmed glasses were perched at a dangerous angle on the end of his nose. I turned on my heel and followed Dr Wassif as he headed out of the ward. He was not tall but I still found it hard to keep pace.

As Dr Wassif strode the corridors, indicating left and right the various departments and facilities available, I could see the hospital was essentially a happy place. Staff smiled, they laughed, they welcomed me. The wards were clean, observation charts were tidily placed and properly completed at the end of each patient's bed. There were no flies or insects, no squashed bed bugs on the walls. No animals were roaming free. For a desert hospital that had long been ignored, undermanned and undersupplied, Tataouine could hold its head in pride.

Yet it was also a place of immense human suffering as the screaming teenager with the shattered thighbone had shown. Despite all the good will, Tataouine Hospital was under extreme pressure. The previous day it had admitted nine casualties, the result of a vehicle coming under fire from pro-Gaddafi forces in western Libya as it had tried to deliver ammunition to a rebel position. Two rebels had been killed outright, while the rest had suffered appalling injuries. In a nearby ward lay a man with his face completely burned, no hair, no eyebrows, huge and swollen lips.

He was barely conscious. His left leg had been shattered below the knee, his condition now so serious that it was unlikely he would make it through the night. Beside him in the same room and only a few feet away lay another casualty, again with a shattered leg, although this time above the knee.

Despite the obvious distress, as I looked at these war wounded I could see how well they were being treated. The burns victim had a breathing tube inserted, monitoring was in place, an intravenous infusion was dripping steadily and a catheter was allowing careful monitoring of his urine output.

Rapidly and efficiently Dr Wassif continued his tour, drifting from bed to bed and room to room like a male version of Florence Nightingale. Mostly we would talk with the patients in French, occasionally in Arabic, although one patient replied in near perfect English when I asked him about his leg. He had not been in the ambushed ammunition vehicle but had been shot by a sniper several days earlier. The bullet had passed through the back of his right thigh, destroying much muscle as it had done so. It had also damaged one of the major nerves to the lower leg, the sciatic nerve, and left the patient without control of his foot. Dr Wassif told me how he had performed an operation to clean the bullet wound but had seen that the sciatic nerve was intact during the operation. This meant that nerve function would most likely return, although it would not be instant. Until then, patience was the order of the day. Patience, of course, was not commonly to be found in an anti-Gaddafi rebel. Mostly they wished to return to the fight as soon as possible. All the same, we left the patient a happy man, as he knew he had a future. As a rough guide, if a nerve is going to recover, it will do so at approximately one millimetre each day. However many millimetres there were between the patient's thigh wound and the foot below would be the number of days it would take the nerve to recover and for proper leg function to return.

To speak a foreign language is an essential part of delivering overseas aid. It is not something for which the British are known. French was a key language in Tataouine as barely anyone spoke English. My own French knowledge had long been gutter based as I confess to being one of the lesser attentive pupils when at school. However, I had already noticed that working in French for twenty-four hours a day was improving my speaking enormously.

Dr Wassif's ward round continued, revealing one tragic story after another. The two-year-old boy with a gunshot wound to the head, yet who was still alive. The fighter whose left arm had been critically injured in a mortar bomb explosion and for whom the only choice had been amputation, the most mutilating of operations and something any surgeon hates to do; the hip that had dislocated but which had been put back in joint. Then there was the mother in tears for her six-year-old daughter who had lost her left foot. The mother had been too terrified to take the child to her local Libyan hospital, only 200 metres from her home, as the shelling had been so severe. She had opted to keep the young girl at home for several days before making an illegal crossing into Tunisia at night to find sanctuary and care in Tataouine. The delay in seeking medical help had led to the loss of her daughter's foot from an overwhelming infection.

While we weaved our way between the patients' beds, moving from ward to ward, Dr Wassif told me the full story of the teenager with the broken thigh. It was a story that brought home to me the importance of my presence in North Africa. The boy had tried to save his family home from forced entry by a small band of soldiers but had failed. As he ran away he had been shot from behind, the high-velocity round destroying much of the bone as it passed through the fragile human frame. He had been left to die, but had not, lurching his way in the back of an open four-wheel drive, a dangerous, 300-kilometre passage of open and exposed desert, to reach Tataouine.

As Dr Wassif finished his ward round, my mind was clear. There was no other sensible decision that could be made. I turned to my new-found colleague and smiled.

'I can help if you wish,' I said, hesitation in my voice. I had sensed that part of the reason for the ward round had been for Dr Wassif to work out whether or not I knew what I was doing and whether I could be of use. I had no idea what he felt, or thought, or might have decided.

I need not have worried. Instantly, Dr Wassif's face broke into the widest of grins. 'Help?' he queried, clear joy in his face. 'Of course you can help. When can you start? How about now?' I saw the tiny tear in the corner of Dr Wassif's eye as he spoke. He was struggling hard not to fully cry. This man, I could see, was at the end of his tether. Too much to do and too little time to do it. Indeed, too little available of just about everything. Tataouine was where I had to be; at least for the moment.

'Not a problem,' I replied. 'It will be a pleasure. Give me an hour or two to find somewhere to sleep and I'll be back.' The relief on Dr Wassif's face was immense. I could sense a surge of energy coursing through his veins, similar to a caffeine shot. For Dr Wassif, this was the relief of Mafeking, Tataouine style.

Outside, Madjid was fast asleep in the Hyundai, hugging his steering wheel as if it was a long-lost friend. I startled him awake by thumping hard on its roof with the flat of my hand. For a brief moment he was disorientated, then he looked up through the half-open window and caught my eye. I reached in to touch his shoulder, aware that he did not see my thump as remotely funny. 'This is it, Madjid,' I said, real enthusiasm in my voice. 'This is most definitely it. There could not be a better place to work. Now it's your turn. Find me somewhere to sleep.' And, typically Madjid, he did.

I was not the only person with interests in Tataouine. The area was fast becoming the hub for all aid programmes wishing to help Libyan refugees. The media were arriving in their droves while many of the major aid agencies were seeking to relocate their northern offices in Zarzis and Tunis to a location further south. There were also a few mystery visitors – tall, muscular, fit-looking individuals with close-cropped hair and the look of backwoodsmen, as they tried to pretend that their khaki camouflage trousers were not military fatigues. To me, they had Special Forces written all over them. The intelligence services were also there in force; America's Central Intelligence Agency, France's Direction Générale de la Sécurité Extérieure, UK's Secret Intelligence Service, even Egypt's Al-Mukhabarat al-Harbeya, at least as best I could tell. They do not say who they are; you cannot expect that. However, most have a penetrating gaze that looks right through you and are clearly a thousand times fitter than the average aid worker. They pack light, move fast and never tell you where they are going or, for that matter, from where they have come. They also appear from nowhere and always catch you off guard.

On one occasion, while struggling up one of the low-lying sandstone mountains that surrounded Tataouine, something I would try for daily exercise, I met a charming but lonely American on its summit. He appeared totally unperturbed by my surprise arrival. It was almost as if I was expected. He was clearly fit, with chest pectorals bulging through his military-style T-shirt. On his left wrist was the largest outdoor watch I had ever seen, complete with altimeter, satellite navigation and stopwatch. It looked the ideal device to have in this land of George Lucas' *Star Wars*.

'Hey! How are you doing?' came the American welcome, his right arm held high as I approached. I was pouring sweat and breathless. My new companion looked totally relaxed. He had either been there for a very long time, I thought in my exhaustion, or was Olympian fit.

Quickly we introduced ourselves, a brief handshake that was all, but then my interrogation began. Why are you here, where are you from, what do you do and where are you going next? I felt slightly as if the police were questioning me. Then the quizzing became more detailed.

Had I seen anything strange? 'Lots,' I replied. 'There's a war on.'

Had I seen any vehicles cross the border? 'Lots,' I replied. 'There's a war on.'

How about armed refugees? Had I seen any of those? 'Lots,' I replied. 'There's a war on.'

Then, as quickly as it had started, the questioning finished. My American companion rose to his feet, stretched back both shoulders with an audible click, checked his mega-watch and then set off at a gentle jog towards the empty desert. He tapped my left shoulder with a calloused palm as he passed, shouting back over his shoulder, 'Thanks! Good to meet you! Have a great day!' Within a half minute he had disappeared from sight, leaving me alone on my mountain.

The mountain was my escape. It was evidently a locally religious place as scattered over its surface were small piles of rock that had been carefully positioned by a human hand to spell religious quotes. *Bismillah* (In the name of God), *Allah akhbar* (God is great) were common, while someone had even constructed a lover's heart. From my mountain's summit was a 360-degree view of the world, a view that appeared to go on forever: to the north from where I had come, to the west where the American superman had disappeared and to the south and east where I could see the occasional flash of reflected sunlight from the windscreen of a vehicle escaping from a ravaged Libya. Far beneath me I could hear the sound of sirens as yet more casualties arrived at Tataouine Hospital from the fighting. Those sirens meant more work for a beleaguered Dr Wassif. Indeed now they meant more work for me.

As I descended from my mountain, at a gentle lope that could in no way match the forever jog of the American, I glanced back towards the south and east, towards the chaos and conflict. Sure, Tataouine was where

I was now and Tataouine had much work to offer, yet south and east, directly into the fighting, was where I had soon to go. For a brief moment I felt fear in my chest, that tight squeeze when you know something is expected of you. Whatever my fears my duty was clear. I needed to be as near to the point of injury as possible, without becoming a casualty, too.

It took me an hour to reach Tataouine Hospital from my vantage point on the mountain; an hour of worry about what I would shortly see. I need not have been concerned. The hospital had, once more, swung into autopilot and was doing what it did best. Casualties were being assessed in the Emergency Department, infusions assembled, injections given, monitors applied, temperatures, pulses and heart recordings taken. Stretchers were squeaking in and out of the X-Ray room, on each one lay a casualty, some in terrible pain while others lay peacefully watching all that was taking place around them. There had been fierce fighting at the Wazin border post to the south-east of Tataouine. Many had been injured and several had died. The frontier was now in rebel hands, the revolutionary flag now flapping gently in what was seen as its rightful position.

Here am I, the battle-scarred surgeon and yet even I am uncertain how a war wound is defined. One might imagine it is the result of a missile, or bullet, or shrapnel or grenade fragment, smashing into the fragile human frame and taking all before it. Tataouine certainly saw a great deal of such things. However, sometimes a so-called war wound can be almost self-sustained. On this occasion one of the seriously injured was a fighter who had been tossed from the back of his Landcruiser like a rag doll as a result of the recoil of his RPG-7, a rocket-propelled grenade launcher of Russian origin. The RPG-7 is the most widely used anti-tank weapon in the world but there is only a fifty-fifty chance of hitting a vehicle target at 200 metres. Stabilising fins also have the strange property of making the flying grenade turn into any crosswind that is blowing, rather than being displaced in the opposite direction as you might expect. When you are holding an RPG-7 and are ready to fire, your mind is totally on hitting your target, not on whether you will be thrown from your launch point onto the desert floor below the moment you squeeze the weapon's trigger. This had happened to the most seriously injured admission that day, a 27-year-old man for whom the hard desert-floor landing had ruptured his right lung and smashed his left thighbone into a myriad of pieces. He had bled extensively from the broken bone, the blood rapidly filling the interior of his thigh and bringing the fighter to the verge of fatal shock. He was being rapidly resuscitated when I arrived. His injury had occurred more than ten hours earlier.

It is not good for a wounded person to lie untreated for too long. War injuries are so unforgiving, largely brought about by the high velocity nature of modern weapons. The speed at which a bullet, or shrapnel fragment, strikes the human frame is critical to the outcome of the patient. The faster the projectile, the greater the damage it will create. A modern rifle can fire a bullet at more than 3,000 miles per hour, roughly four times the speed of sound. As the bullet strikes human tissue, all the energy the projectile possesses is transmitted to the skin, and muscle, and tendons, and bone. Tissues can be damaged a huge distance away from the point of entry of a bullet. Furthermore, there is a so-called cavitation effect deep inside the body, which sucks in debris and bacteria from the surface of the skin. Then, as the bullet exits, it leaves an enormous hole behind. This is why high velocity wounds so frequently become infected and why patients die from that most horrible of illnesses, gas gangrene. This was a major cause of death during World War I.

Generally, a surgeon will not close or sew up a bullet wound when the patient is first seen after being shot. This is asking for trouble, as it traps the lethal gas gangrene bacteria beneath the skin and allows them to multiply. The bacteria hate oxygen, so the best treatment is for the surgeon to make the bullet wound larger, not smaller, a process called 'laying open' the wound. All dead tissue is removed. On one occasion, during the Sarajevo siege in the mid-1990s, I laid open a bullet track of a soldier from the top of one buttock to just above his ankle, an incision almost three feet long. The tissue destruction created by the single bullet had been immense yet the end result some three weeks after surgery was excellent. The principle is to lay a wound open first of all and then go back a few days later to close it. This delay is referred to as DPC, or delayed primary closure. It is a lifesaving treatment, simply because the gas gangrene bacteria hate it.

The low velocity projectile, however, is a different beast. This would generally come from a weapon such as a pistol, which will have a much shorter range than a rifle. Clint Eastwood's .44 Magnum handgun, for example, would be difficult to use at ranges over 100 metres. It can still kill a patient but does not have the same cavitation effect as its high velocity cousin. As a consequence, contamination is not such a problem and gas gangrene less common. Sometimes low velocity wounds can be closed without being laid open. However, often a surgeon will not know whether a wound has been caused by a high velocity or low velocity projectile, so it is better to err on the side of caution and assume everything is high velocity.

This type of surgery is far removed from the techniques used by most surgeons during peacetime. Outside conflict zones, gas gangrene is generally not a problem and wounds can often be closed when they are first seen, although clearly after they have been surgically cleaned. This is the major difference between war surgery and everything else. Infection during times of conflict is a real killer. Everything a surgeon does aims to reduce this risk.

The fighter injured by his own RPG-7 needed surgery fast. He was going to die without it. Yet his operation was a surgical nightmare, a time I will remember for the rest of my days. The 27-year-old was well built and muscular but he bled and bled and bled. Any tissue I touched, almost with any instrument, seemed to bleed of its own free will. It took six hours of sweat, extreme worry, and almost tears to reconstruct the shattered thighbone. However, by the end I had inserted a long metal rod down the length of the thighbone in order to stabilise the broken bone. The moment a surgeon stabilises a break, the bleeding will often stop. This happened with the fighter. I was lucky that day. The hospital was almost running out of its stock of blood transfusions; there was just one bag left.

To work in conflict areas a surgeon must be prepared to improvise as it is not only blood transfusions that can be in short supply. Tataouine Hospital was short of many things - instruments, surgical swabs, stitches, anaesthetic – almost anything a surgeon might normally require. Because of this, it was commonplace for a patient, or their relatives, to be asked to buy the necessary rods, screws, plates and washers from a nearby surgical instrument shop before surgery was undertaken. The southern Tunisians used such things in the same way as we might use supermarkets back home for food. However, for this casualty this was not possible. He had no relatives in Tunisia and, anyway, had no money to spend. He just wanted to stay alive.

So I had to use what was available rather than what might have been ideal. The thighbone was secured with a rod that was too long, the screws were those designed for use in the forearm rather than the leg, while the instruments had certainly seen better days. The forceps – surgical tweezers – grasped nothing and the needles were as blunt as blunt can be. The drill was a hammer drill from a nearby do-it-yourself store and the X-Ray machine I used to check the bone's position during surgery leaked radiation like a sieve. This was improvisation in the true sense of the word but it was improvisation that worked. I felt immensely proud to see the fighter back in his bed after surgery, his leg now straight, his bleeding controlled. Although he still had his breathing tube in place and was therefore unable to speak, he gave a huge smile and firmly shook my hand. His eyes were happy, glistening brightly. He was truly grateful to be alive.

The staff at Tataouine Hospital were brilliant. Because of their remote location they would undertake procedures that would normally be the sole domain of specialists in the larger cities. The anaesthetist for the thighbone operation was a nurse, not a doctor. I have worked with many anaesthetists over the years and the Tataouine anaesthetic nurse was up there with the best of them. To give a general anaesthetic in the presence of a ruptured lung is hugely challenging and not without danger. To do that while a patient is also bleeding furiously is a quantum leap of danger beyond that. The staff simply saw what was required and then acted appropriately. Rules, regulations and paperwork did not concern them. To the staff of Tataouine Hospital there was only one thing that mattered, the patient. Any doctor will tell you, that is how it should be.

* * *

Chapter 26

War Changes You

Tataouine Hospital was only one part of my function in North Africa. Libya still beckoned. My aim was to create a casualty evacuation chain. In conflict it is unlikely that a wounded fighter can be fully treated, from beginning to end, by one establishment. Normally, a casualty will be treated initially at the point of wounding by his fellow soldiers, the so-called buddy-buddy system. Then he will be taken to the nearest medical facility where basic life-saving surgery can be found. It is likely this first facility will be near to the action and, as a result, be a dangerous place to work. There the casualty will stay until it is safe to move along the evacuation chain to a place where more advanced surgery can be offered. In this case that was Tataouine.

I still had to create the first part of the chain, the part that would begin as near to the battlefield as possible and the problem we had actually come to solve. That meant entering Libya. Staying in Tunisia would not do. That also meant persuading London that this was reasonable, persuading colleagues who had never shot or been shot at, and who had never seen a friend die by their side. The hesitation of my briefer in London before I flew to North Africa was still fresh in my mind. 'Find somewhere safe and secure,' she had said. Some hope, I thought as yet another six casualties were wheeled through the front doors of Tataouine Hospital. Some hope indeed.

No one ever had trouble entering a war zone. Plenty had trouble leaving. Ask any Special Forces soldier, particularly a sniper, and they will tell you that the first thing in their minds when planning to enter enemy territory is, 'How do I escape if it all goes wrong?' You cannot rely on Lady Luck when it comes to warfare, as one day she will let you down. Planning is all.

To the south-east of Tataouine lies the town of Dehiba, the last decent habitation before the narrow tarmacked road enters Libya through the Wazin border crossing, four kilometres away. The route from Tataouine to Dehiba was a largely straight, narrow tarmacked road that carried very little traffic even in pre-conflict days. It carried even less once the fighting started. Our journey took ninety minutes of Madjid's fast driving, flashing past salt pans, camel farms and the exotic sandstone village of Ksar Ouled Debbab, a major tourist lure in more normal times. Despite fighting less than an hour away, the occasional four-by-four, laden with wealthy French, would still visit the place.

Four military checkpoints barred the way between Tataouine and Dehiba, soldiers armed with high velocity weapons glaring at us with suspicion at each one. The passport, but predominantly Madjid, saw us through safely. The route passed through the military town of Remada, home also to 3,000 tented refugees, before leading into the small town of Dehiba itself.

Dehiba's life revolved around a tiny central roundabout with an equally small café to one side. The café was a seedy place – shadowy, dusty and desperately in need of decoration - I instantly christened it the Graham Greene, after the well-known English author who had been known for his espionage fiction and who, in real life, had tried to kill himself several times by Russian roulette. In Dehiba's Graham Greene café, much legal and illegal business took place. Refugees arranged accommodation, money was changed, assassinations plotted, illegal border crossings finalised, while copious coffee was drunk.

'It's good, Dr Richard,' Madjid said as I stepped from the car into the stifling heat outside. 'Perhaps I can come with you when you go into Libya?'

'Let's see,' I replied. 'I need to meet with these folk first.'

You could not even contemplate drinking decaffeinated coffee in southern Tunisia. Their coffee was as strong, bitter and reviving as it looked. As thick as treacle, a thin scum on its surface, you would feel its stimulating kick within seconds of the first sip. My role in the Graham Greene café was not to plot an assassination but to meet two individuals. Both were charming, both well informed and both had crossed the Libyan frontier that morning specifically to meet with me. I needed to know how to cross the border with minimum risk and, more importantly, how to return intact. I needed to see those in whose hands I would place my security and perhaps my life. I needed to see them and they needed to see me.

One might imagine that in areas of conflict the tall, fit and muscular individual would prevail. The two men who had slipped quietly across the border that morning to reach the Graham Greene were none of these things. Neither looked as if he could sprint ten metres let alone a hundred and both clearly enjoyed their food. Neither, I thought, would be able to shoot their way out of trouble as I saw them catch their breath after mounting the half-dozen steps leading to the café's rear veranda. Yet both were the epitome of charm. The eldest, perhaps in his mid-forties, was Ahmad, a major bigwig in the Libyan health system. Although dressed in a very Western way, off-white shirt, dark grey trousers with loosely fitting leather-look belt, he was unquestionably a Berber.

Off-white shirts and crumpled grey trousers seemed to be standard dress for most North African officials. A further reason, I thought, that Madjid might have another life outside driving. He was dressed just like the archetypal official.

In the Graham Greene, the second man I had come to meet was Basam. Dressed almost identically in the attire of a North African official, he had the addition of a thick cotton photographer's waistcoat, pockets dotted everywhere and emblazoned with a logo in faded Arab script. Basam had one of the most pronounced limps I had ever seen, most likely from childhood hip disease. However, he was also one of the kindest, finest, supportive men I had ever met. We rapidly discovered a common bond as we had both spent part of our childhoods in Greece. With a liberal sprinkling of Greek '*Kalimera sas*' ('Good morning') and '*Ti kaneis*' ('How are you') supplemented by lengthy Arab greetings that bless the welfare of everything from health, work and wives to camels, goats and family, we were soon down to business.

This was a gold dust meeting if there ever was one. Within minutes we had agreed a plan of action, something that would have taken the administrators in Zarzis a lifetime to decide. Basam was someone I could trust and he, I could tell, trusted me. Quietly he said, out of any earshot, that he would happily act as a *passeur*. All it would need was a telephone call from me. Furthermore his services were for free.

In addition to the Graham Greene, Dehiba was dominated by a refugee camp that was steadily increasing in size. Most of the aid agencies were represented. The Tunisian military were also there in force, busy manning the border and laying barbed wire in order to prevent the conflict from spilling across the frontier. Already, some of Gaddafi's rockets had landed in Dehiba from western Libya, although whether by accident or design was difficult to say.

The journey back to Tataouine that evening was largely in silence. No *surya*, no intense religious discussions with Madjid reminding me repeatedly that Jesus could only have been a prophet. There was no way, he had insisted, that Jesus could have been the Son of God. It was not the occasion to argue, when I was so far from my own country and surrounded by a population in a deeply religious mood.

Once back in Tataouine it did not take me long to realise how impossible it would be to persuade London that I needed to cross the border. My telephone calls with them were lessons in frustration. More meetings were suggested, more talking, more delays. Meanwhile casualties were still flooding across the frontier into Tataouine. To a surgeon's eye, these casualties would have benefited from proper surgery as near to the point of wounding as possible. In some cases it was taking them a week to cross the border. A week lying with an open wound makes it almost impossible for a surgeon to achieve a decent end result, however talented he may be. I had to move fast and needed to complete the treatment chain as soon as possible. I was there to set it up and set it up I would do. I was about to make myself very unpopular with London.

We moved the very next day, unexpectedly helped by a team from Al Jazeera Television whom I met in the lobby of a nearby Tataouine hotel. They had just returned from a brief cross-border visit into Libya and had filed a most impressive report from the front line. Conflict journalists are a hardy breed, perhaps even slightly unhinged. The risks they take to file their stories are sometimes more than extreme. The agency had lost a cameraman, shot through the heart near Benghazi, only four weeks earlier. Meanwhile two other journalists had been killed less than two days earlier by an RPG-7 in Misrata. With the Tataouine team was a burly and likeable Scot, clearly ex-military, who was acting as their security adviser. A few minutes with him and my view was clarified. Yes, there were risks to entering Libya but they were not daft. At that moment the rebels controlled the Wazin frontier crossing but for how long was anyone's guess. I would have to be quick. Five minutes' later I was on the telephone, this time not to London but to Basam, my *passeur*.

However often you do it, however experienced you may be, entering a war zone is stressful. I have lost count how many times I have been through that sleeplessness, the worry that I might never return. The moment you cross that line, that frontier, that fence, whatever it may be, the rules change. Suddenly nothing is predictable, nothing and no one can be trusted, around that invisible corner can be a friend, or enemy, perhaps a roadblock, or perhaps a sudden death. War zones are trouble, they are always so, and need a special psychology to enter. Not everyone has that psychology. Experience helps, but only a little. You need to spend time coming to terms with yourself. How you do it is up to you. Disappear into a darkened room, perhaps go for a walk, take to the bottle, chain smoke, or simply talk to your God. Whatever your choice, you need to dress rehearse your fear, practise what you will do when that terror comes for real. It is always unexpected, always in a form you cannot predict or describe, and always you have to think on your feet. Terror drives out logical thought. It can turn the hardiest individual into a jelly-like mess, it can make the pacifist a maniac. War changes you, and not always for the better.

*   *   *

Chapter 27

Border Crossing

The drive back to Dehiba, south from Tataouine, was once more largely silent. Madjid had been very disappointed when I had told him that he would not be coming into Libya with me.

'But these are my people!' he had protested.

'Your people?' For a moment I thought he was about to confess that he worked for Gaddafi.

'Libyans, yes. We are like brothers. We have been this close for many years.' Madjid held the palms of his hands together. 'Tunisia loves Libya,' he continued. 'At least the people do, whatever our Government might say.'

'It's too dangerous, Madjid,' I replied. 'If I am killed or captured, I will need someone to rescue me. You'll do that for me, won't you?'

'OK, then,' Madjid added. 'But you take care.'

The five road blocks we encountered on the way to Dehiba came and went, passports were produced and returned, smiles given, handshakes made. Madjid was in fine form and working well despite his disappointment.

Dehiba was bustling with activity as usual. Our first stop was a small, cream-coloured bungalow on the outskirts of the town. This was the office and home of the IMC. I walked in, knocking gently on the half-open front door. Beyond, I could see an IMC team in deep discussion with a major aid bigwig who was on a whistle-stop tour of the area. The floor was held by the head of the IMC emergency response, who looked up briefly as I entered, nodding her head gently to acknowledge my arrival as she spoke to her visitors.

'We have received information about pro-Gaddafi activity here,' came the words as she pointed a ball pen towards the Google Earth map on her screen.

'We believe mines are being laid here.' The ball pen moved again.

'And here.' It moved again.

'Casualties are making it across the border,' she continued, 'but travel is often unsafe and the unofficial routes are being closed rapidly. It may soon be impossible to cross the frontier in this region at all.' The ball pen made its final flourish across the screen before taking its place on the dark wooden table beside the computer. The IMC head looked directly at the bigwig. I could see her words had taken effect. What she had said, in essence, was that crossing the border was a crazy thing to do and becoming crazier by the hour.

I quietly left the shadowed room as the bigwig was asking his questions. If I were to enter Libya at all, I thought, it would have to be soon, very soon. Even this evening could be too late.

The Graham Greene was busy that morning. At each of its tiny circular tables sat small groups of men, mostly under the age of forty, deep in discussion, heads bowed closely together, voices low, concentration evident. Others stood shoulder to shoulder beside the café's counter. Negotiations were clearly underway. Occasionally I could see money change hands, slid slowly across a table from one individual to another. Border crossings were being arranged and changed, cargoes negotiated, security assured.

The whitewashed, chipped concrete veranda was as busy as the café's interior. Every table was taken and as far as I could tell there was not a spare chair to be found. A young man, perhaps in his late twenties, smiled as he proffered me his chair. Yet behind the smile I could see the eyes. They were hard; steely brown, bright and powerful. These eyes I had seen before, at least eyes like them. They were the eyes of a fighter, of a man who lives life on the edge. I looked beyond him, towards his three companions seated around their plastic table. I could see the hard outline of handguns in their lightweight jacket pockets. These were fit young men, motivated and cunning. The Libyan rebels had come to Dehiba.

As I took my seat on the rickety chair, the café's owner placed a glass of local tea on the low veranda wall beside me. This was not tea such as I might drink back home. This was a thick, concentrated dark liquid, served in a hot, hot glass, with four sugar lumps. I telephoned Basam. He answered almost immediately and within minutes I saw his familiar frame limp up the rear steps onto the veranda. He was, as always, smiling.

Today and unusually for him, Basam looked impatient. 'We must go soon,' he said, pointing to his watch. 'The border is open but I do not know for how long. Please come. There is word that Gaddafi will attack at any moment. He is only ten kilometres away from where we are headed.'

Briefly I glanced towards my still steaming tea, hoping to down it hastily before departing, but reluctantly decided I should get going. I followed Basam as he nimbly hobbled down the veranda steps towards the battered and scratched green Landcruiser that was waiting patiently outside. On the far side of the road I could see Madjid leaning against the front wing of the Hyundai, talking earnestly to a group of four men.

'I'm off now Madjid,' I said. 'Not sure when I'll be back. Actually, I'm not sure if I'll be back at all.'

'Good luck, Dr Richard,' came the reply. I will be in Dehiba until you return. I'll leave a note behind the counter at the café so that you will always know where I am. What do you call that place? Gr…Gra…Graaaam Grin?'

I laughed. There were some words that Madjid's Arab tongue simply could not master and Graham Greene were two of them.

'I'll teach you when I return, Madjid. That's a promise.'

With that I jogged back across the road to the waiting Landcruiser.

I was squashed tightly into the back seat of the Toyota. To my front was an elderly Berber driver, to his right sat one of his friends. Basam was in another vehicle. He leaned through the open window and waved.

'Bye, Dr Richard,' he said, smiling broadly.

'Bye? Are you not coming?' Instantly my suspicions prickled.

'Do not worry. I will be in the vehicle behind.'

Quietly I shook my head, scolding myself. How could I do this? I had just climbed into a car on the edge of a war zone with a driver I had never before met on the advice of a smiling Libyan, Basam, whom I had first seen only a few days before. I had no real idea of where I was going, or how I would get there. I certainly had no idea how I would get out. I had placed my faith totally in Basam and my ability to be a judge of character. On that judgement my safety would depend. I hoped I was right.

From Dehiba it is the shortest of drives to the Wazin border crossing, which now lay open thanks to the repeated efforts of the rebel forces, although for how long it would stay in rebel hands was anyone's guess. The crossing point was chaos. Only three vehicles were entering Libya at that moment, our small two-vehicle convoy and the team from Al Jazeera. But there were more than 300 waiting to come out. As far I could see was a single line of traffic stretching into the distance. One by one the cars were moved forward, one by one they were searched, and one by one the occupants were asked why they wished to leave Libya.

I wanted to shout 'Isn't it obvious?' but remained in control. Never attract attention in a war zone. Join the shadows and stay there.

It was here that the real value of Basam became clear. Slowly he walked up the line of waiting traffic, shaking hands with almost everyone. He smiled and laughed and slapped people's backs. They laughed in return. The sleepy border post official took my passport from Basam as if it was a gold-studded item and I was instantly waved through. Basam was clearly a Libyan version of Madjid. I might have made it through without Basam but it would have taken a very long time indeed. Those few Greek words, spoken at haste in the back of a smoke-filled café, had bought me a pile of privilege.

We set off into Libya itself as a small, two-vehicle convoy, my Landcruiser in front, Basam's immediately behind. He was almost attached to our rear bumper. Once into Libya the mood changed. Rebel forces manned the country's border post; all of them young men. These were the so-called *thuuwar*, or revolutionaries. Some wore desert fatigues and some were bearded, with the air of a conflict veteran. The majority were fresh-faced young men, carrying not-so-fresh weapons. I saw Belgian FNs, Armalites and Kalashnikovs. I even saw a .410 shotgun with a kitchen knife taped to its barrel as a bayonet. Nowhere did I see a grenade and nowhere did I see any evidence of digging in, at least not at the border. These were amateurs, in the truest sense of the word. Everywhere fluttered the red, black and green flag of the Libyan rebel forces, the so-called National Transitional Council, their motto, 'Freedom! Justice! Democracy!'

Despite the fighters' obvious enthusiasm, they looked disorganised. I could see no officer types, or senior NCOs. What, oh what, I thought, are this lot going to do when they come under fire? Where do they run? Where do they hide? What are their arcs of fire? In fact, are any of the weapons I can see even loaded?

Our objective was Nalut, first town in and forty-five minutes from the border. The Berber driver took the journey at extraordinary speed. The speedometer, which I could see still worked, barely fell below 120 kilometres per hour. He would swerve this way and that on the tarmacked road, sometimes on the right, sometimes on the left, through the barren and lifeless landscape. Basam mostly kept up but on occasion would briefly fall behind. Ahead, all I could see was mile upon mile of empty expanse strewn with rock, light brown dirt and natural rubble. I caught occasional glimpses of the northerly Jefara Plain below and to our left, picturesque gorges cutting deeply into the Nafusa Mountains.

Driving fast when in exposed areas is clearly essential in a war zone. You do not wish to remain a sniper's target for long. I remained largely silent, partly because my driver could not understand me anyway and partly because I was deep in personal thought. I was an Englishman now in hazardous territory. I may have been medical, I may have had the best intentions in the world, but did I truly think that my humanitarian motives would cut any ice at all at a Gaddafi roadblock? My Government was busy bombing throughout the land. What a wonderful prize I would be. I doubted that I would remain either free or alive for long and leaned back as far as I could in order to take futile cover behind the inadequate door pillar to my left.

I had no body armour, no helmet and, with an ex-military mind, could see plenty of locations for a vehicle ambush. Abrupt bends in the road where even our Berber driver had to slow, small cuttings that were perfect for a camouflaged machine gunner to fire from barely a twenty-metre distance, interspersed by vast expanses of flat nothing where even the most disinterested sniper could have a go.

My vehicle had no markings, nor did Basam's behind. In war zones any moving item is seen by some as fair game. Ask the Serbian snipers in Sarajevo, or the Taliban in Helmand, or even the Israelis in southern Lebanon, how much trouble they took to identify friend from foe when looking down their telescopic sights. The sniper fears for his or her life too. Anything that moves is a target.

As he drove, the driver's turban blew violently in the wind that streamed in through his half-open window. He would frequently turn to talk to his colleague, who sat in the front passenger seat, both of them shouting to be heard. Each time the driver turned to speak, so the vehicle would swerve violently and each time he came to a corner he appeared to increase rather than decrease speed. The Landcruiser would pitch this way and that, swaying perilously on every corner. At times it would be on only two wheels. Squashed rigidly in the back seat, I laughed briefly to myself. The greatest risk I had so far run in Libya was the Berber driving.

Our route passed through the Nafusa Mountains. This was not the first time the region had been a trouble spot for Gaddafi. The people in this area are a Berber folk known as the Amazigh, who speak a minority language that they hold dear, called Tamazight. The word *amazigh* means 'free man' in Tamazight, which perhaps sets the scene for the attitudes of the local people. It had long been forbidden by Tripoli that Tamazight should be taught in the local schools. Meanwhile, children were not permitted Amazigh names, only Arab ones would do. The three Nafusa towns of Nalut, Az Zintan and Yefren were effectively under siege by Gaddafi, who was making strong efforts to cut the passage of refugees and supplies between Libya and Tunisia. It was almost as if opportunity was being taken for a form of ethnic cleansing. Diesel was being poured into water wells, cows, goats and sheep were being slaughtered and many young Amazigh men had simply disappeared, victims of the early morning knock on the door. No one knew to where they had been taken, or whether they were even still alive. Enforced disappearances, the official term for this, were increasing steadily.

The Wazin border crossing was being hotly contested as a result. The road along which I lurched was the main way in and out, what the military would call a Main Supply Route, or MSR. I was lucky to be able to use it that day. If Basam's information was correct, Wazin would not be staying in rebel hands for long. Then the only way out would be across the sieve-like illegal frontier, being steadily mined by Gaddafi.

Desert travel can be extremely rapid, as my Berber driver was showing, so it is possible for forces to assault enemy positions many miles away in a very short time. The knowledge that pro-Gaddafi forces were ten kilometres east of Nalut, my eventual destination, was no security. They could travel that distance in as many minutes. It is for this reason that in desert warfare, positions can change hands very rapidly and it is not unusual for a town, or village, perhaps only a mound of rubble, to change hands three, four or even five times in one day. You must be able to move fast in desert warfare. Blink and you can be in trouble.

As we hurtled towards Nalut, at times almost reaching take-off speed, I passed occasional camouflaged Landcruisers manned by young men dressed in a variety of uniforms. Sometimes they wore no uniform at all, just a pair of jeans and a T-shirt. Camouflage was normally mud, or at least the desert equivalent, streaked down the side of a chipped vehicle's residual paintwork. It was remarkably effective at blending the *thuuwar* transport into the background.

The scattered buildings I also passed showed no sign of blast damage, something I was accustomed to seeing in other war zones. Probably, I thought, this was because NATO had largely destroyed Gaddafi's armour, so small arms were the only real weapons he was able to use.

Despite the environment, despite my earlier concerns, the lurching movements of the Landcruiser were making me relax. I began to feel sleepy and could sense my eyes begin to close. Then, almost instantly, that changed. I was awake and alert. The Landcruiser was entering yet another road cutting, mounds of desert rubble to either side restricting my view so that I could only see in front and behind. Despite the strong sun I was suddenly thrust into shade. It felt sinister. I saw the driver put two hands to his wheel, perhaps the first time he had done this since leaving the border, and then the Landcruiser slowed rapidly as it entered a sharp right-hand bend. Immediately after the apex of the bend was the roadblock - sudden, unexpected and unavoidable – a fortified roadblock bristling with armed men. Slightly to my left I could see the AK47 in the bearded soldier's hands rise to his shoulder, the barrel now pointing in my direction. Who was this, I thought, *thuuwar* or Gaddafi?

The roadblock had been well positioned, at a T-junction surrounded by rubble mounds. Large piles of rock had been carefully placed across the road so any approaching vehicle had to slow rapidly to avoid them. A debris-filled oil drum stood in the centre of the junction and from it leaned a drunken and tattered flag. I squinted through the grime-caked windscreen and then sighed audibly. It was a rebel flag, not Gaddafi. We were likely to make it through.

*   *   *

Chapter 28

Roadblock

When surrounded by armed men you cannot afford to alarm them in the slightest way. Slowly I wound down my window to show who I was, clearly an unarmed visitor.

Seeing my face, and glancing towards Basam's vehicle to our rear, the bearded soldier immediately lowered his AK47, nodded and gave me a broad, welcoming smile. Either side, and arranged haphazardly around the T-junction, were other rebel fighters. They were dressed as irregulars; uniform on one, jeans on another, headgear here, no headgear there. There was no conformity, the only feature bonding these young fighters being their desire to see Gaddafi go. Nowhere did I see a helmet and certainly no body armour. Apart from basic weapons and enthusiasm as their defence, these men were hugely exposed. To me they were the bravest of the brave. Particularly with Gaddafi only minutes away.

For many of the fighters, they had been thrust into an unexpected career change by the conflict, and with barely any notice. Peacetime dentists had now become military cooks, postmen had become snipers and dustmen were now clearing mines. The bond between them all was clear. At that roadblock I felt, for a brief moment, an enormous sense of privilege. I was being allowed to enter this tight-knit rebel family as a friend, based entirely on the say-so of Basam.

Straining, I glanced through the tiny rear window behind me, to see Basam leaning out of his black Landcruiser and talking enthusiastically to a taller, broader individual who seemed to be in charge. The leader type was gesticulating wildly, yet it appeared to be a friendly gesturing, not threatening. Then the gesticulations gave way to laughter, the rebel leader thumping the roof of Basam's four-by-four with his hand. I heard Basam then shout, in a tongue I could not understand, and my Berber driver immediately floored the accelerator pedal and we were away, turning hard left, with Basam hot on our tail.

For the first time since I had entered Libya, I began to sense military professionalism around me. Despite their rag-tag appearance, the fighters at the roadblock had an air of authority. As we entered this final stage of our journey, it was very clear the *thuuwar* were taking the defence of Nalut seriously. Slightly beyond the roadblock we passed a large, bright yellow mechanical digger parked to one side of the road, beside it the product of its hard labour. Two massive trenches, ten metres wide and the same deep, extended at right angles from each side of the road for at least 100 metres. These were tank traps. Immediately beside the trenches was parked the massive articulated lorry that could be driven across the road itself to completely bar the way. This would force any enemy vehicle, whatever its size, to drive around the obstacle area. They would not survive for long. At the far end of each trench I could see the twin protruding barrels of a Toyota-mounted heavy machine gun. This was well dug in. The weapon was the ZU-23-2, a weapon of Soviet origin, designed more than fifty years ago to take on low-flying targets and armour. It has a decent range, in excess of 2.5 kilometres, and can punch a hole through armour up to thirty millimetres thick.

The modern military term for these improvised, armed vehicles is a 'technical', a word first used to describe a makeshift fighting vehicle in the Somali Civil War that started in the early 1990s. In fact, lighter vehicles have long been used for desert conflicts. Perhaps the originals were those used by the Long Range Desert Group, eventually to become the fledgling British Special Air Service, in the deserts of North Africa, including Libya, during World War II. Irregular forces throughout the world have long cherished technicals. In some respects they are a sign of the power of an individual warlord or tribal leader. The more technicals you have the more influential you are likely to be.

Beyond the tank traps, to our left I could see abandoned armour, again of Soviet origin. There was a BMP-1, the world's first mass-produced infantry fighting vehicle, while beyond lay the lifeless form of a Soviet T-55 tank, the most produced tank in history.

That was the outer cordon of defence for Nalut. Hard core and professional, ready for anything Gaddafi might deliver. Three hundred metres further on was an inner cordon. This time there was no trench, no tank trap, no dug-in emplacement, no articulated lorry or digger. Two large and irregular concrete blocks lay in the centre of the road, forcing my driver to weave first to the right, then to the left. On the far side of the makeshift barrier sat three fighters. I smiled briefly at them as we passed. They smiled back, one raising his hand lazily in welcome as he saw my clearly non-Arab face. He was elderly, perhaps sixty, maybe more. His two colleagues were also beyond their first flush of youth. This was the Dad's Army of the *thuuwar*. There was no doubting their courage but Nalut's inner cordon did not inspire confidence. Clearly the focus of the city's defence was its outer layer. If Gaddafi ever broke through the outer cordon I doubted he would have much trouble reaching the town's centre.

Once beyond the sleepy inner cordon we entered Nalut proper. The town was a veritable Marie Celeste, almost totally silent and remarkably intact. The original population of 100,000 had largely fled, leaving behind a hard-core, mainly male populace of about 7,000. Most, in one form or another, were involved with the fighting. The streets were empty, bar the occasional pickup or camouflaged Landcruiser dashing noisily past, weaponry ostentatiously positioned. In its centre lay an abandoned roundabout in the middle of which was a pile of rubble, remnants of a statue of the Gaddafi Green Book, now destroyed and burned by the local people.

The Green Book was Gaddafi's attempt to produce something similar to the Thoughts of Chairman Mao, or even Hitler's Mein Kampf. Children were taught from it while Colonel Gaddafi would use quotes from the text almost daily. For a freedom-seeking people such as the Amazigh of Nalut, The Green Book was a red rag to a bull. Down came the statue at the first opportunity, an act repeated in towns throughout Libya.

The Nalut protest was supplemented by the creation of Radio Free Nalut, broadcasting to the region on FM in the Tamazight language. However quiet the city's streets might have appeared, behind its walls was a huge undercurrent of rebellion.

Without warning, the Landcruiser turned hard right, through a small archway and into the arrivals area of what I could only assume was Nalut Hospital. The Berber driver brought the vehicle to a jerking halt, with Basam's black Landcruiser doing the same behind. I tumbled from my peapod seat into the fresh air, stretched my legs to return their circulation, pulled back my shoulders with an audible clunk and looked around at my new environment. We had made it through. Now it was down to business.

*   *   *

Chapter 29

Unsung Heroes

Nalut Hospital was once a thriving establishment and was still trying to maintain a semblance of normality. It was almost a Tataouine lookalike. Imagine a low, whitewashed, two-storey building stretched out right and left before you, its portico entrance dead centre, and you have it. The hospital could manage almost 200 beds, several operating theatres, and staff who were as multinational as one might find. There were nurses from Libya, Bangladesh and Egypt, some from Sri Lanka and China, too. There were surgeons from North Korea and Tunisia, and other staff who were Czechoslovak, Polish, French and Italian. There were several whose nationality I could not identify. This could have been the world's most cosmopolitan city, I thought, as I made my way from room to room, department to department, trying to establish how I, the latest addition to Nalut's healthcare, could help in any way. I talked with everyone and anyone I could find.

But there were very few patients. With the massive depopulation created by the conflict, all routine medical and surgical activity had ceased. There were no hernias and hip replacements, testicular lumps and ingrowing toenails and there was certainly no gynaecology or obstetrics. All that had departed for Tunisia many days earlier, leaving behind an emergency trauma service only evidenced by the many willing healthcare workers waiting for the occasional war injury.

With war you cannot tell what is needed, nor how frequently or severe. You can sometimes sit for days with nothing to do, at other times you are rushed off your feet. Nalut Hospital was a perfect example of this. The surgeons there with whom I spoke had been largely twiddling their thumbs, waiting for work to arrive. When it did so, it would appear with frightening speed, so they had to be alert and ready to act often with little more than five minutes' warning.

For many of the hospital's staff, I could not understand why they stayed. Their workload was not huge, the border was now temporarily open, so why not escape? I asked a Bangladeshi nurse.

'But where would I go?' came the reply.

'Back home,' I replied. 'Back to Bangladesh.'

The nurse looked horrified. 'To Bangladesh!' she exclaimed. 'I cannot go there. I am a Hindu. I am safer here than with the Muslims in my own country. Anyway, the route between here and Tunisia is extremely dangerous. Many people have been killed.'

So she had decided to stay and to take her chances with her nursing colleagues in Nalut. If she had fled Libya into the arms of the United Nations, positioned immediately across the Tunisian frontier, she would have been returned to Bangladesh. She would not have been allowed to stay in Tunisia.

The same story applied to the two charming North Korean surgeons, who would walk the hospital's corridors doing whatever work they could. Their English was non-existent, as was their knowledge of any of the planet's languages other than North Korea's Chosonmal tongue. Spoken communication with them was impossible. Yet through creative sign language, I established they could not return to North Korea, indeed had been forbidden from returning, for fear they would spread the word of revolution throughout their parent land.

There was a heroic quality to all these people, a heroism that would never be recognised by the world or by authority. No medals for them, no knighthoods, not even special pay. No films, biographies, or documentaries about what they had done, or would do, or the dangers they ran. Most had been there before the war, although some had more recently crossed the frontier illegally, often at night, frequently evading minefields, and occasionally under fire. They had come to Nalut driven by a force that few other than medical folk can understand. It is a sort of mixture of caring, of passion, of wonder and of a desire to do good. If you have a talent, if you have ability, then you must place it where it can do its best. Despite their individual difficulties, despite the knowledge that Gaddafi's forces could come round the corner at any moment, the hospital staff were a happy group; an impromptu war-created team. I felt very much the outsider even if I was welcomed as a long-lost friend.

Sometimes, of course, there are other reasons why a healthcare worker may be found in the back of beyond. This is not often a subject one broaches with a colleague when away from home. There is an almost unwritten taboo about discussing matters domestic. Mostly I could not say whether an aid relief colleague is married or unmarried, has children, is gay, straight, or even upside down. Yet whenever I have been sufficiently brave to broach the subject, I have often found tales of domestic mayhem. By my reckoning, a good proportion of individuals who seek to work in these troublesome parts of the globe are escaping from something. They wish to clear their minds, or the air, perhaps to become invisible for a period.

From time to time something hits you, overpowers you. Normally I am a fairly hard-hearted guy, at least they tell me I am, but my time on the Intensive Care Unit of Nalut Hospital changed me that day. It was the three patients lying in their beds, each dripped and catheterised, each drifting in and out of consciousness, and each a young man barely into his mid-twenties. These were pro-Gaddafi soldiers, not *thuuwar*. A fourth lay in the hospital's morgue covered by a shroud.

For all I could tell they were related. They looked identical, well built and muscular, despite being patients under intensive care. They were not mercenaries and were clearly Libyan. Their short-cropped hair made them intensely military-looking and they had manifestly been fighting for something in which they believed. They were the result of a major contact ten kilometres east of Nalut two days earlier, between the *thuuwar* and Gaddafi. The pro-Gaddafi forces were sometimes called *alkata'ib*. For them, there had been 450 fighters, for the *thuuwar* 250. The end result had been five casualties, all from the *alkata'ib*. One had died in the field, one in Nalut Hospital, which left the three young fighters on intensive care. Their colleagues had left them to die on the battlefield. Rumour had it that Gaddafi did not encourage casualties to return to Tripoli as it was bad for morale. For this reason, I was told, it was not unknown for *alkata'ib* wounded to be despatched on the field. However, on this occasion the *thuuwar* had come to the rescue of their foe. They say that the Arabs invented chivalry and no better example was there than this. Three young men left to die and yet rescued by their enemy - truly remarkable.

To sustain five casualties from a total of 700 fighters is significant if you are one of the five but a tiny number when considering the number of men involved. This was evidence of NATO's efforts, destroying much of Gaddafi's heavy armour and confining him to the use of small arms, although some missiles did remain. With little high explosive available, shrapnel injuries were uncommon. Normally, for example in World Wars I and II, Korea or Vietnam, two-thirds of combat wounds were caused by shrapnel, no more than a quarter by bullets. In Libya's Nafusa Mountains, the lack of high explosive meant that these figures could be reversed. The bulk of injuries were bullet-created, the casualty count being reduced as a result. This was despite the clear death wish of some of the fighters, largely *thuuwar*, who seemed not to mind at all if they were wounded or killed.

During one contact between *thuuwar* and *alkata'ib* a few days earlier, an Associated Press cameraman had filmed the entire battle at considerable risk to himself. The final footage showed none of the *thuuwar* in body armour or helmet and an appalling application of basic field craft. One fighter was calmly eating a sandwich under fire, bullets flying in all directions and several striking the ground within inches of him. He appeared not to care. Another fighter, totally unarmed, had remained on his feet throughout the final assault. His arms outstretched, he walked slowly towards the Gaddafi position, praying loudly throughout. It was as if he was saying, 'Kill me if you dare.' He survived.

Before every attack, before any risk was taken, those involved would cry, '*Allah akhbar* (God is great)'. You could not visit the Libyan conflict without feeling that out there somewhere, well out of sight, was a greater power. These people had total faith in their Maker. If they survived, they survived. If they died, they died. If they were wounded, well they would prefer to have died, but it was all up to their Maker. A far greater honour was attached to death than to almost anything else in life.

In the hospital's Intensive Care Unit the young man to my left had been gut shot. Such injuries are almost universally fatal but he had been saved by a visiting Tunisian surgeon who had stopped the life-threatening bleeding, removed damaged bowel and performed what is known as a temporary colostomy. This is where the end of the large intestine is disconnected from the rectum and anus and brought out through the abdominal wall so that all the faeces go into a colostomy bag. Sometimes this is a permanent requirement and is often performed for cancer victims during peacetime but the same operation may be used to rest a damaged bowel after injury. Once the injured intestine had recovered, the surgeon would disconnect the colostomy and reconnect the bowel. I could see that this young man, severely injured though he may have been, was going to survive.

To my front was his friend, at least that was my presumption. He had been shot through the humerus, the upper arm bone, which had been totally shattered. Another surgeon had expertly fixed this, although had been able to do nothing about the nerve damage that lay around the broken bone. Despite this, surgery had gone well, although to expect the young man's arm ever to function normally again was unreasonable. There was no hope of that. Despite surviving his injuries, the injured arm would affect his employability for life. That was presuming Gaddafi allowed him to survive, or if he eventually made it back to Tripoli.

To my right lay the third casualty. He had survived gunshot wounds to the groin and shinbone thanks to the work of the Nalut surgeons. Yet they had only been able to complete half the job. The hospital did not have sufficient equipment. What was needed was an external fixator. This is a Meccano-like device where thick steel pins are screwed directly into the bone through the skin and are left protruding. The outer ends of the steel pins are then connected together by a strong metal bar. This so-called external fixator keeps the shattered bone aligned so that healing can take place over time. It is possible to adjust the position of the broken bone simply by readjusting the external bar, something that is easily done painlessly and without anaesthetic.

External fixators come in many shapes and sizes and are widely used in conflict zones. I had already used many in Tataouine. Yet Nalut Hospital had used its last one and the young pro-Gaddafi soldier remained only partially treated as a result. It was distressing to see. The soldier could not be evacuated to Tunisia, as he would be unlikely to survive when surrounded by thousands of *thuuwar*-supporting refugees. He certainly could not go to Tripoli as an enforced disappearance beckoned if he did. No, the external fixator would have to come to him and that meant another dangerous dash to Tunisia.

I found Basam just outside the hospital's main doors, smiling, laughing and talking with a group of local men. He was centre stage. Seeing my concerned expression he stopped mid-sentence and hobbled across to me. His colleagues watched his every move. Quickly, I explained to Basam the desperate need for external fixators and that the soldier on the Intensive Care Unit was essentially untreatable without one. I also explained that Nalut would be a perfect place to work and that my casualty chain was now complete. First patch-up after wounding would be in Nalut, the second would be in Tataouine.

Basam listened carefully. I could tell he was pleased that something could be done for the pro-Gaddafi soldier and that surgical support for war wounded would continue in Nalut. Yet there was also uneasiness about him, a discomfort I could not explain; until it was his turn to speak. Then it became clear. Basam had been waiting patiently, not saying a word, while I had prattled on. With me now silent, he leaned across, almost whispering in my ear.

'I was about to come and find you, Dr Richard,' he said. 'Gaddafi is trying a pincer movement and wants to cut the supply route. My people tell me he is only a few hours away. You can stay if you want to – you should be safe in Nalut. But if you want to leave, you must move quickly.'

For a while I did not know what to say. 'Do I stay or do I go?' I thought. I glanced at my watch as if it would give the advice I required. It did not. I looked to the sky. That did not help me either.

To stay in Nalut was unquestionably the safer option. It would take a major, armoured assault to dislodge the outer cordon and the only armour I had seen had been abandoned. The *thuuwar* technicals had been well dug in and the tank traps, even if there were no tanks, would have stopped anything on four wheels in an instant. Admittedly, if Gaddafi did break through the outer cordon and made it to central Nalut, I was in trouble. Ex-SAS and clearly English, I would be a gift to any pro-Gaddafi unit. Even if I was not shot on the spot, I could see myself being paraded through the streets of Tripoli, beamed to every television screen in the world, as an example of UK espionage. That had already happened to one of my former colleagues in Zimbabwe. London had not helped him and I doubted they would help me. The same risk would not apply to the other staff at Nalut Hospital. A UK passport can be a wonderful thing but in war-torn Libya it was a warrant for imprisonment, interrogation or execution.

On the other hand, to cross the border again, with Gaddafi so very close, would be extremely dangerous. We would be in full view of any advancing Gaddafi troops and a perfect target for snipers. There was no cover from fire at all between Nalut and the hotly disputed border. Out there the only thing between instant death and me was an open Toyota window and the skills of a Berber driver.

The answer soon became clear. I was tempted to stay, but I would be a functionless surgeon if I did. The hospital had largely run out of supplies, the pro-Gaddafi soldier being a prime example. Without an external fixator he was untreatable and if any further wounded arrived they would be untreatable too. Nalut needed equipment and drugs and it needed them fast. Whatever the risks I had to cross the border once more to be sure Nalut received the equipment and drugs it needed. Only then could the place function and only then could lives continue to be saved. I would have to take my chances once more in that disputed zone between the outer cordon and the border. To stay where I was in Nalut was not an option.

'Let's go, Basam,' I said. I indicated the hospital behind me. 'They are desperately short of equipment in there. Any form of decent surgery is impossible. Patients are bound to die as a result. We must cross to Tunisia, find the equipment, and deliver it back here as soon as we can.'

Basam nodded and then smiled, placing his hand on my shoulder as he spoke. 'We are so glad you have come to help us, Dr Richard. The people of Nalut are grateful. Now let us cross that border while there is still a chance.'

No surprise then, for the return journey, that my Berber driver increased rather than decreased speed in a way that I had thought was impossible. I was still squashed into the back seat, watching in horror as the driver controlled the vehicle with his knees while drinking a can of fizz with one hand and violently gesticulating to his Berber colleague with the other. Basam's Landcruiser, once again, was immediately behind. At the *thuuwar* roadblock the fighters were on obvious high alert, tense, on edge, their eyes flicking rapidly in all directions. They were handling their weapons nervously.

'Go! Go! You must go! Quickly!' I heard the lead rebel shout, this time in Arabic rather than Tamazight, through our window. My Toyota shot forwards once more, thumping my head forcefully against the tiny cabin window behind. Five hundred metres beyond the roadblock we turned off the road and headed cross-country towards the escarpment that led down to the northerly Jefara Plain. Despite his half empty can of beer and his now one hand on the wheel, I was relieved to note the Berber driver made sure not to skyline his vehicle. The Gaddafi snipers were known to be good. Way beneath me there was much movement. Dust kicked up from the wheels of speeding technicals, puffs of smoke gave evidence of the few remaining missiles being fired and striking home. War was approaching and headed towards me fast. Delay was not an option.

There is a problem with using *passeurs*, even ones as capable as Basam.

Not all have military training. They rely on their wits and charm, as well as an incredible social network for their information. However, military tactics are not always their strong point and social networks can be so easily penetrated by the enemy. The problem stood out that day, when we used the same Wazin border crossing to return to Tunisia as we had used to enter Libya. That would have been forbidden in my SAS days. Never use the same routes in and out. You are asking for trouble if you do as the enemy are waiting for it. Many years earlier the IRA had murdered a good family friend because he had used the same route to and from work each morning. He had made it easy for them and received a bullet through the head for doing so.

Yet squeezed into the back of the speeding Toyota, and with Basam so tightly behind that our bumpers almost touched, I was committed to the methods of a Libyan *passeur*. There was no way my Berber driver was slowing down. When we had dived off cross-country I thought we would be headed towards a different border crossing but we were not. Within a half-kilometre the Toyota had swung back onto the Main Supply Route as we hurtled westwards.

'Shit!' I thought. The locals are taking me back out along the same route.

But by then it was too late. The Gaddafi forces were to our right and heading fast in the same direction. It was almost a matter of who would reach Wazin first. I tried to shrink myself down in the Toyota's back seat but to make my six-foot frame disappear was impossible. This was a highly dangerous situation. To my right I could see the puffs of smoke come nearer. Gaddafi was not far away.

All around us the *thuuwar* were readying themselves for the action that was about to take place. I could hear the sound of small arms fire and the occasional crump as a missile struck home.

We made it by a whisker. Somehow I made it back into Tunisia that day while still using that same border crossing. The *Allah akhbar* mentality of my *passeurs* had done the trick, though God only knows how. Gaddafi's *alkata'ib* took and closed the crossing only a few hours later. Basam's source of intelligence, whatever or whoever that was, had been correct. Basam, too, had shown himself to be totally trustworthy, not always a common finding on the edge of a war zone.

Basam's final words to me as we parted company at the frontier were clear. 'Let me know when you need to cross again,' he said, 'although we will probably need to use a different route.' I nodded and then I smiled, slapping him gently on the shoulder as I spoke. 'Now you tell me about different routes, my friend! Now you tell me!' Together we laughed.

The moment I re-entered Dehiba I called Madjid. He answered after the first ring.

'Richard, Richard!' he began. I noticed the 'Dr' had come out of my name but saw that more as a compliment than a liberty. 'How did it go?' he added.

'Fine,' I replied. 'But I have some urgent work to do. Where are you?'

'Where do you think?' came a slightly jovial reply. 'The Gr...Gra...Graaaam Grin of course.'

'Madjid, can't you pronounce the name any better than that? You've had ages to practise.'

'You teach me,' came the reply. 'I am here when you are ready.'

Our journey back to Tataouine passed in a flash, although Madjid never did learn to pronounce the name Graham Greene, however many times I tried to teach him. We stopped at Tataouine Hospital so that I could seek out Dr Wassif. He was hard at work in the operating theatre completing the amputation of a leg in a young child who had stepped on a landmine several days earlier. The wound was filled with grit, sand and dirt, the tissues completely destroyed. There was no way that leg was going to survive, whatever surgical magic might be available. Amputation, that awful operation of last resort and something I try hard to avoid, was the only way forward.

'What about you?' I asked Dr Wassif as he tied the final stitch on the now clean amputation stump. 'Will you be staying?'

'Of course,' he replied. 'This is what I do. When it is over, then perhaps I will leave.'

The evacuation chain, my primary task, was almost complete. At least it would be once Nalut Hospital was properly equipped. Nalut would patch and mend the injured as soon after wounding as possible and hold them until it was safe to cross the border. Basam and his *passeur* colleagues would then transport the wounded to Tataouine where more advanced surgery could be offered. From a small office in Tataouine Hospital I immersed myself in satellite telephone calls, text messages and emails with Zarzis and London. Two hours later the job was done. Merlin had pulled out all the stops, surgical teams were on their way and equipment by the ton had been ordered.

However, I did have one major, personal commitment still to honour – the leg of the pro-Gaddafi soldier. Perhaps it is age, perhaps experience, perhaps nothing more than exhaustion, but somehow that young man had reached my inner core. Despite a career dealing with conflict and disaster in so many different forms, the *alkata'ib* soldier lying untreated on Nalut's Intensive Care Unit had brought home to me the futility of war. Brother does shoot brother, children are orphaned, whole families and livelihoods are ripped apart.

Tired, I rose to my feet and left the tiny office, heading towards the equipment store of Tataouine Hospital. It was darkening outside, the hospital corridors were largely silent, although from the distant operating theatre suite I could hear the rhythmic sound of an anaesthetic ventilator maintaining life while Dr Wassif operated on yet another casualty. The equipment store was unmanned, so I rapidly scanned the items stacked neatly on its shelves. Even here, equipment was in short supply, but in one far corner I saw the small metal box, no more than 18 inches square, marked clearly with the words "External Fixator". Quickly and quietly I opened the box to check that its contents were complete. Satisfied that nothing was missing I picked up the box and turned to leave. My next step was to seek out someone in authority. So immersed was I in my task that I had not heard the gentle footsteps behind me. However, I did hear the quiet cough.

'Can I help, Dr Richard?' said the voice. I turned to see the theatre manager, a thin woman of medium height. She was looking puzzled.

'If you can,' I replied. I nodded towards the metal equipment box that I now held in both hands. 'This external fixator. I would like to send it to Nalut.'

'Who is the patient?' she asked.

'Who? What do you mean?'

'Anti-Gaddafi or pro-Gaddafi?'

'A young man,' I replied. 'A young man in trouble. Does it really matter to which side he belongs?'

The woman hesitated. I could see her thinking. For a moment I felt she would lecture me on the rights and wrongs of supporting one side or another. She looked hard at me, her brown eyes holding a firm gaze. I knew that Tataouine Hospital was largely filled at that time with anti-Gaddafi rebels. Few pro-Gaddafi fighters made it that far alive.

For what seemed an eternity our eyes locked. Then the brown eyes glanced downwards as the woman spoke. 'You are right, Dr Richard. It does not matter to which side he belongs. Give that box to me. There is a *thuuwar* vehicle crossing the border tonight, headed for Nalut.'

Within forty-eight hours the external fixator had found its way to the pro-Gaddafi soldier with the broken shinbone and, when last heard of, he had offered his services to the rebel forces, as had his two colleagues. There was no way that any of the three wished to return to Tripoli. The defection rate from *alkata'ib* to *thuuwar* was considerable. Only rarely was it the other way. Medical equipment and staff passed to and fro across the border for many weeks thereafter, sometimes legally, sometimes illegally, sometimes by day and sometimes by night. Basam, and his fellow *passeurs*, never received the recognition they were due. Yet these unsung heroes probably saved more lives than any other agency involved in the conflict. They perhaps rescued more souls than the NATO campaign, or Gaddafi, in his madness, destroyed. In great contrast, and to his eternal credit, Basam achieved his objectives without ever firing a shot.

*   *   *

Afterword

Homecoming

Four stories, four different situations. Yet one thing they have in common. The homecoming.

Disasters and wars can happen so quickly. One minute is normality; the next there is chaos. To help you must respond the same way. If your heart wishes to go, then you go. If there is doubt, then you stay. But your colleagues, friends and family are those who are left behind. They say they understand but do not fully do so. They say they wish to help but do not know how.

For those who love you, disasters and conflicts can be difficult times. They follow every news bulletin; they remain glued to the spot. They do not sleep, they do not go out and they eat barely a morcel. Each time an aid worker is wounded or dies, it is you. Each time someone is kidnapped, it is you, too. They talk about you when you are away and make presumptions that are incorrect. They say you look sick when in fact you are well. They say you look well when in fact you are ailing.

However, it is those you leave behind – the abandoned - who perhaps deserve most praise. With a wave of your hand you are away to some pestilent place on the planet. Yet the abandoned do not know if they will ever see you again, although they do know your life insurance is worthless. When the telephone rings it could be you talking cheerily of disaster. Or, perhaps it is a voice saying you are missing without trace.

Then there are those who are selfish, those who refuse to understand and those who prefer to disapprove. The elderly couple that criticised my unshaven appearance after Haiti. I sat near their restaurant table after three weeks without proper food. The patient who complained because Kashmir had disrupted her appointment. Or, the colleague who simply said I was an attention-seeker gone wrong.

When I return, I prefer not to talk immediately of my adventures. It takes me time, often weeks, to settle down. There are some experiences from which I will never recover and there are those that lead to the dreams, the anxiety and the recurring nightmare. When I return I also realise I am fortunate and that problems I once thought large are actually tiny. We live in a world where brother should help brother, sister should side with sister and where all mankind should pull as one.

Yet of what am I most proud? Perhaps it is the opportunity to make a difference, a difference when people need it most. How can I compare a clinic of fifteen patients in gentle England to 3,000 casualties screaming helplessly in some foreign field? I am older now. I have seen a lot, I have done a lot, yet there is still much more to do. My bag is packed, my arm sore from preparatory inoculations. The box of antimalarials is still in date. Meanwhile I continue working, my telephone is on and I wait. I wait for the call. The call that means I must leave loved ones once more, and that I should apologise to so many for what I am about to do. I tell them I will be back, as soon as I can, that I am doing what I believe to be right and they should not worry. I tell them there are people out there, desperate people, folk without a future who need our help. When my turn comes, as it surely will, I can only hope that I, too, have a future.

* * *